# The Maid I Hired Recently Is Mysterious

4

Wakame Konbu

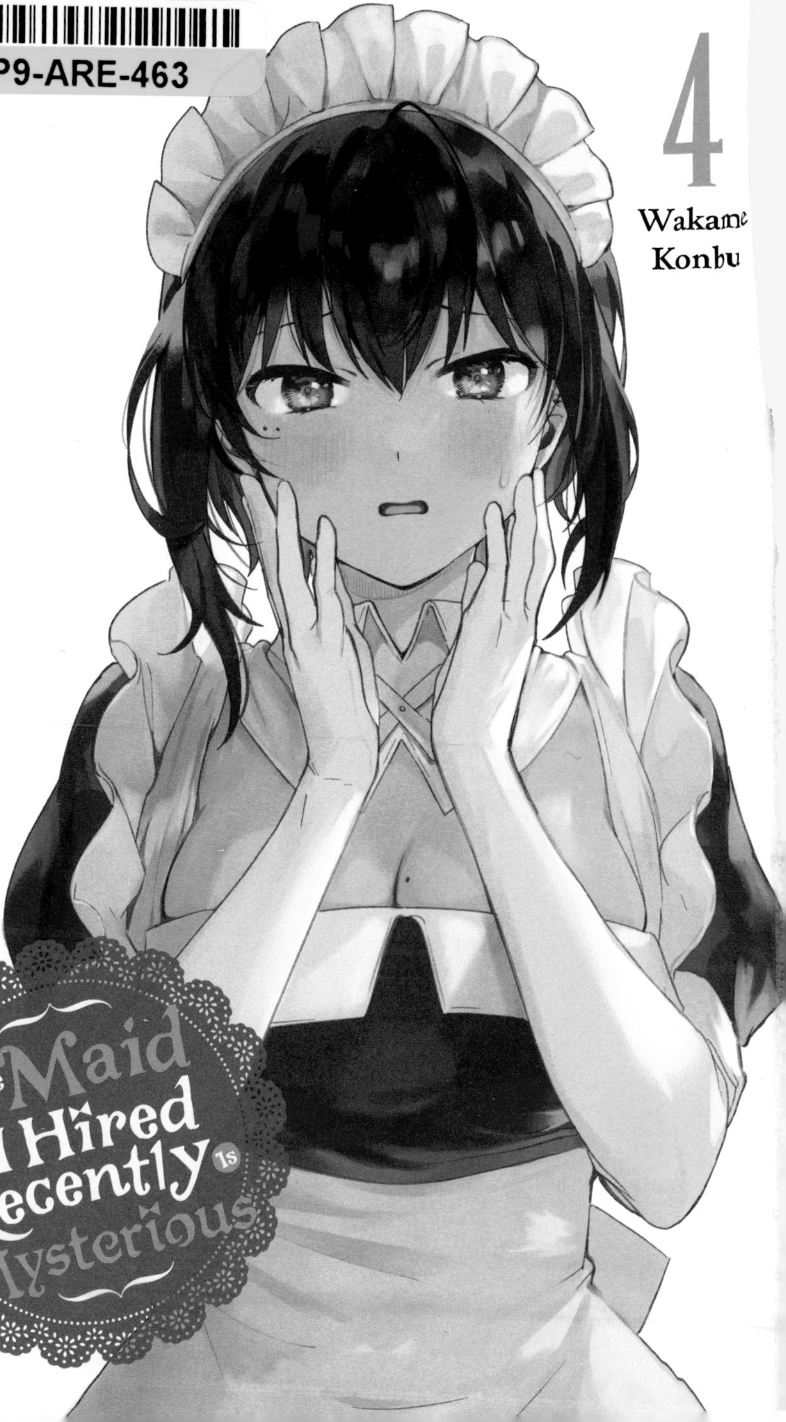

# CONTENTS

The Maid I Hired Recently
Is Mysterious

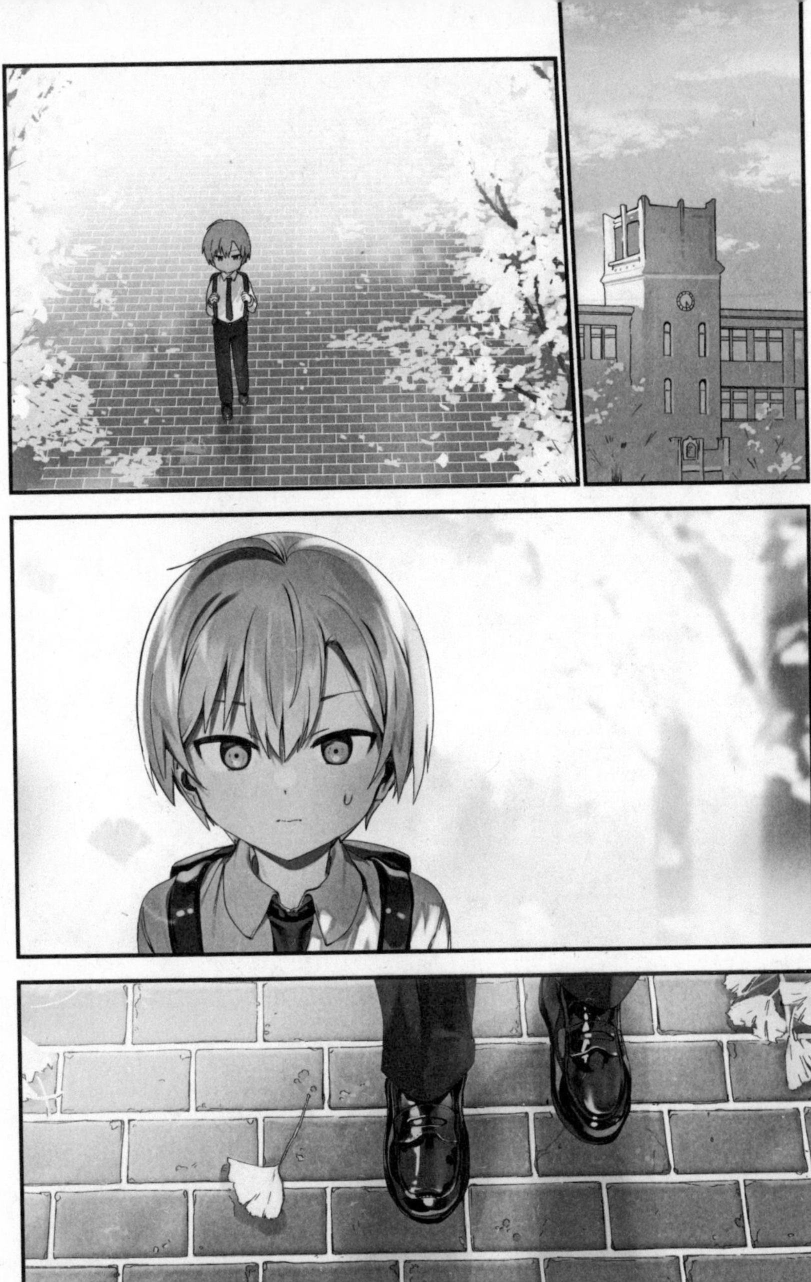

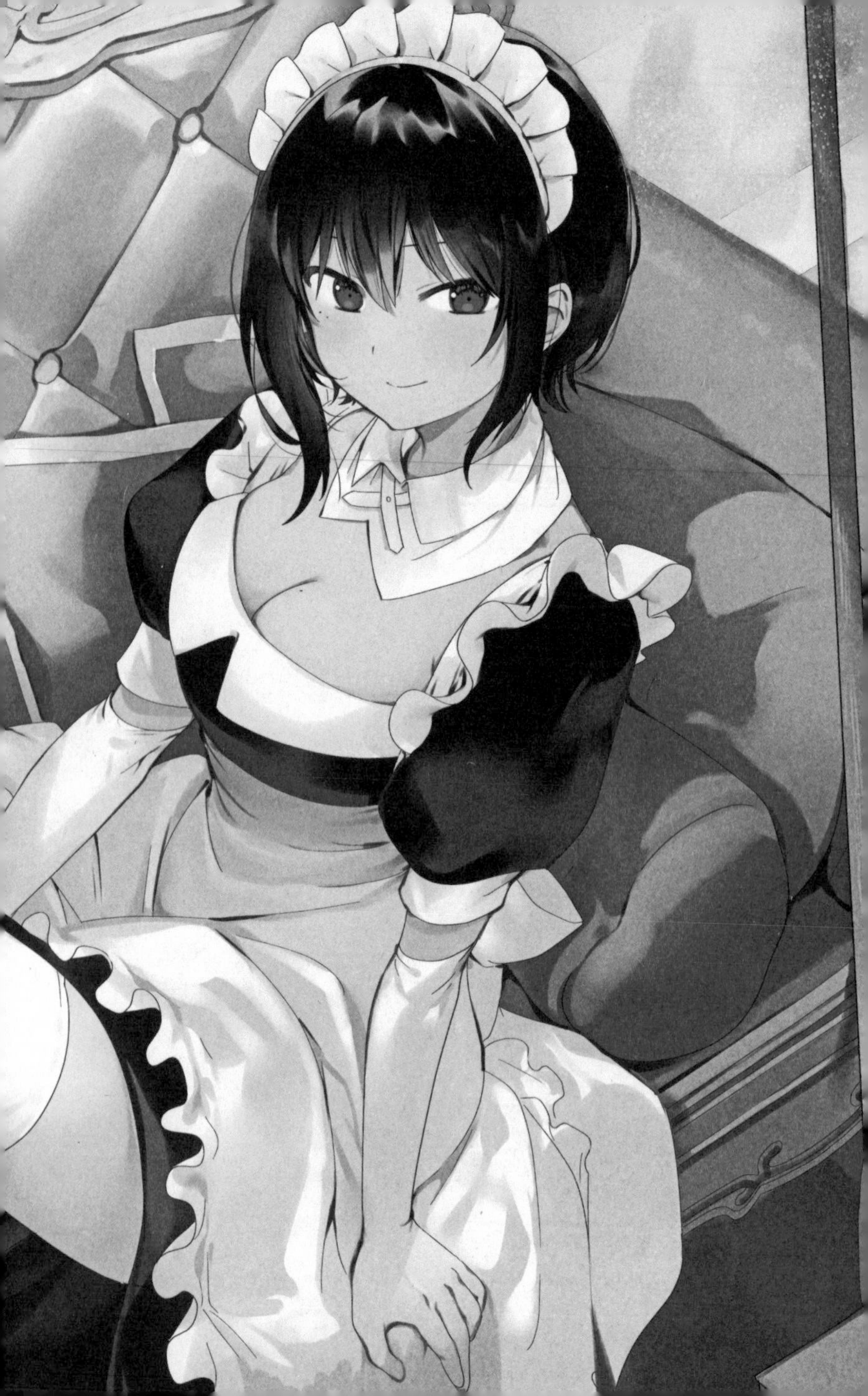

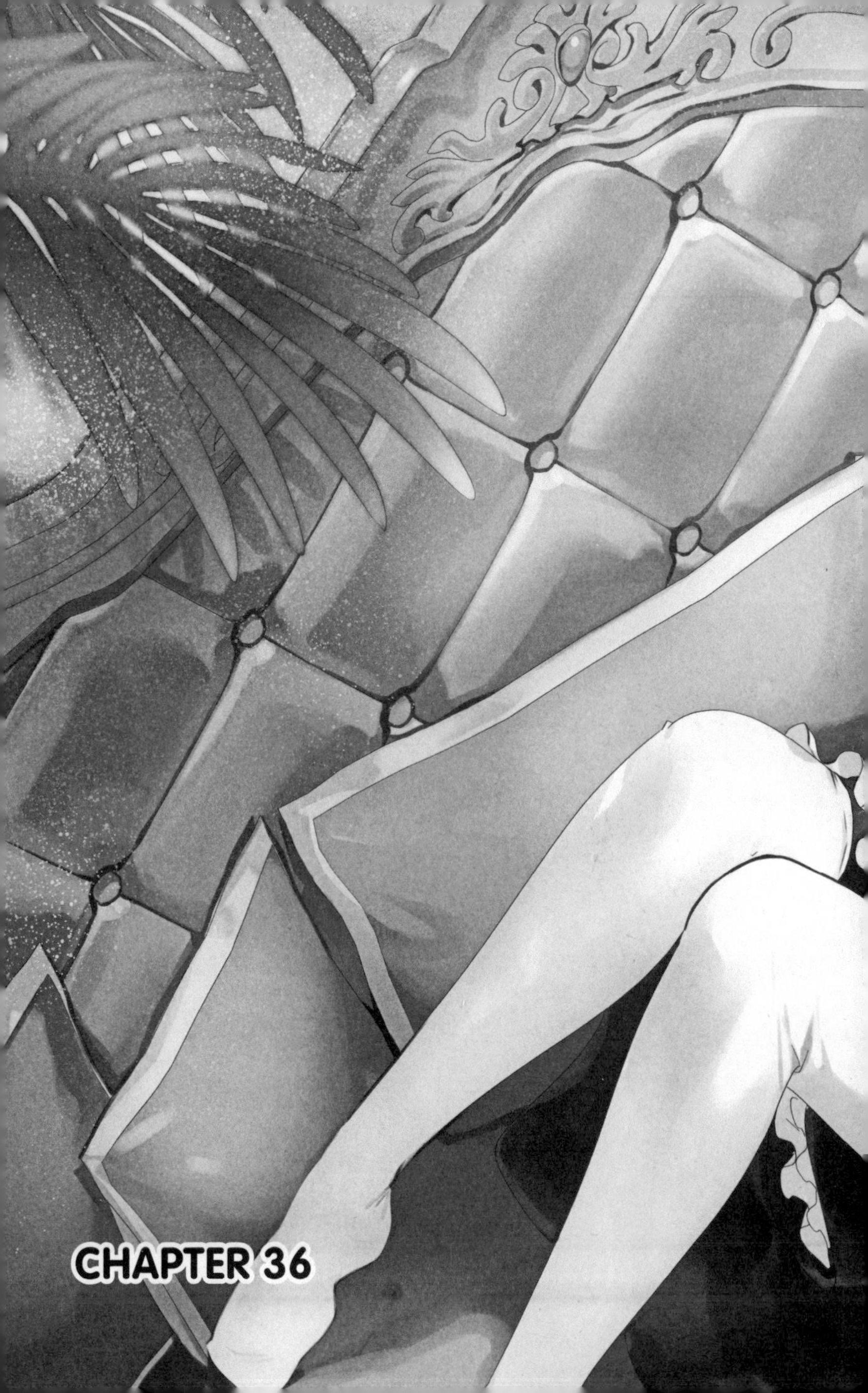
CHAPTER 36

The Maid I Hired Recently Is Mysterious

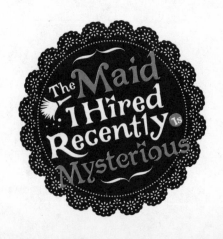

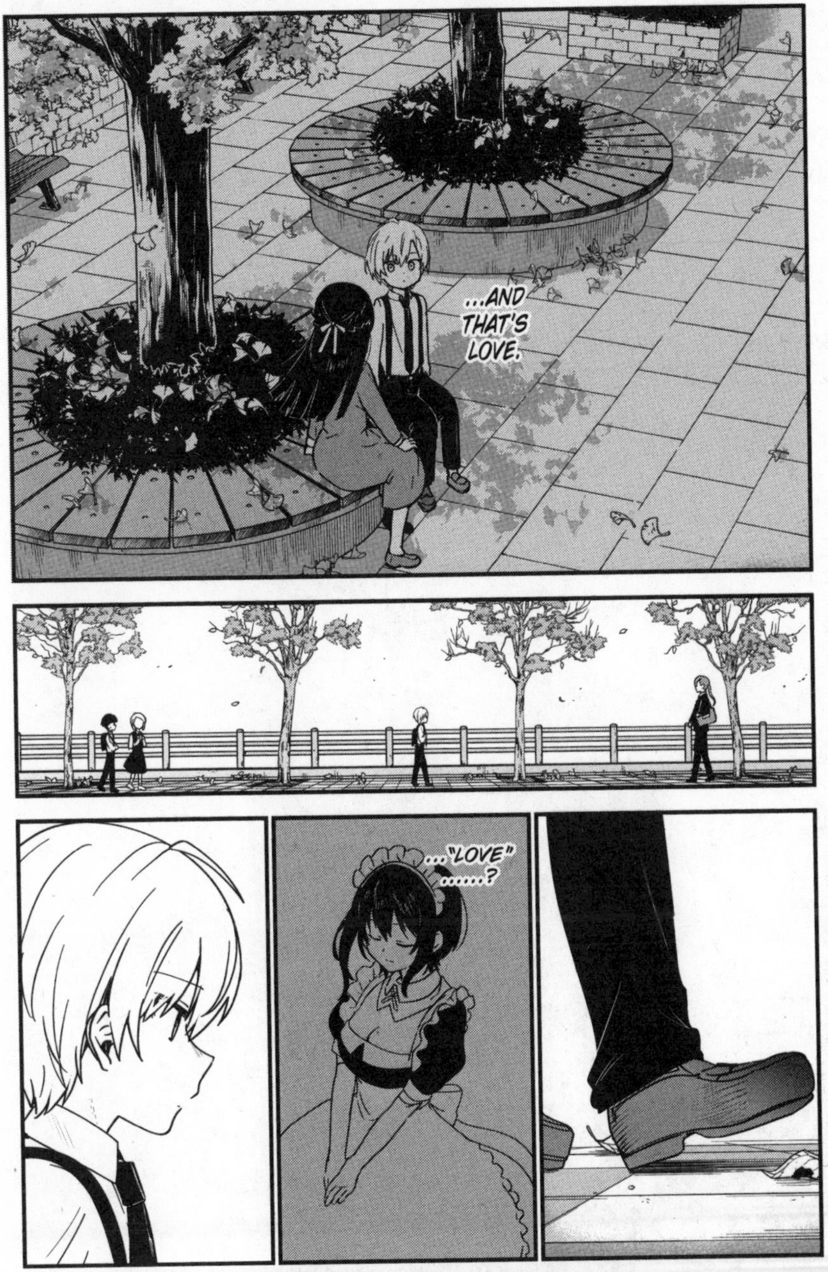
...AND THAT'S LOVE.
..."LOVE" ......?

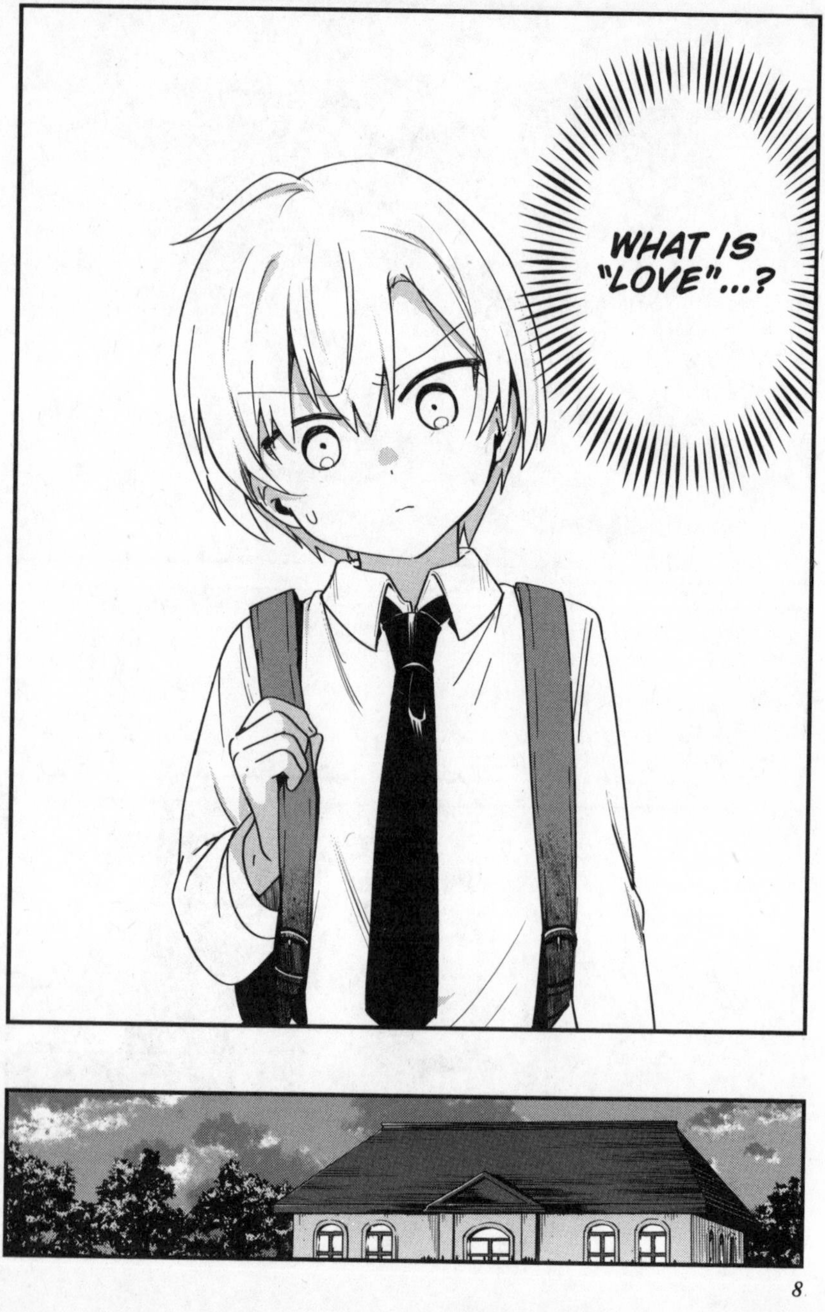
WHAT IS "LOVE"...?

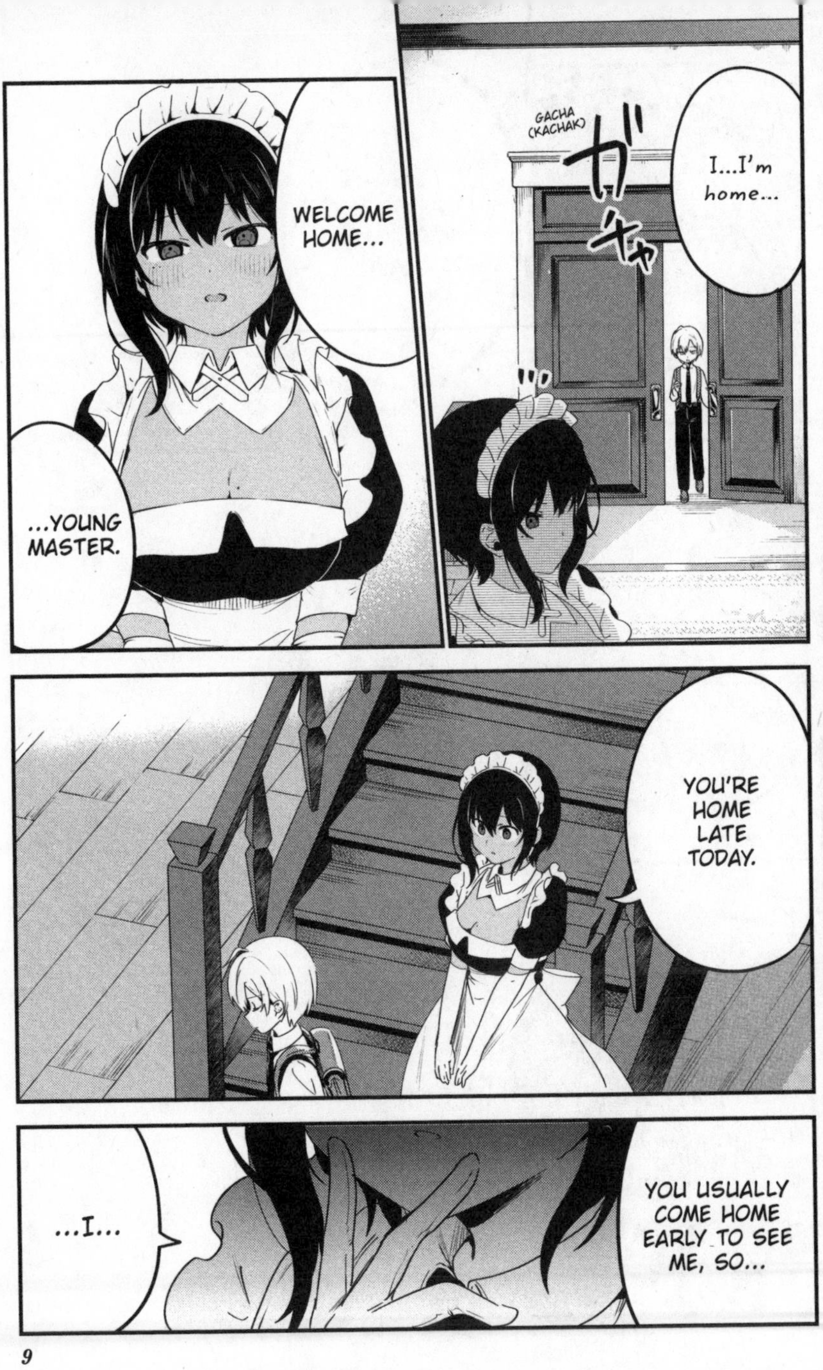
GACHA (KACHAK)
I...I'm home...
WELCOME HOME...
...YOUNG MASTER.
YOU'RE HOME LATE TODAY.
YOU USUALLY COME HOME EARLY TO SEE ME, SO...
...I...

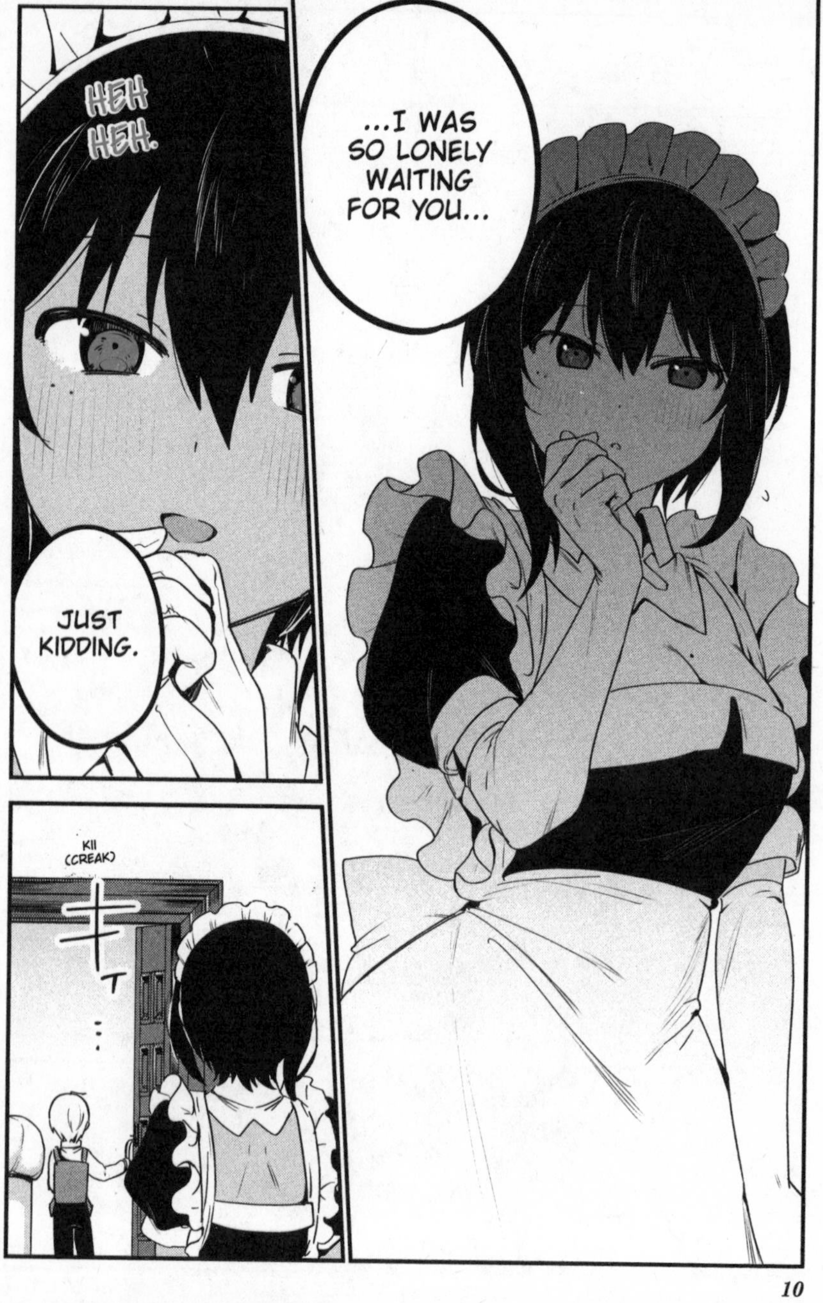
...I WAS SO LONELY WAITING FOR YOU...
HEH HEH.
JUST KIDDING.
KII (CREAK)
...

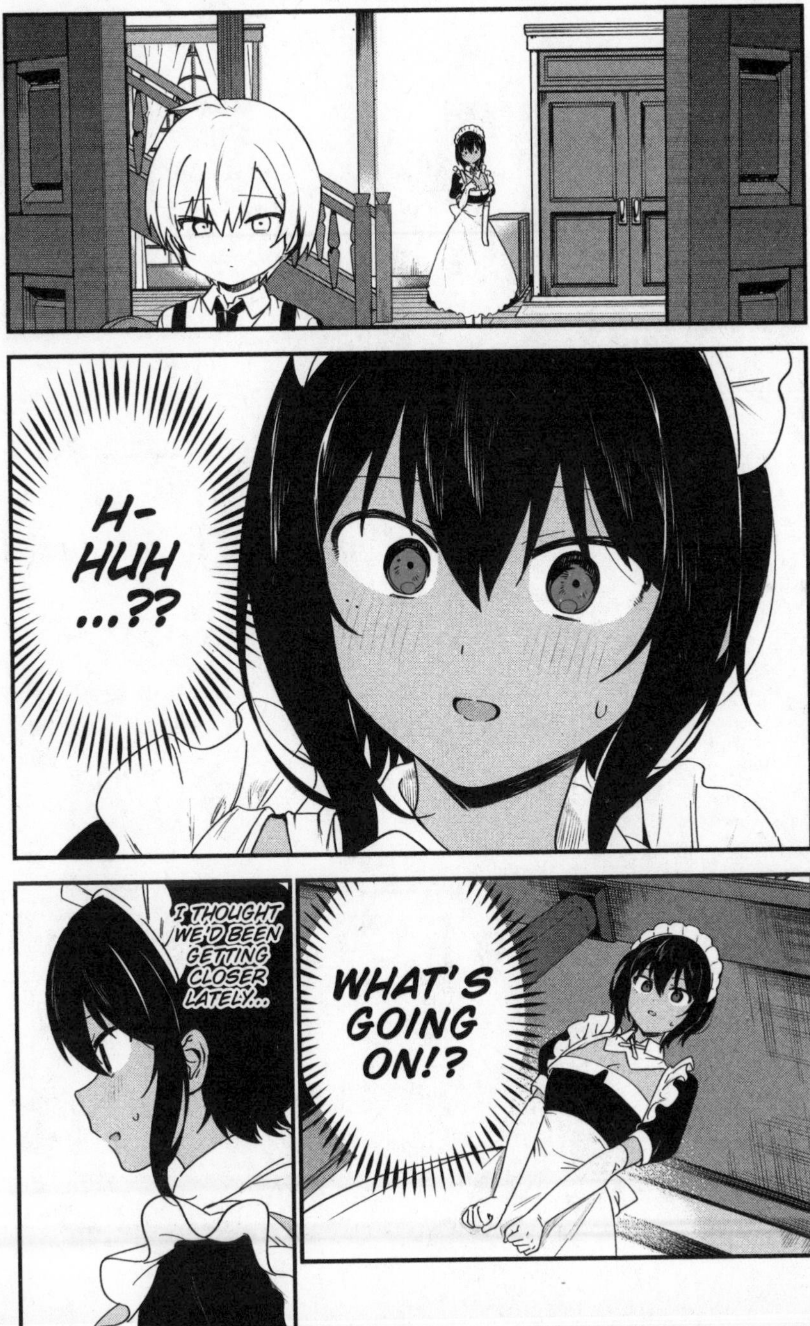
H-HUH...??
WHAT'S GOING ON!?
I THOUGHT WE'D BEEN GETTING CLOSER LATELY...

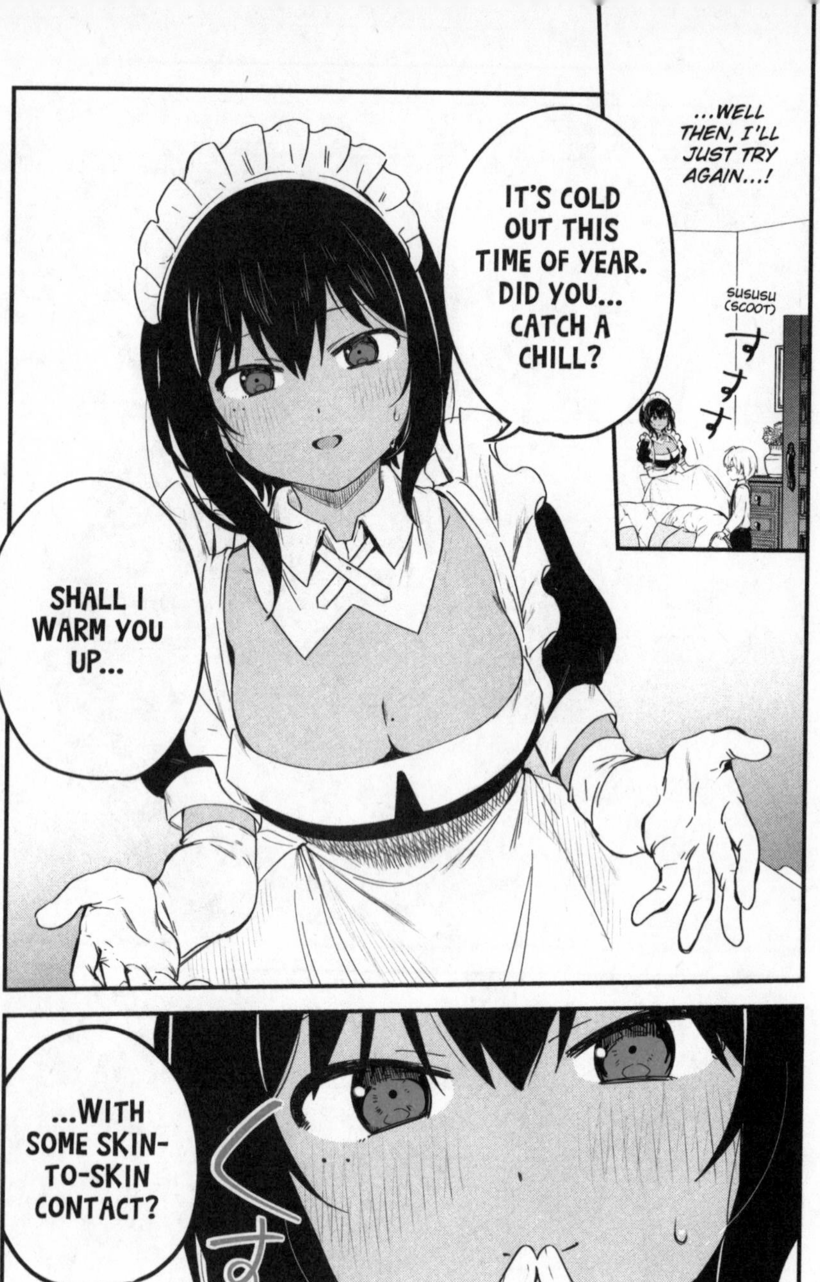
...WELL THEN, I'LL JUST TRY AGAIN...!
SUSUSU (SCOOT)
IT'S COLD OUT THIS TIME OF YEAR. DID YOU... CATCH A CHILL?
SHALL I WARM YOU UP...
...WITH SOME SKIN-TO-SKIN CONTACT?
KUSU (GIGGLE)

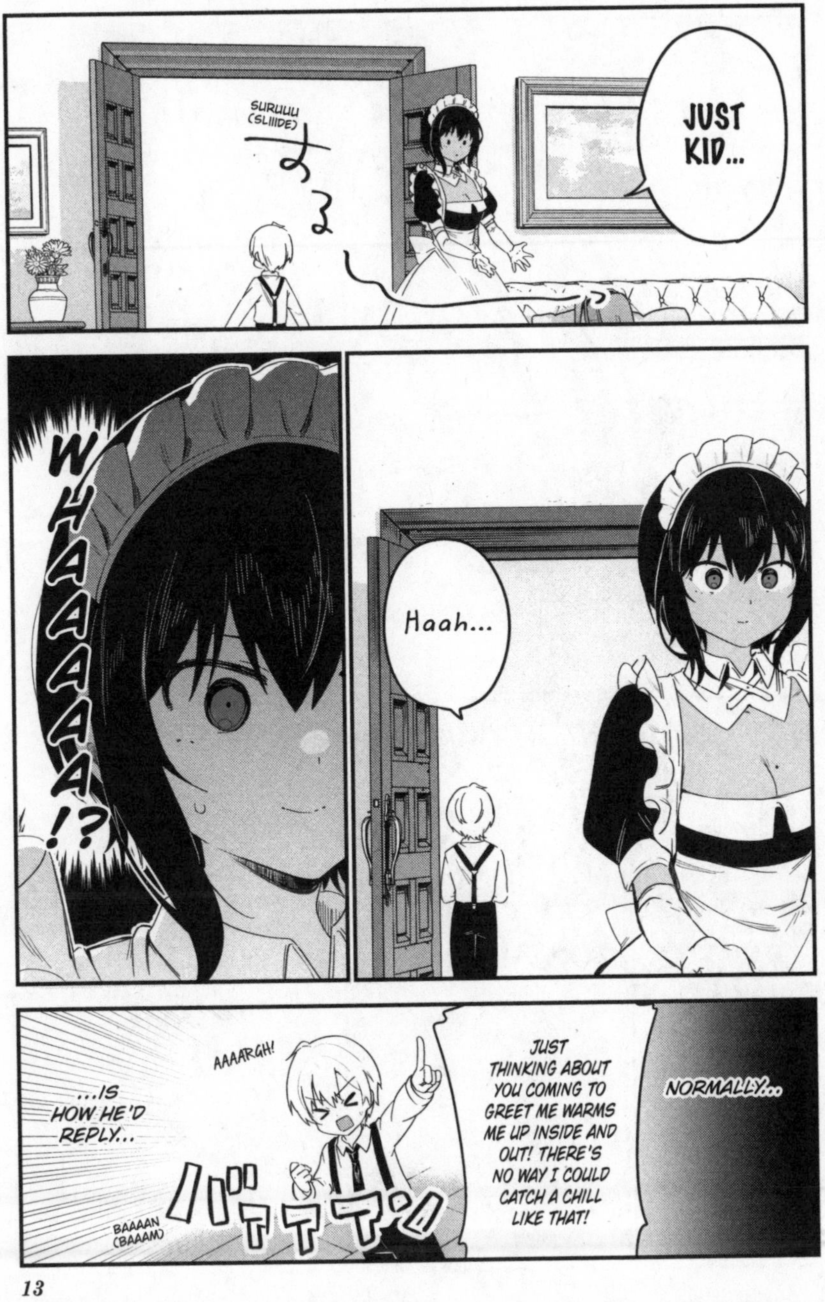
JUST KID...
SURUUU (SLIIIDE)
Haah...
WHAAAAAAA!?
NORMALLY...
JUST THINKING ABOUT YOU COMING TO GREET ME WARMS ME UP INSIDE AND OUT! THERE'S NO WAY I COULD CATCH A CHILL LIKE THAT!
AAAARGH!
...IS HOW HE'D REPLY...
BAAAAN (BAAAM)

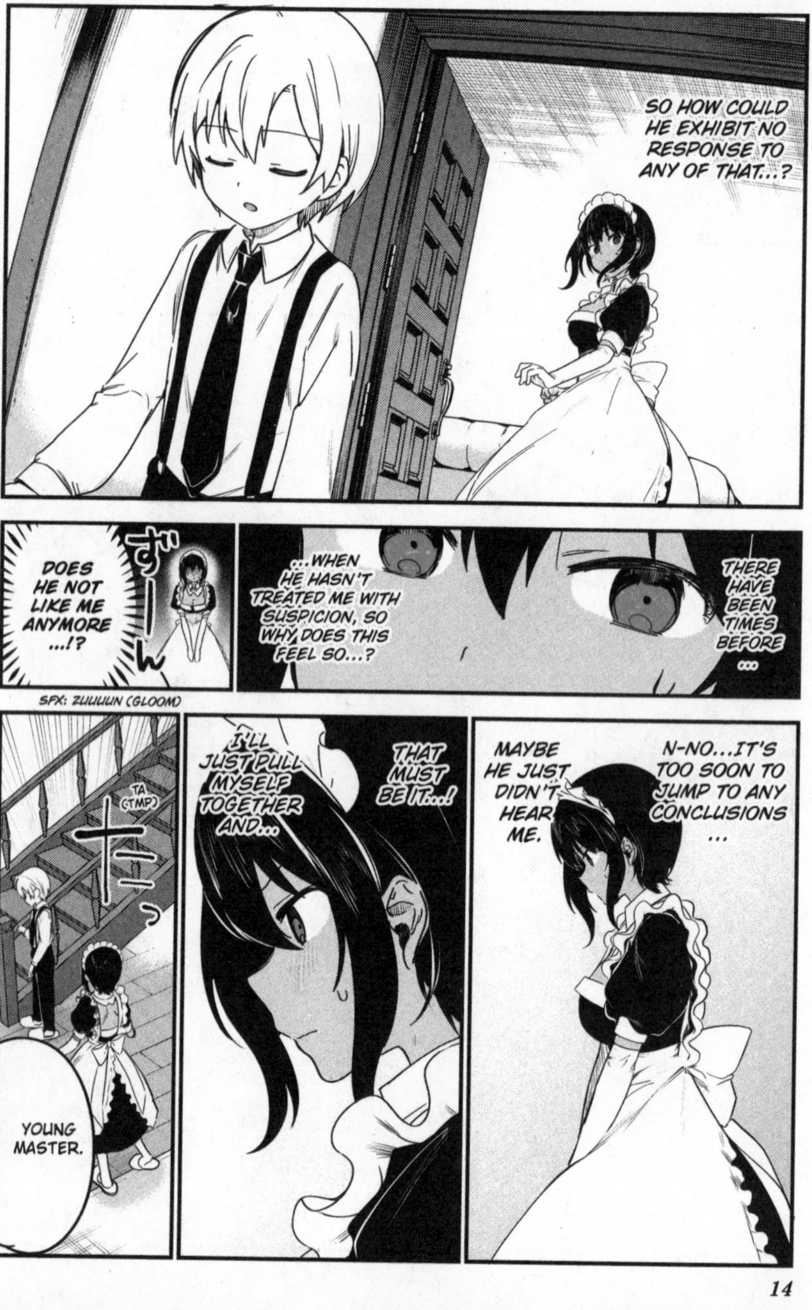
SO HOW COULD HE EXHIBIT NO RESPONSE TO ANY OF THAT...?
THERE HAVE BEEN TIMES BEFORE...
...WHEN HE HASN'T TREATED ME WITH SUSPICION, SO WHY DOES THIS FEEL SO...?
ずーん
DOES HE NOT LIKE ME ANYMORE...!?
SFX: ZUUUUN (GLOOM)
N-NO...IT'S TOO SOON TO JUMP TO ANY CONCLUSIONS...
MAYBE HE JUST DIDN'T HEAR ME.
THAT MUST BE IT...!
I'LL JUST PULL MYSELF TOGETHER AND...
たーっ
TA (TMP)
YOUNG MASTER.

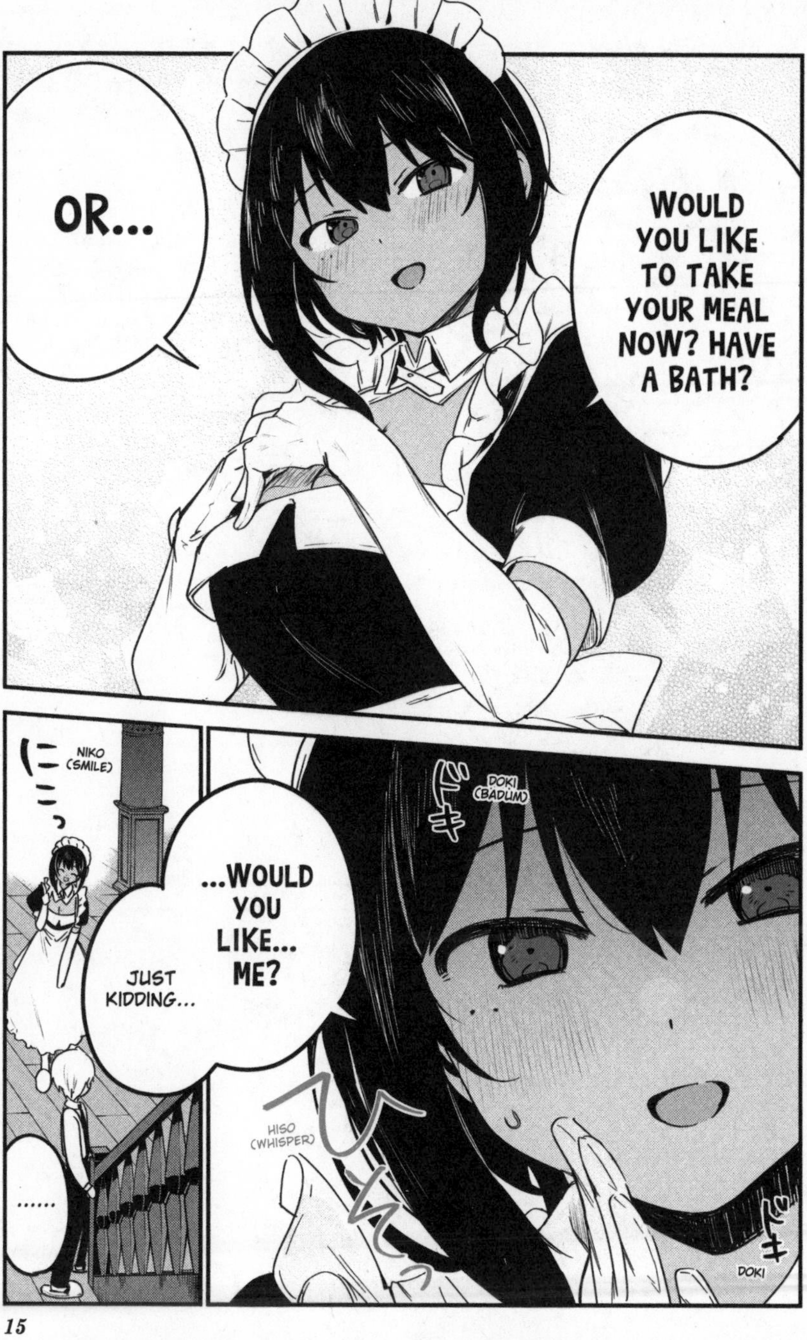
WOULD YOU LIKE TO TAKE YOUR MEAL NOW? HAVE A BATH?
OR...
DOKI (BADUM)
...WOULD YOU LIKE... ME?
JUST KIDDING...
HISO (WHISPER)
DOKI
NIKO (SMILE)
......

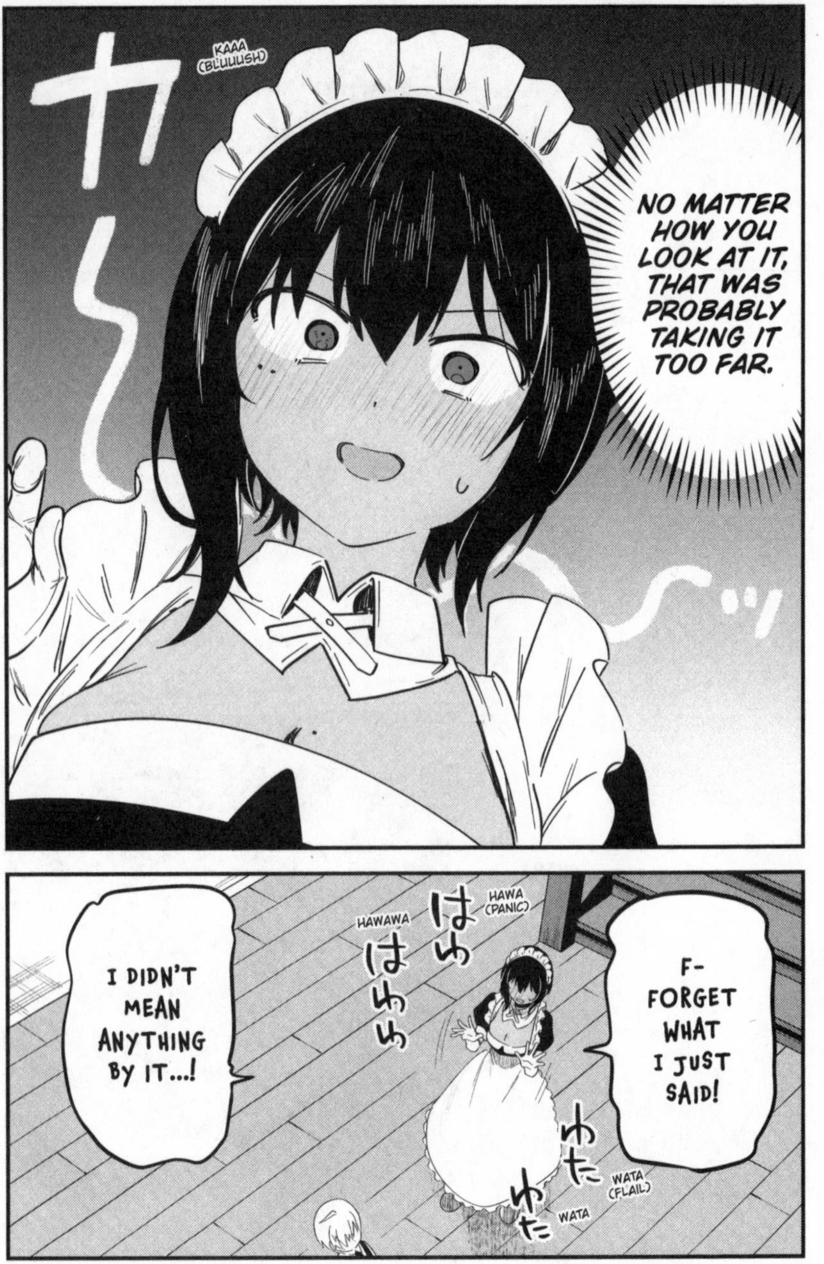
NO MATTER HOW YOU LOOK AT IT, THAT WAS PROBABLY TAKING IT TOO FAR.
KAAA (BLUUUSH)
F-FORGET WHAT I JUST SAID!
HAWA (PANIC)
HAWAWA
WATA (FLAIL)
WATA
I DIDN'T MEAN ANYTHING BY IT...!

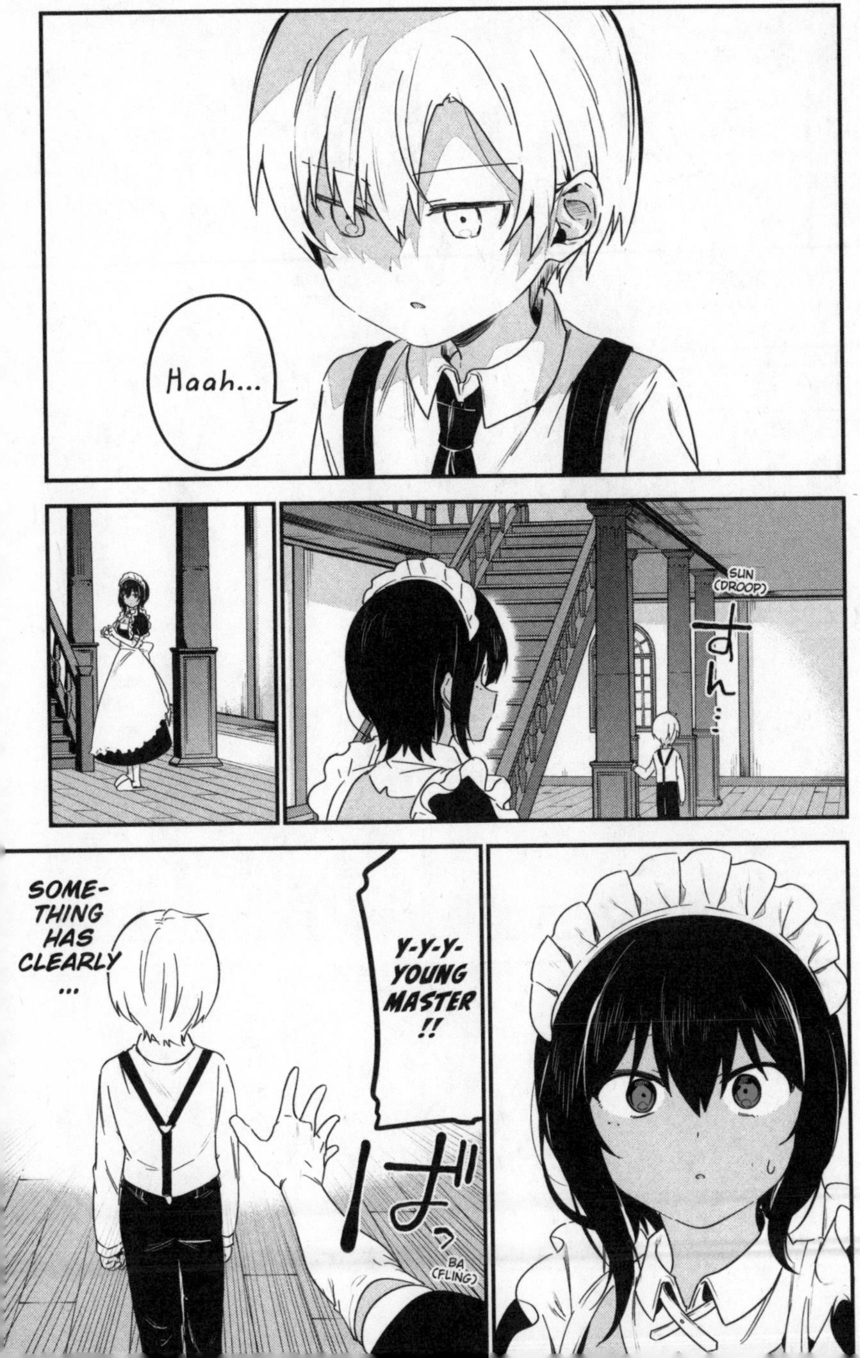
Haaah...
すん…
SUN (DROOP)
Y-Y-Y-YOUNG MASTER!!
SOME-THING HAS CLEARLY...
ばっ
BA (FLING)

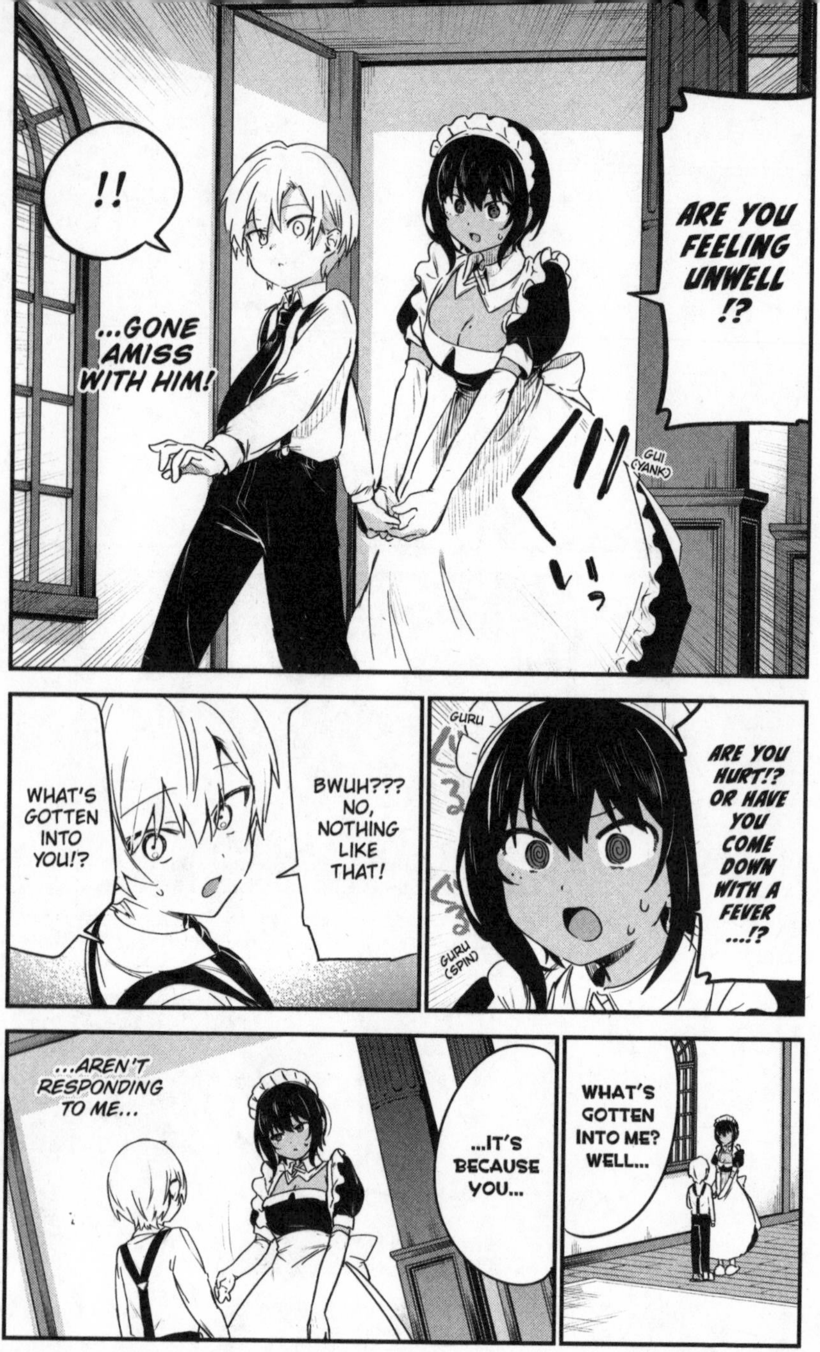
ARE YOU FEELING UNWELL!?
GUI (YANK)
!!
...GONE AMISS WITH HIM!
GURU
ARE YOU HURT!? OR HAVE YOU COME DOWN WITH A FEVER...!?
GURU (SPIN)
BWUH??? NO, NOTHING LIKE THAT!
WHAT'S GOTTEN INTO YOU!?
WHAT'S GOTTEN INTO ME? WELL...
...IT'S BECAUSE YOU...
...AREN'T RESPONDING TO ME...

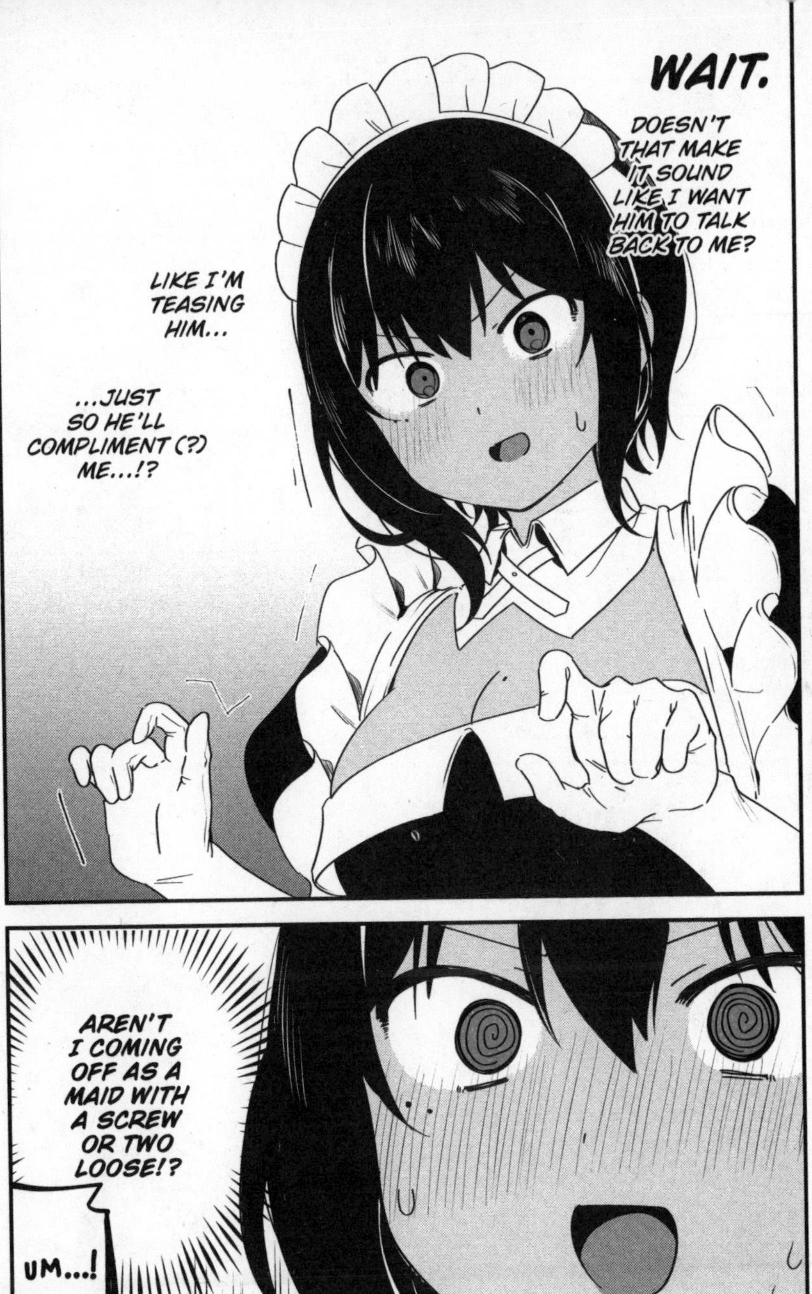
WAIT.
DOESN'T THAT MAKE IT SOUND LIKE I WANT HIM TO TALK BACK TO ME?
LIKE I'M TEASING HIM...
...JUST SO HE'LL COMPLIMENT (?) ME...!?
AREN'T I COMING OFF AS A MAID WITH A SCREW OR TWO LOOSE!?
UM...!

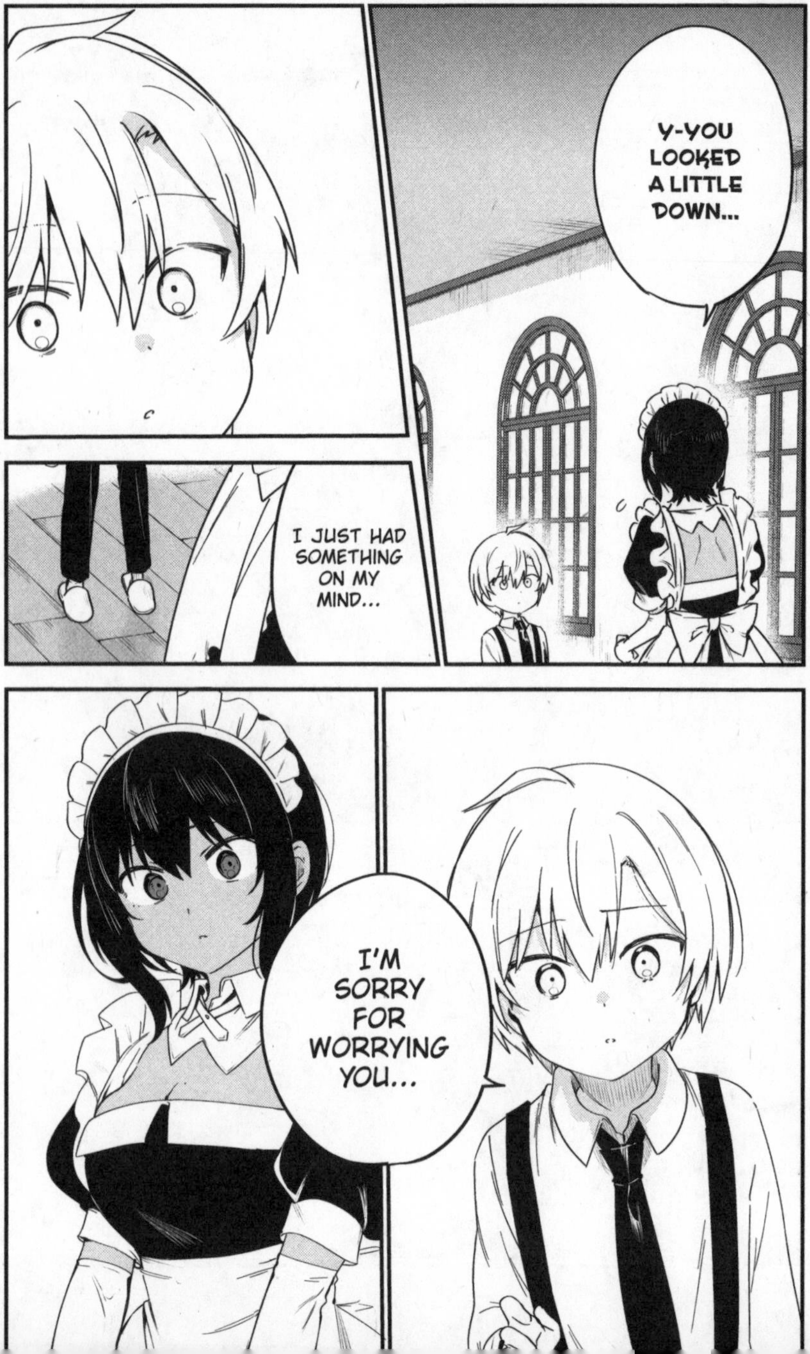
Y-YOU LOOKED A LITTLE DOWN...
I JUST HAD SOMETHING ON MY MIND...
I'M SORRY FOR WORRYING YOU...

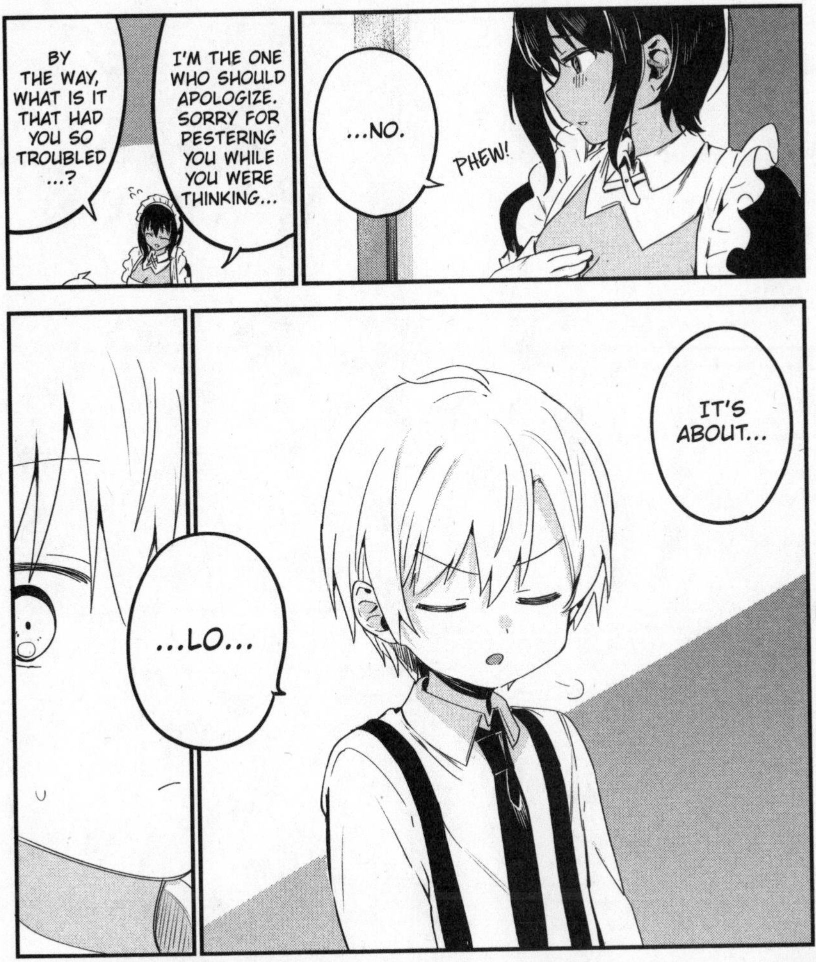
...NO.
PHEW!
I'M THE ONE WHO SHOULD APOLOGIZE. SORRY FOR PESTERING YOU WHILE YOU WERE THINKING...
BY THE WAY, WHAT IS IT THAT HAD YOU SO TROUBLED ...?
IT'S ABOUT...
...LO...
LO...?
......

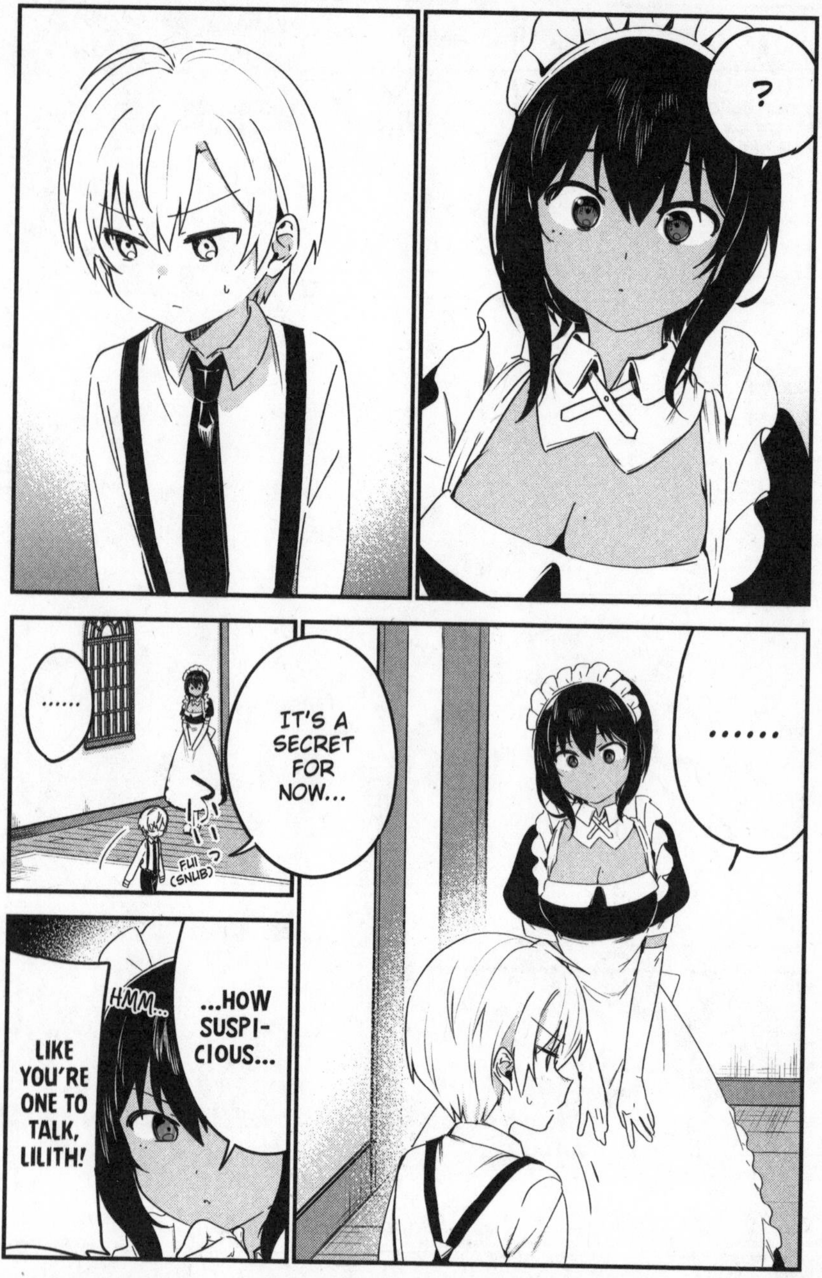
?
......
IT'S A SECRET FOR NOW...
FUI (SNUB)
......
...HOW SUSPI-CIOUS...
HMM...
LIKE YOU'RE ONE TO TALK, LILITH!

The Maid I Hired Recently Is Mysterious

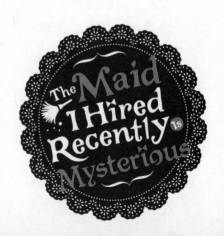

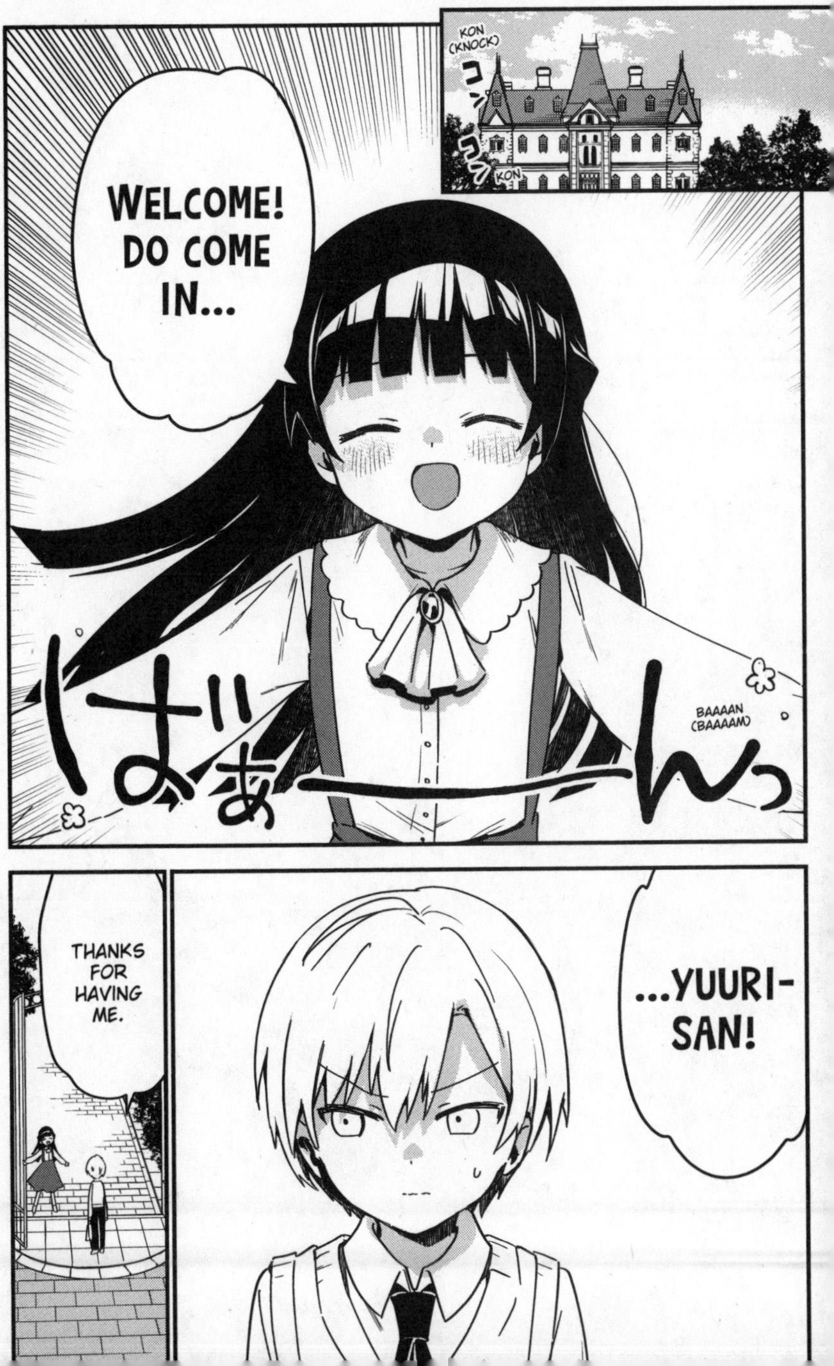
KON (KNOCK)
コン
コン
KON
WELCOME! DO COME IN...
ぱぁーーんっ
BAAAAN (BAAAAM)
...YUURI-SAN!
THANKS FOR HAVING ME.

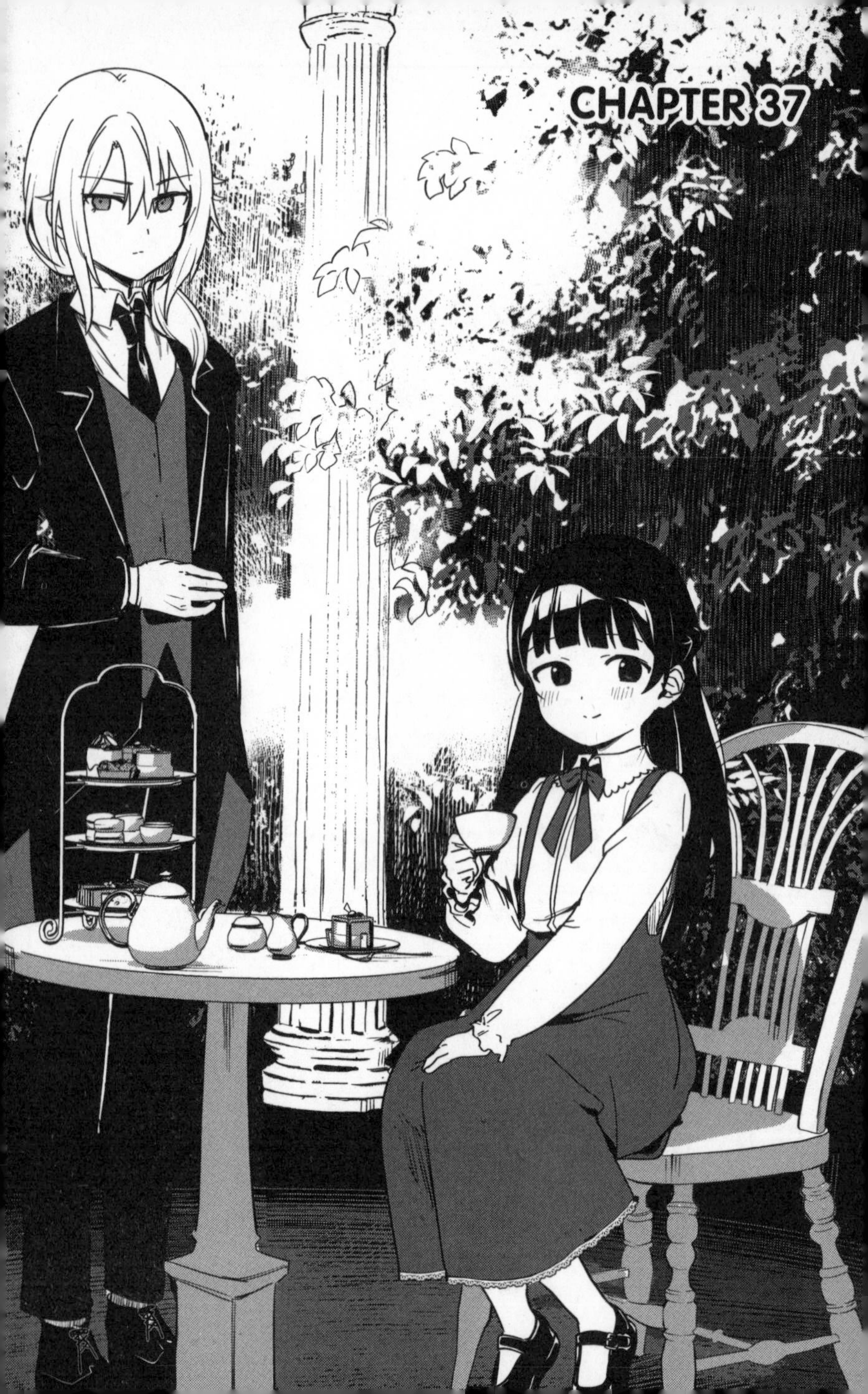
CHAPTER 37

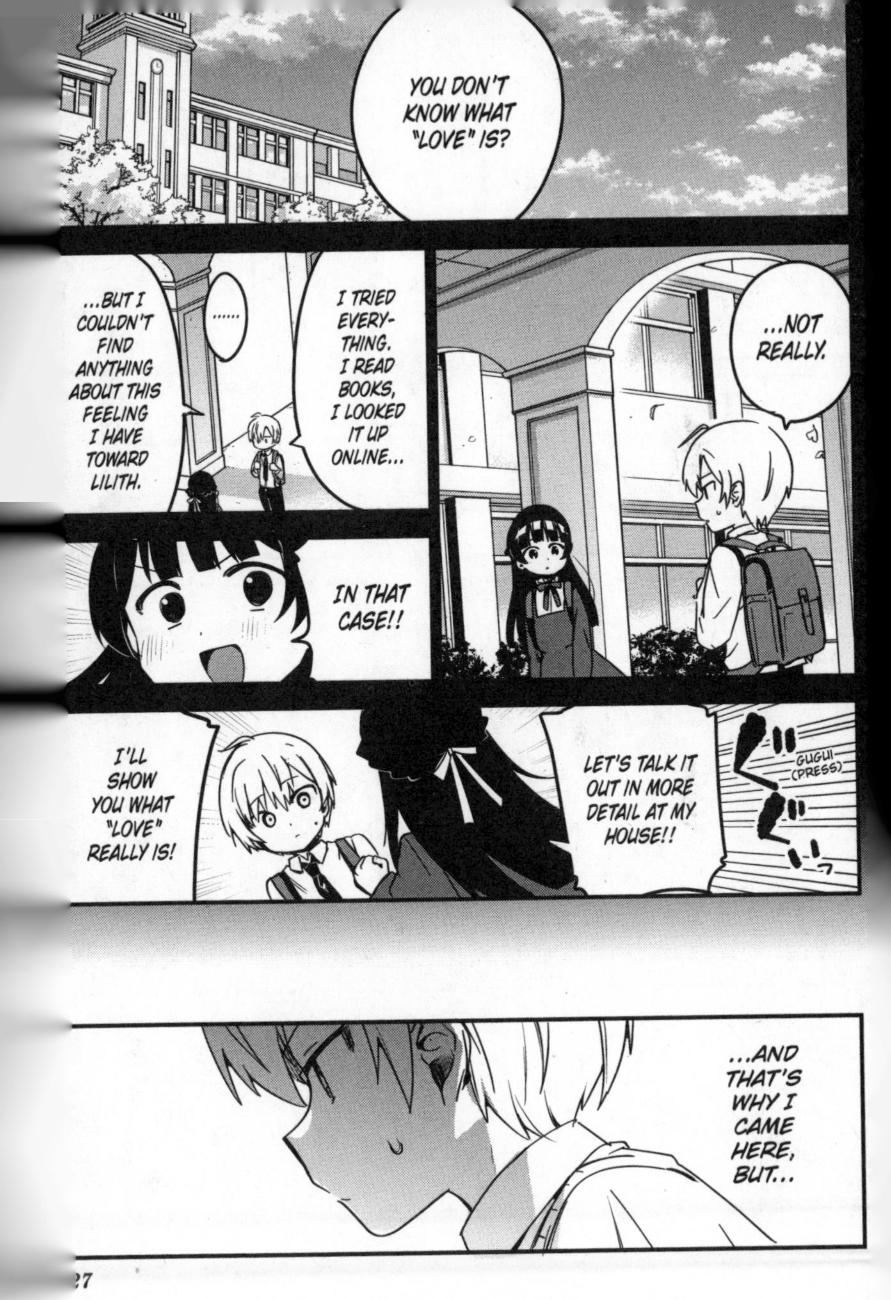
YOU DON'T KNOW WHAT "LOVE" IS?
...NOT REALLY.
I TRIED EVERYTHING. I READ BOOKS, I LOOKED IT UP ONLINE...
......
...BUT I COULDN'T FIND ANYTHING ABOUT THIS FEELING I HAVE TOWARD LILITH.
IN THAT CASE!!
GUGUI (PRESS)
LET'S TALK IT OUT IN MORE DETAIL AT MY HOUSE!!
I'LL SHOW YOU WHAT "LOVE" REALLY IS!
...AND THAT'S WHY I CAME HERE, BUT...

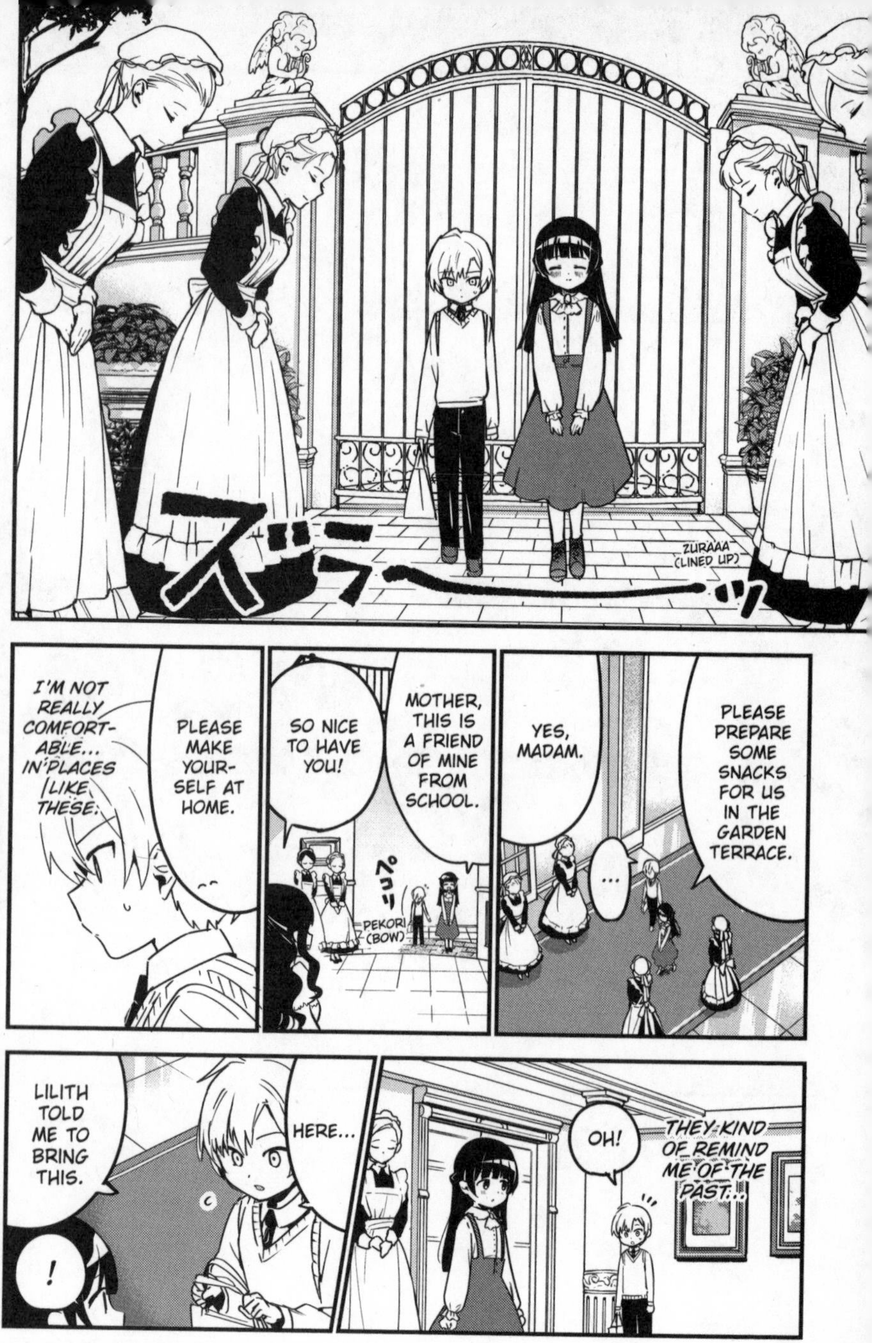
ZURAAA (LINED UP)
PLEASE PREPARE SOME SNACKS FOR US IN THE GARDEN TERRACE.
YES, MADAM.
...
MOTHER, THIS IS A FRIEND OF MINE FROM SCHOOL.
SO NICE TO HAVE YOU!
PEKORI (BOW)
PLEASE MAKE YOUR-SELF AT HOME.
I'M NOT REALLY COMFORT-ABLE... IN PLACES LIKE THESE.
THEY KIND OF REMIND ME OF THE PAST...
OH!
HERE...
LILITH TOLD ME TO BRING THIS.
!

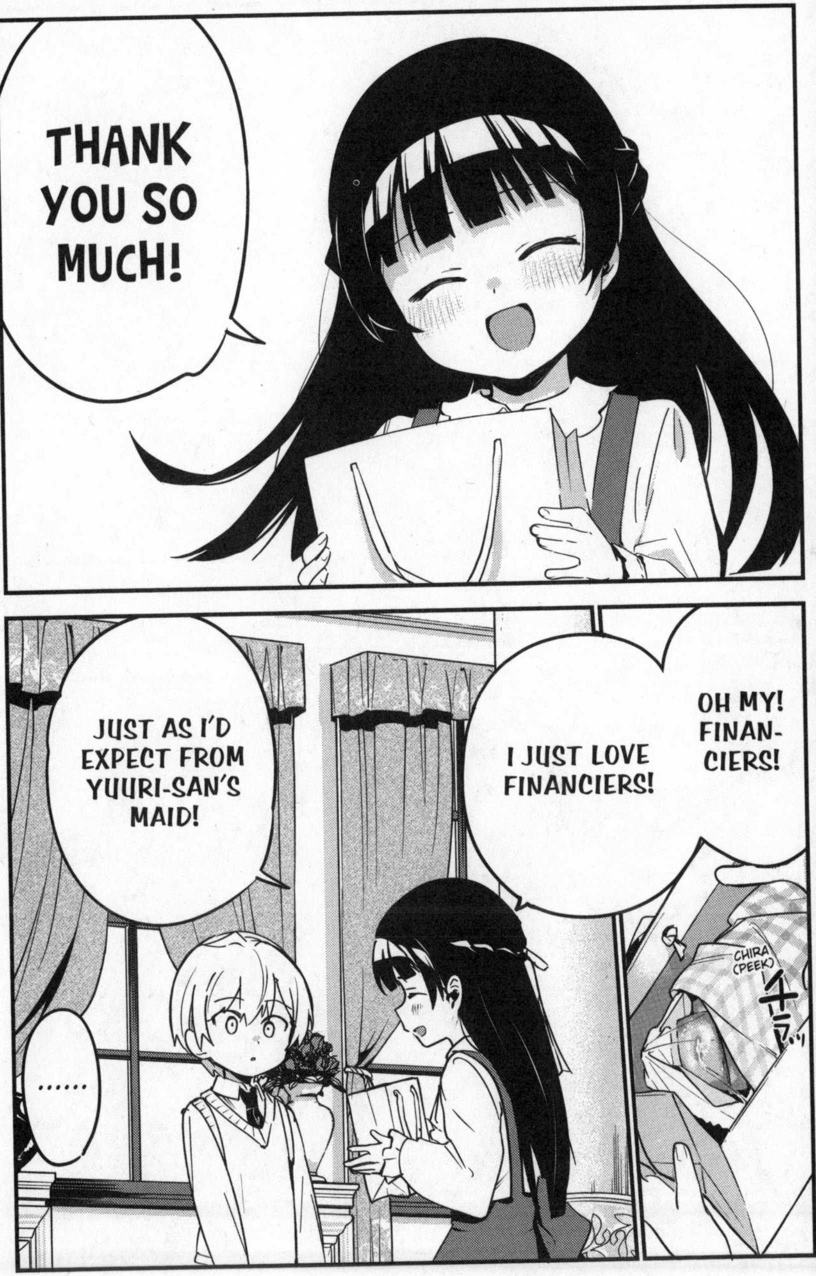
THANK YOU SO MUCH!
OH MY! FINAN-CIERS!
CHIRA (PEEK)
チラッ
I JUST LOVE FINANCIERS!
JUST AS I'D EXPECT FROM YUURI-SAN'S MAID!
......

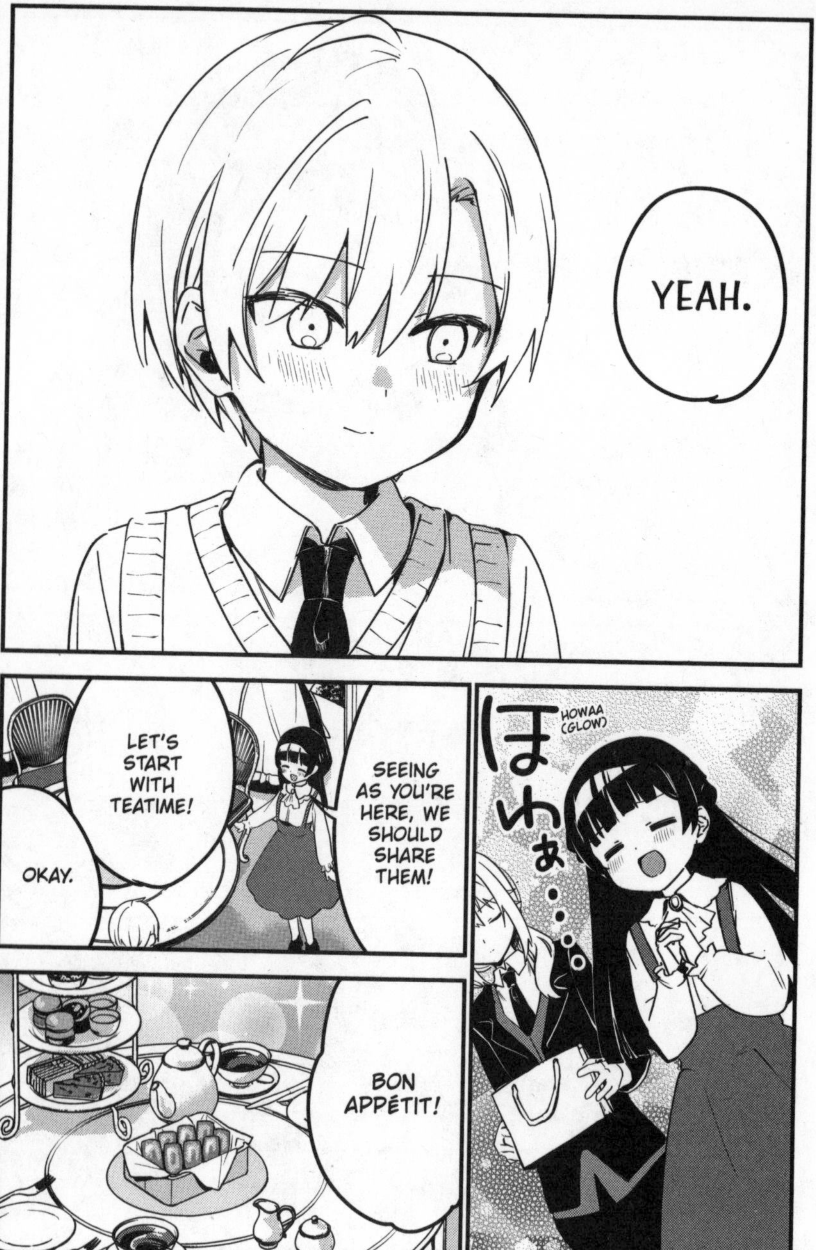
YEAH.
ほわぁ…
HOWAA (GLOW)
SEEING AS YOU'RE HERE, WE SHOULD SHARE THEM!
LET'S START WITH TEATIME!
OKAY.
BON APPÉTIT!

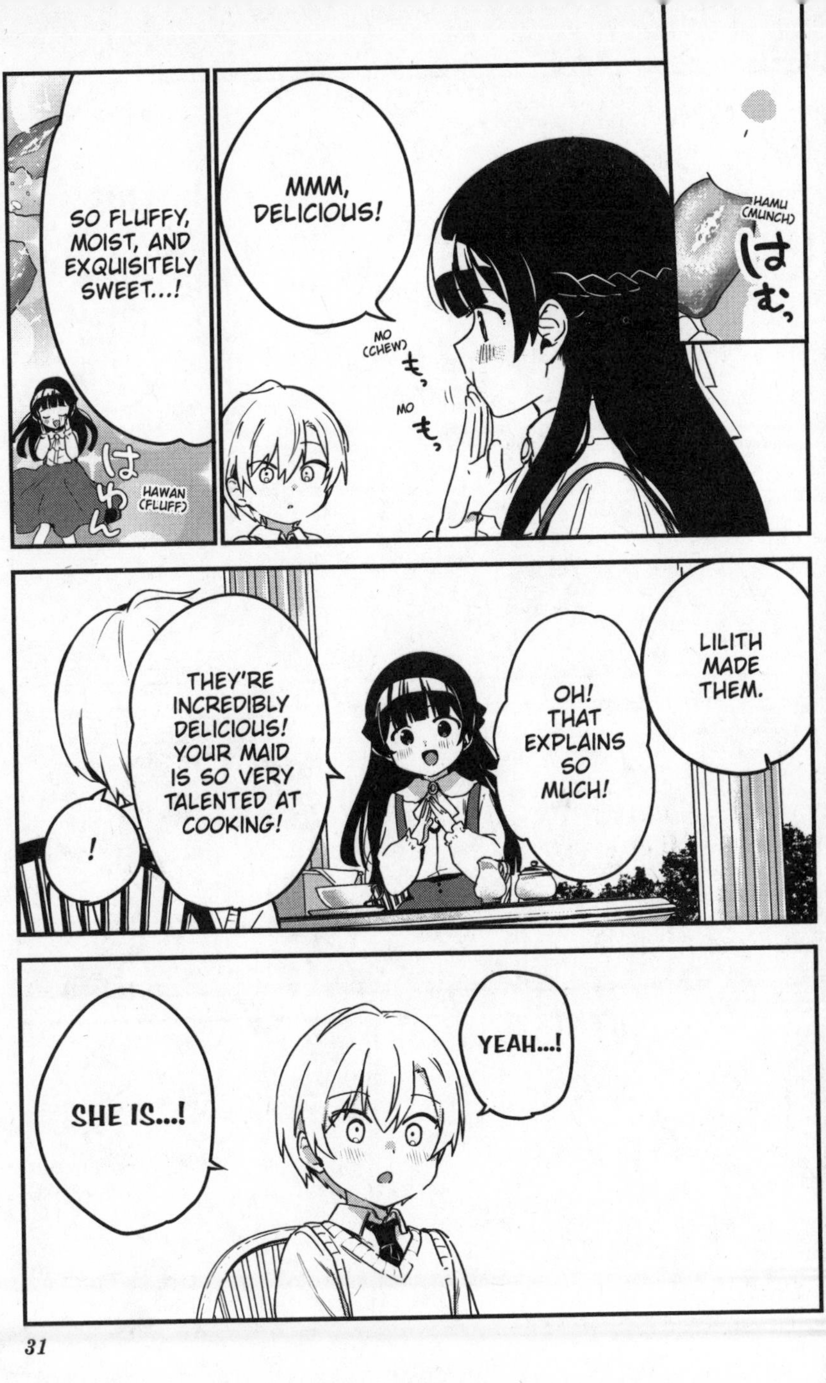
HAMU (MUNCH)
はむっ
MMM, DELICIOUS!
MO (CHEW)
もっ
MO
もっ
SO FLUFFY, MOIST, AND EXQUISITELY SWEET...!
はわん
HAWAN (FLUFF)
LILITH MADE THEM.
OH! THAT EXPLAINS SO MUCH!
THEY'RE INCREDIBLY DELICIOUS! YOUR MAID IS SO VERY TALENTED AT COOKING!
!
YEAH...!
SHE IS...!

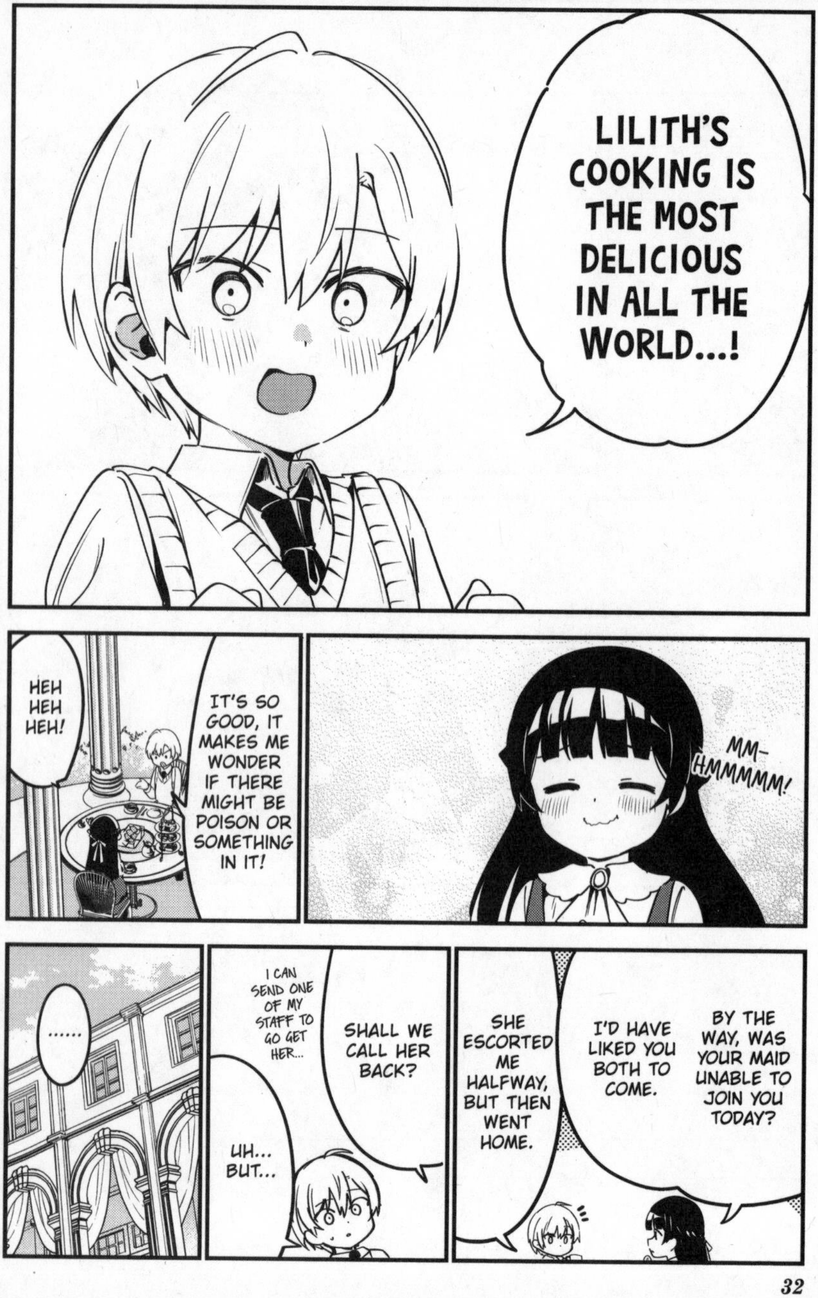
LILITH'S COOKING IS THE MOST DELICIOUS IN ALL THE WORLD...!
MM-HMMMMM!
IT'S SO GOOD, IT MAKES ME WONDER IF THERE MIGHT BE POISON OR SOMETHING IN IT!
HEH HEH HEH!
BY THE WAY, WAS YOUR MAID UNABLE TO JOIN YOU TODAY?
I'D HAVE LIKED YOU BOTH TO COME.
SHE ESCORTED ME HALFWAY, BUT THEN WENT HOME.
SHALL WE CALL HER BACK?
I CAN SEND ONE OF MY STAFF TO GO GET HER...
UH... BUT...
......

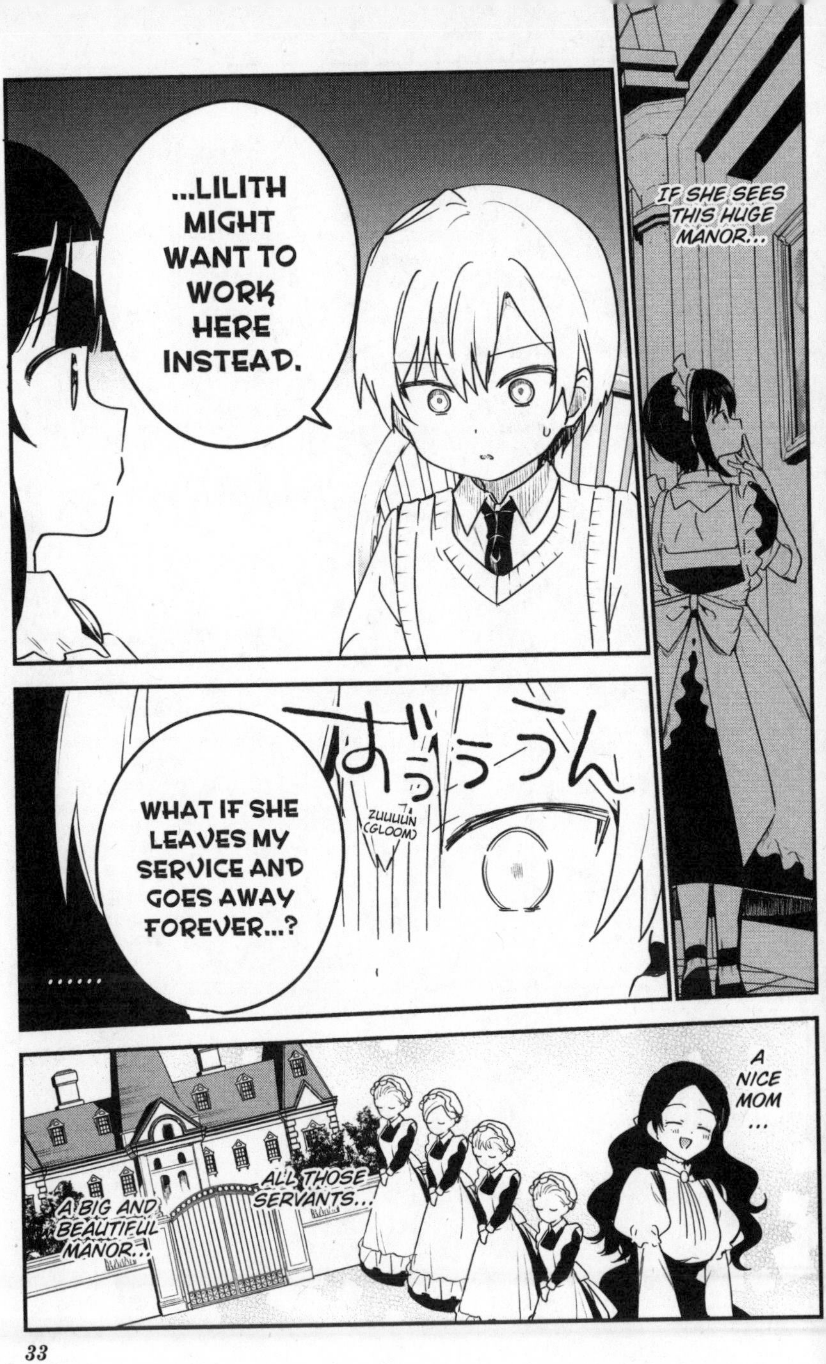
IF SHE SEES THIS HUGE MANOR...
...LILITH MIGHT WANT TO WORK HERE INSTEAD.
ずぅぅうん
ZUUUUN (GLOOM)
WHAT IF SHE LEAVES MY SERVICE AND GOES AWAY FOREVER...?
......
A NICE MOM...
ALL THOSE SERVANTS...
A BIG AND BEAUTIFUL MANOR...

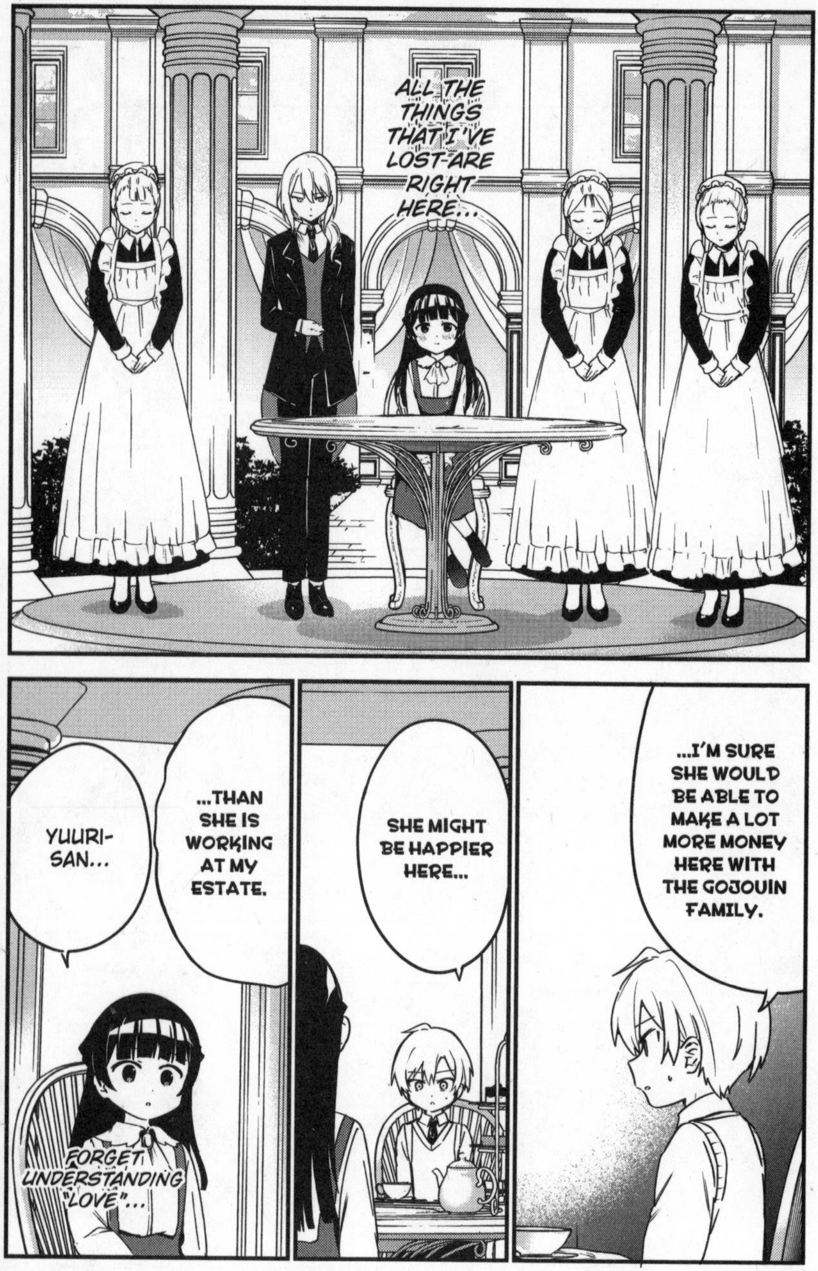
ALL THE THINGS THAT I'VE LOST ARE RIGHT HERE...
...I'M SURE SHE WOULD BE ABLE TO MAKE A LOT MORE MONEY HERE WITH THE GOJOUIN FAMILY.
SHE MIGHT BE HAPPIER HERE...
...THAN SHE IS WORKING AT MY ESTATE.
YUURI-SAN...
FORGET UNDERSTANDING "LOVE"...

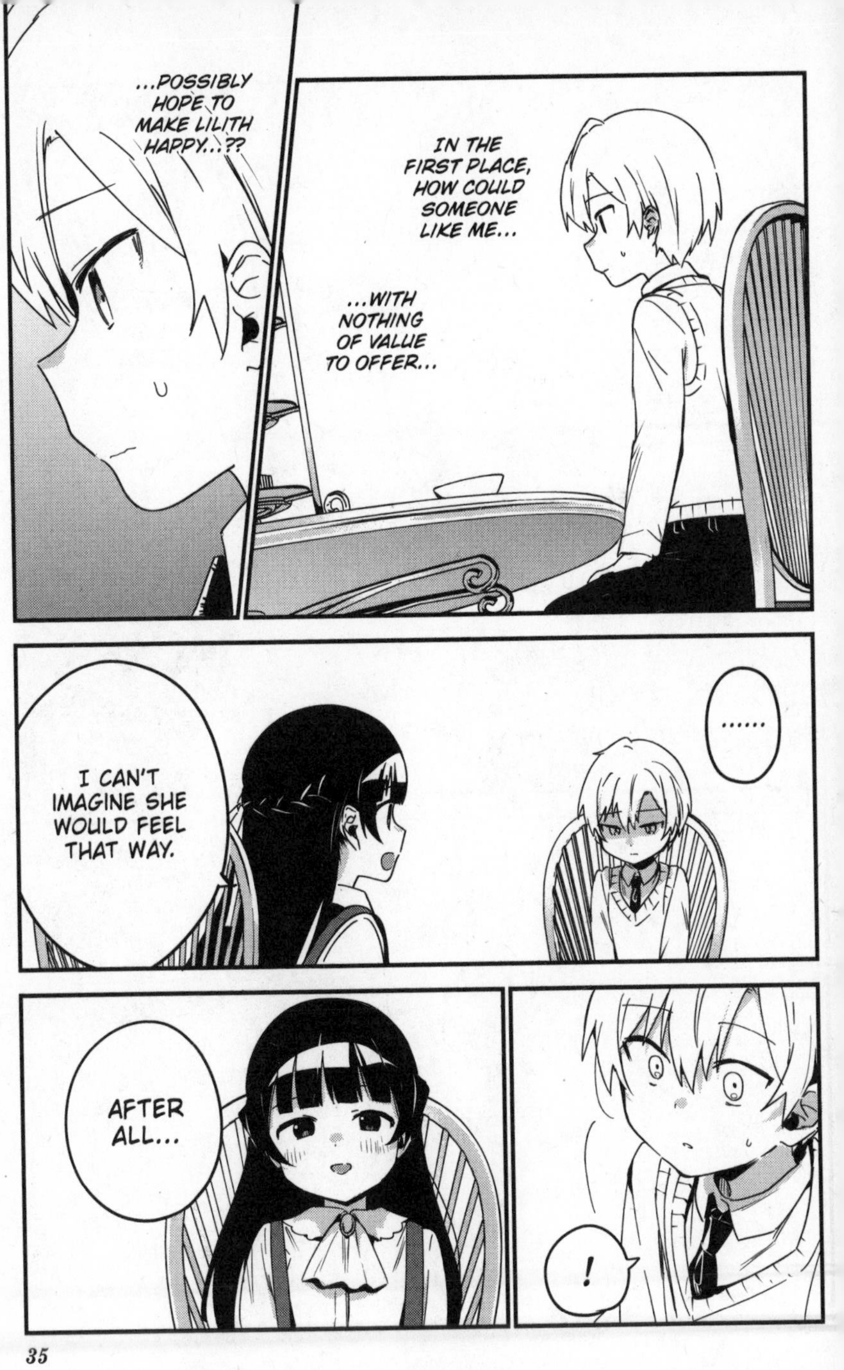
IN THE FIRST PLACE, HOW COULD SOMEONE LIKE ME...
...WITH NOTHING OF VALUE TO OFFER...
...POSSIBLY HOPE TO MAKE LILITH HAPPY...??
......
I CAN'T IMAGINE SHE WOULD FEEL THAT WAY.
!
AFTER ALL...

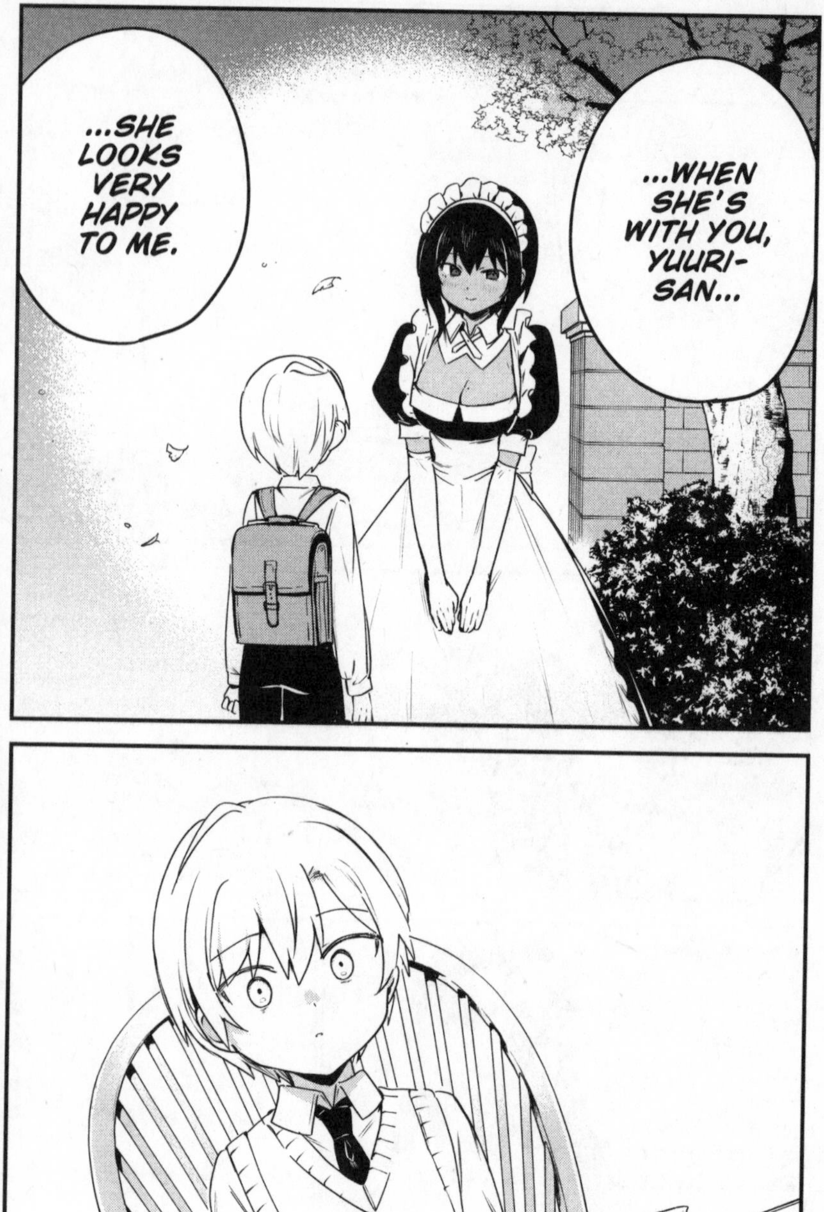
...WHEN SHE'S WITH YOU, YUURI-SAN...
...SHE LOOKS VERY HAPPY TO ME.

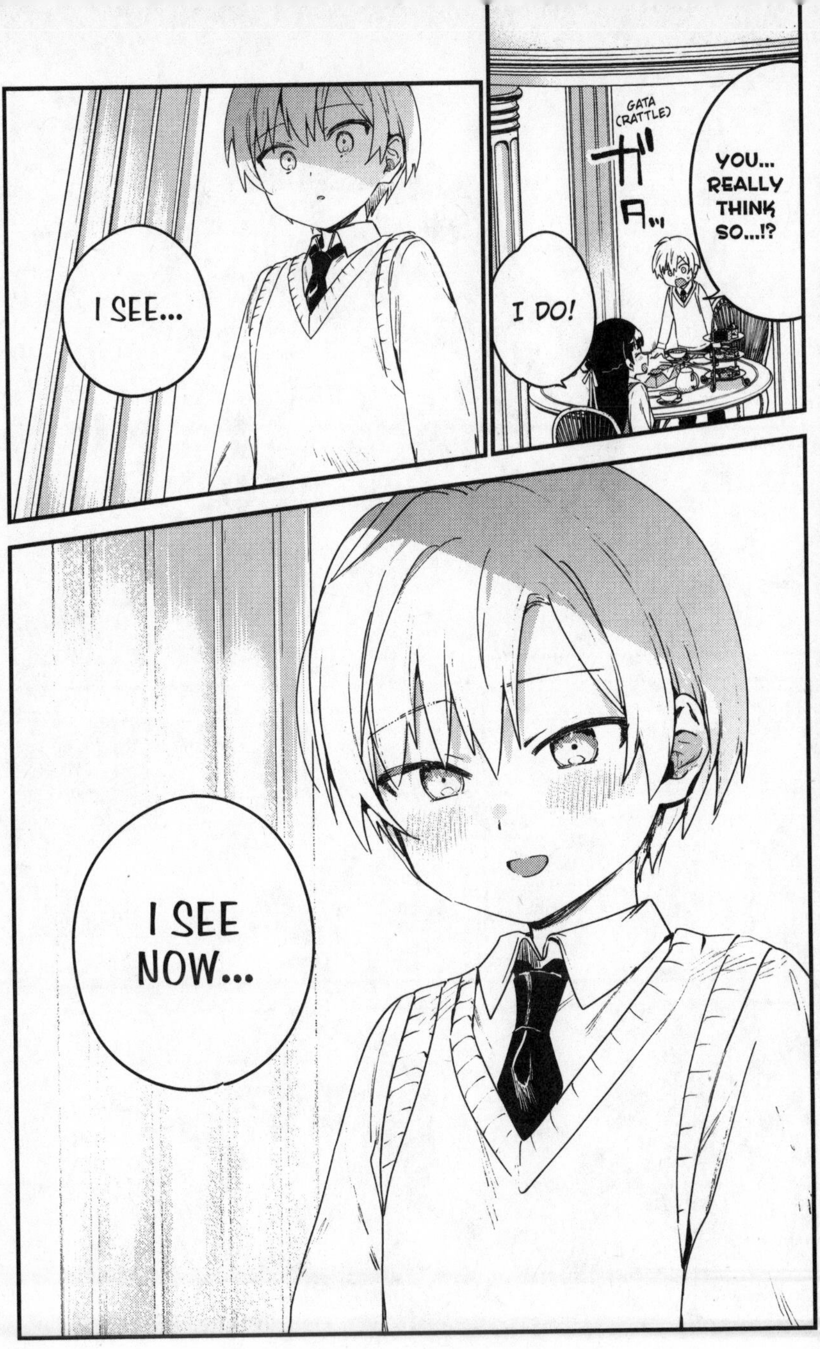
YOU... REALLY THINK SO...!?
GATA (RATTLE)
ガタ…
I DO!
I SEE...
I SEE NOW...

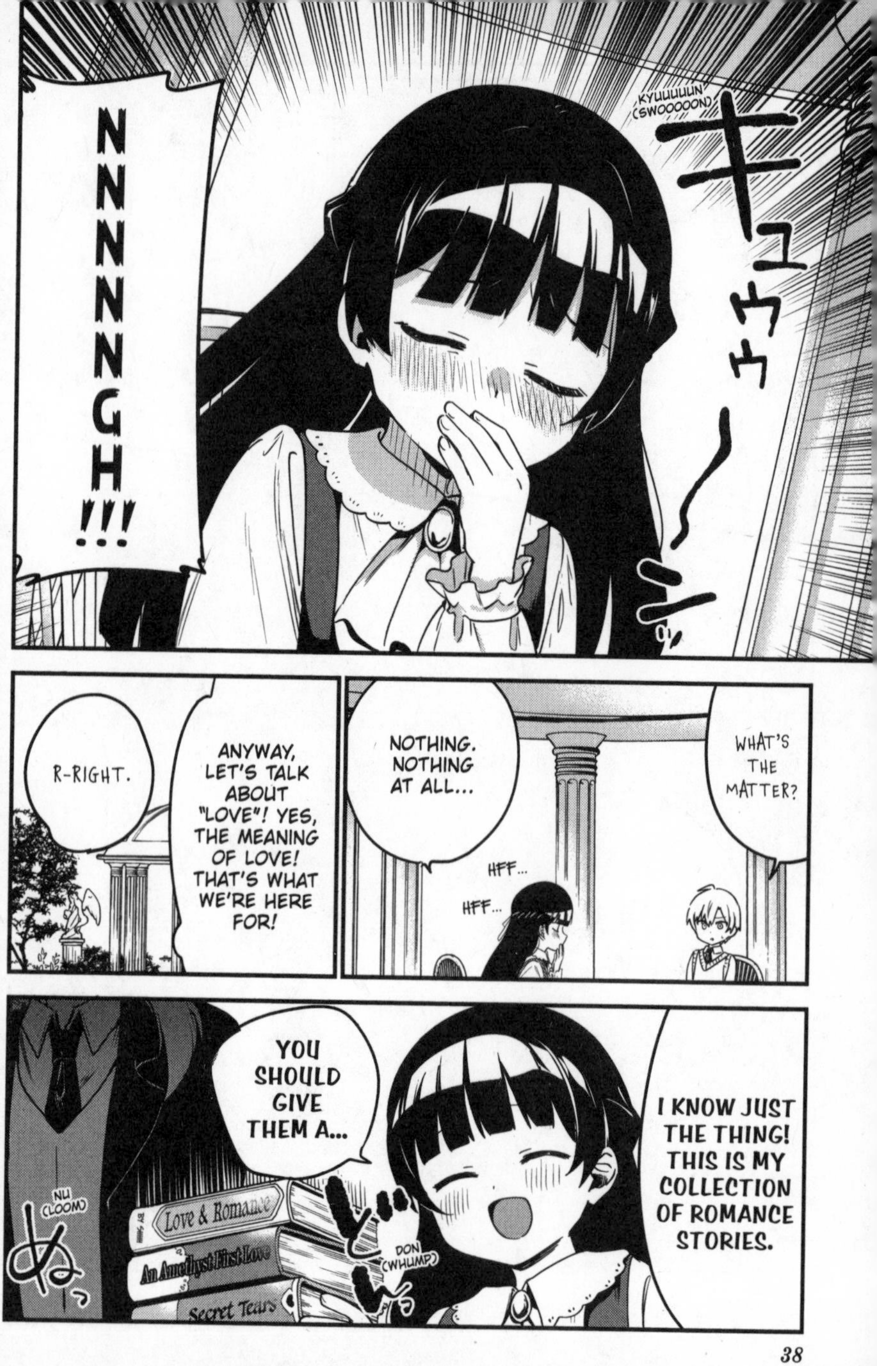
KYUUUUUUN (SWOOOOOON)
キュウ～ン
NNNNNGH!!!
WHAT'S THE MATTER?
NOTHING. NOTHING AT ALL...
HFF...
HFF...
ANYWAY, LET'S TALK ABOUT "LOVE"! YES, THE MEANING OF LOVE! THAT'S WHAT WE'RE HERE FOR!
R-RIGHT.
I KNOW JUST THE THING! THIS IS MY COLLECTION OF ROMANCE STORIES.
DON (WHUMP)
Love & Romance
An Amethyst First Love
Secret Tears
YOU SHOULD GIVE THEM A...
NU (LOOM)

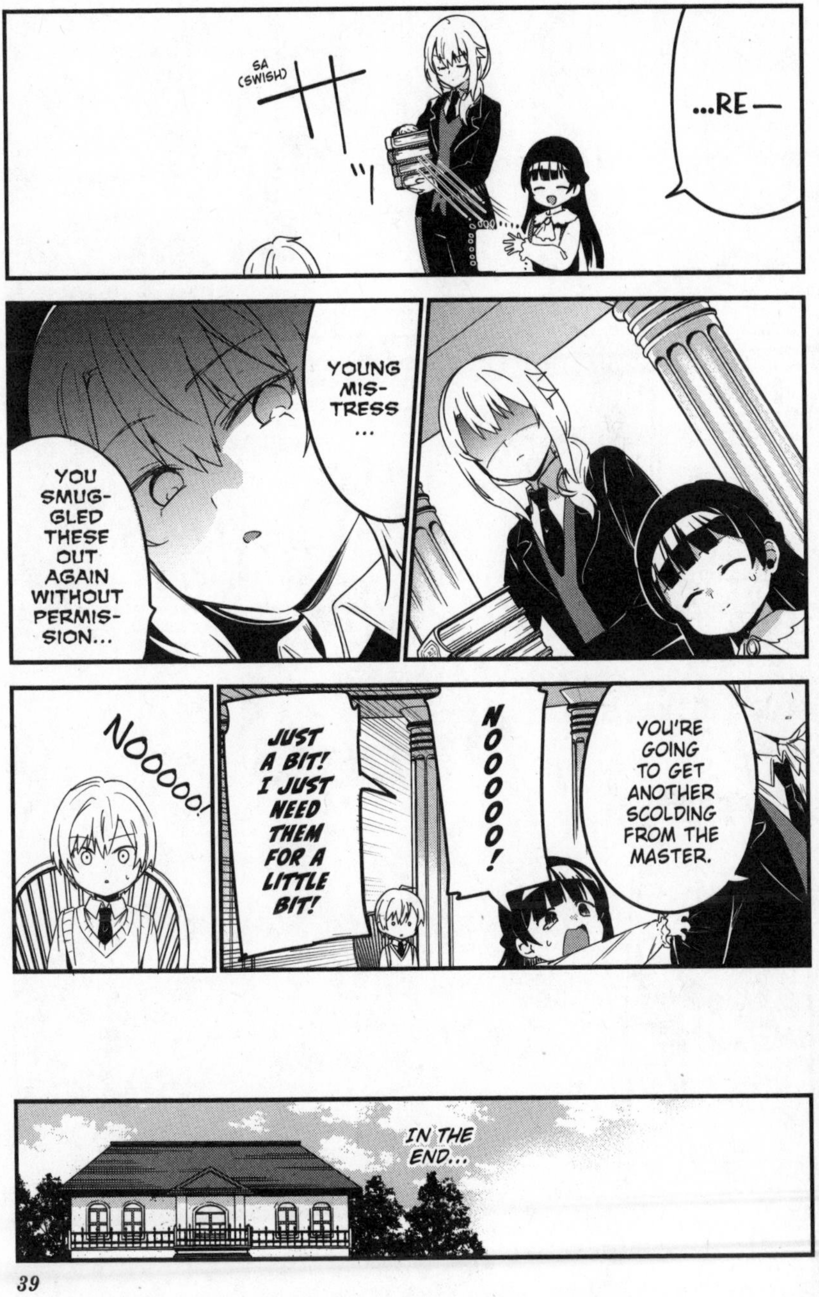
...RE—
SA (SWISH)
YOUNG MISTRESS...
YOU SMUGGLED THESE OUT AGAIN WITHOUT PERMISSION...
YOU'RE GOING TO GET ANOTHER SCOLDING FROM THE MASTER.
NOOOOOO!
JUST A BIT! I JUST NEED THEM FOR A LITTLE BIT!
NOOOOOO!
IN THE END...

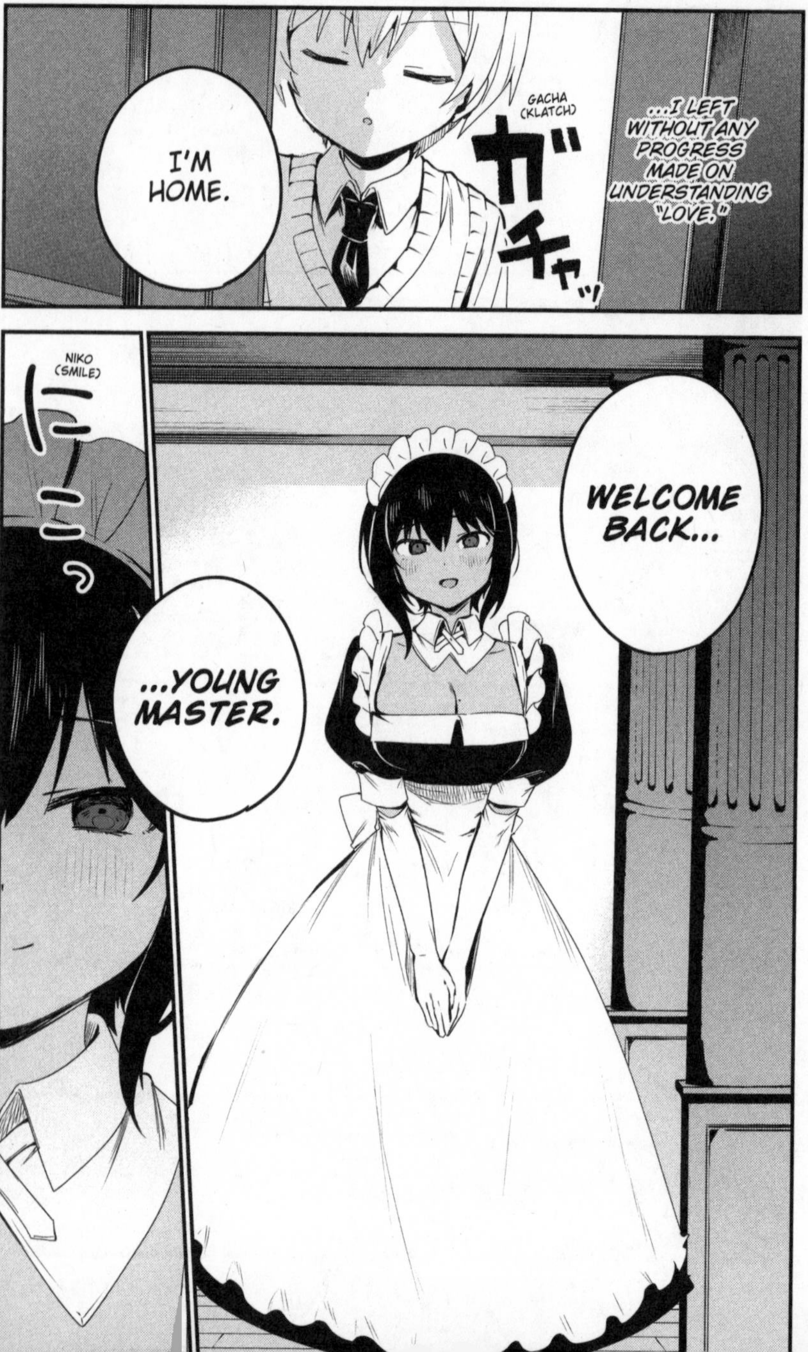
...I LEFT WITHOUT ANY PROGRESS MADE ON UNDERSTANDING "LOVE."
GACHA (KLATCH)
I'M HOME.
WELCOME BACK...
NIKO (SMILE)
...YOUNG MASTER.

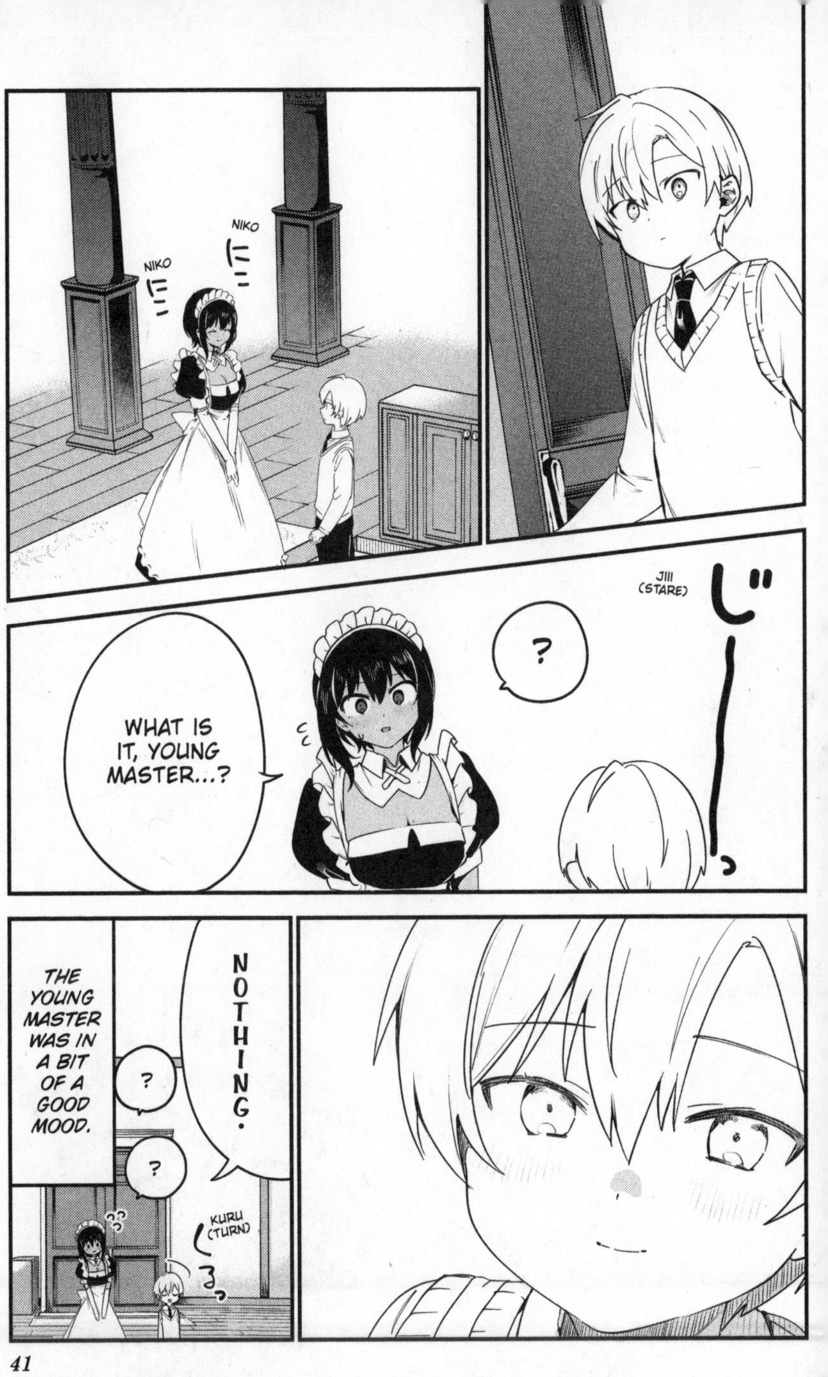
NIKO
NIKO
JIII (STARE)
?
WHAT IS IT, YOUNG MASTER...?
NOTHING.
?
THE YOUNG MASTER WAS IN A BIT OF A GOOD MOOD.
?
KURU (TURN)

The Maid I Hired Recently Is Mysterious

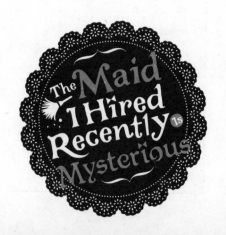

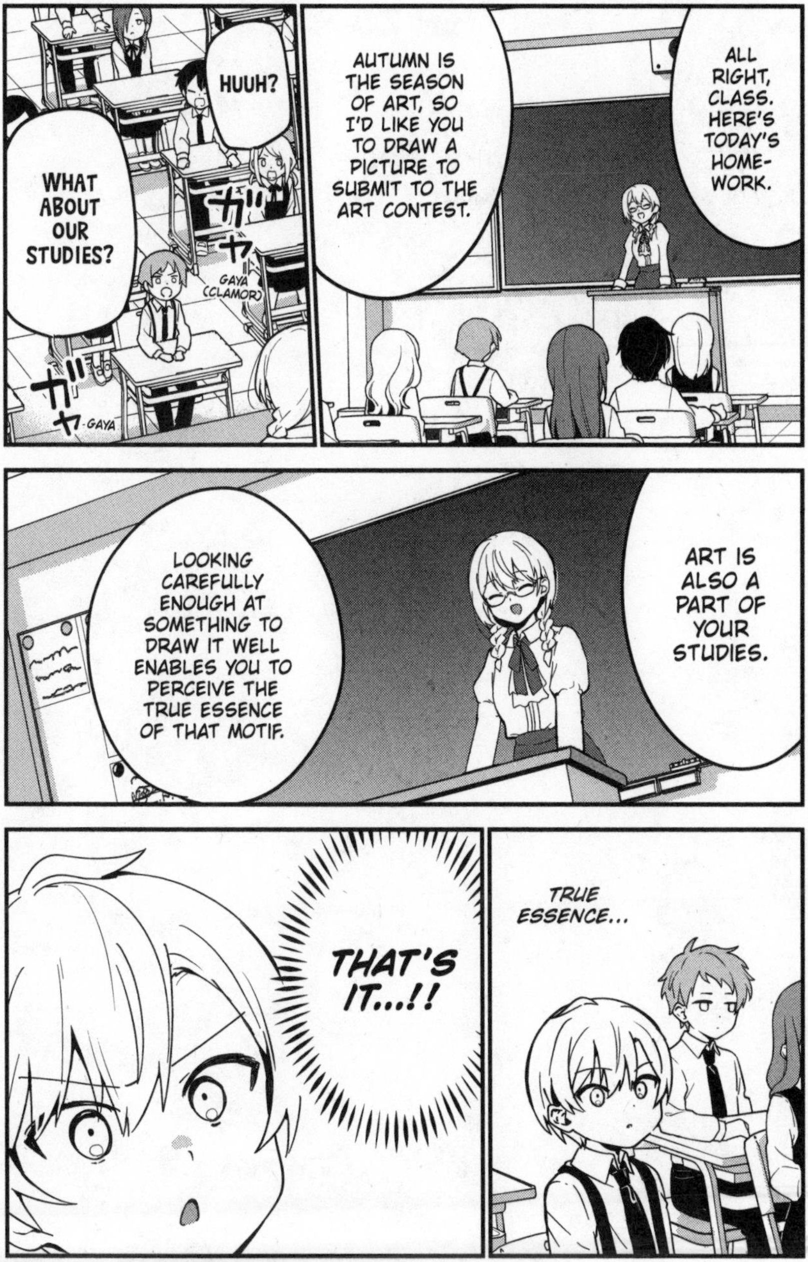
ALL RIGHT, CLASS. HERE'S TODAY'S HOMEWORK.
AUTUMN IS THE SEASON OF ART, SO I'D LIKE YOU TO DRAW A PICTURE TO SUBMIT TO THE ART CONTEST.
HUUH?
ガヤ
GAYA (CLAMOR)
WHAT ABOUT OUR STUDIES?
ガヤ -GAYA
ART IS ALSO A PART OF YOUR STUDIES.
LOOKING CAREFULLY ENOUGH AT SOMETHING TO DRAW IT WELL ENABLES YOU TO PERCEIVE THE TRUE ESSENCE OF THAT MOTIF.
TRUE ESSENCE...
THAT'S IT...!!

# CHAPTER 38

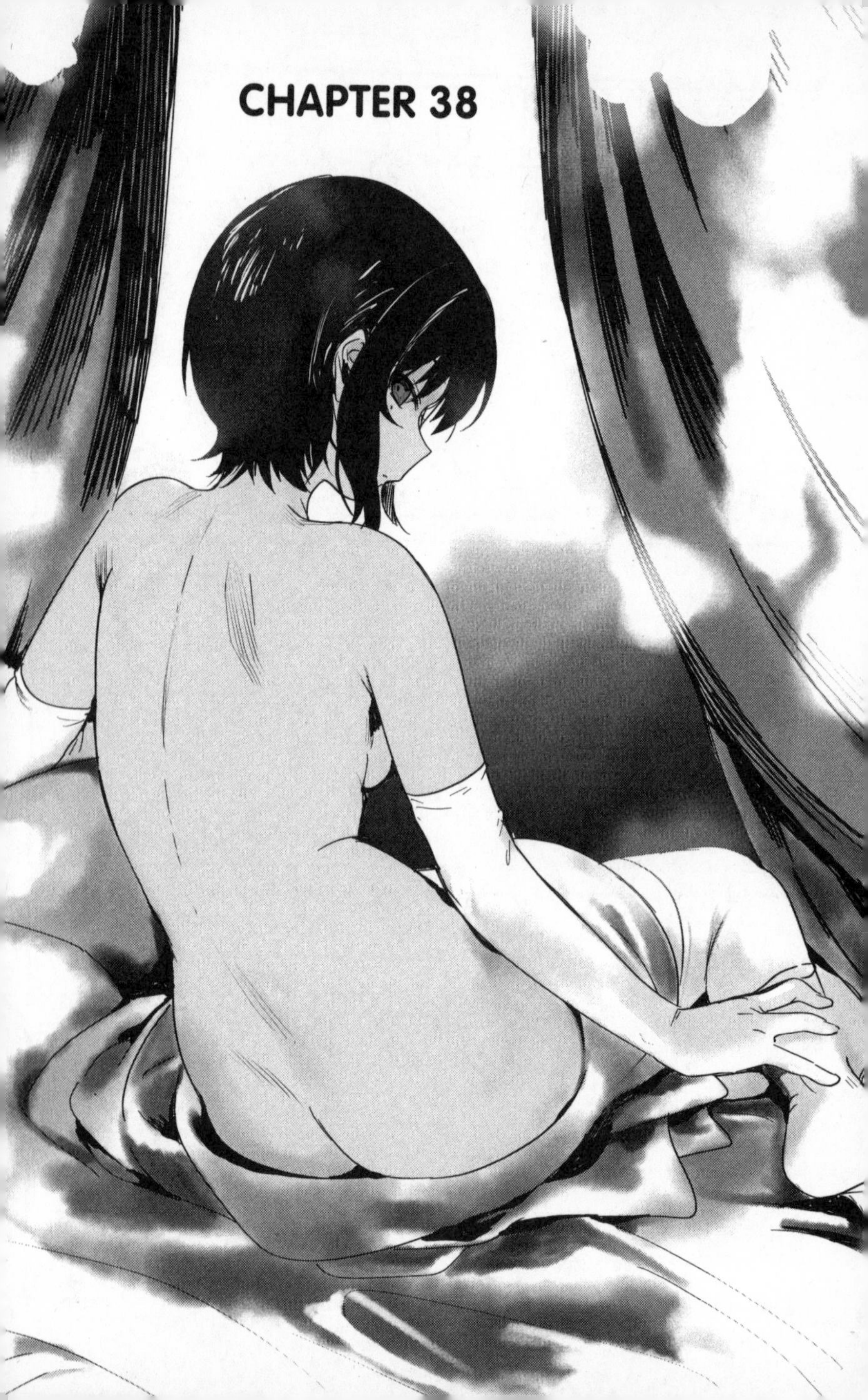

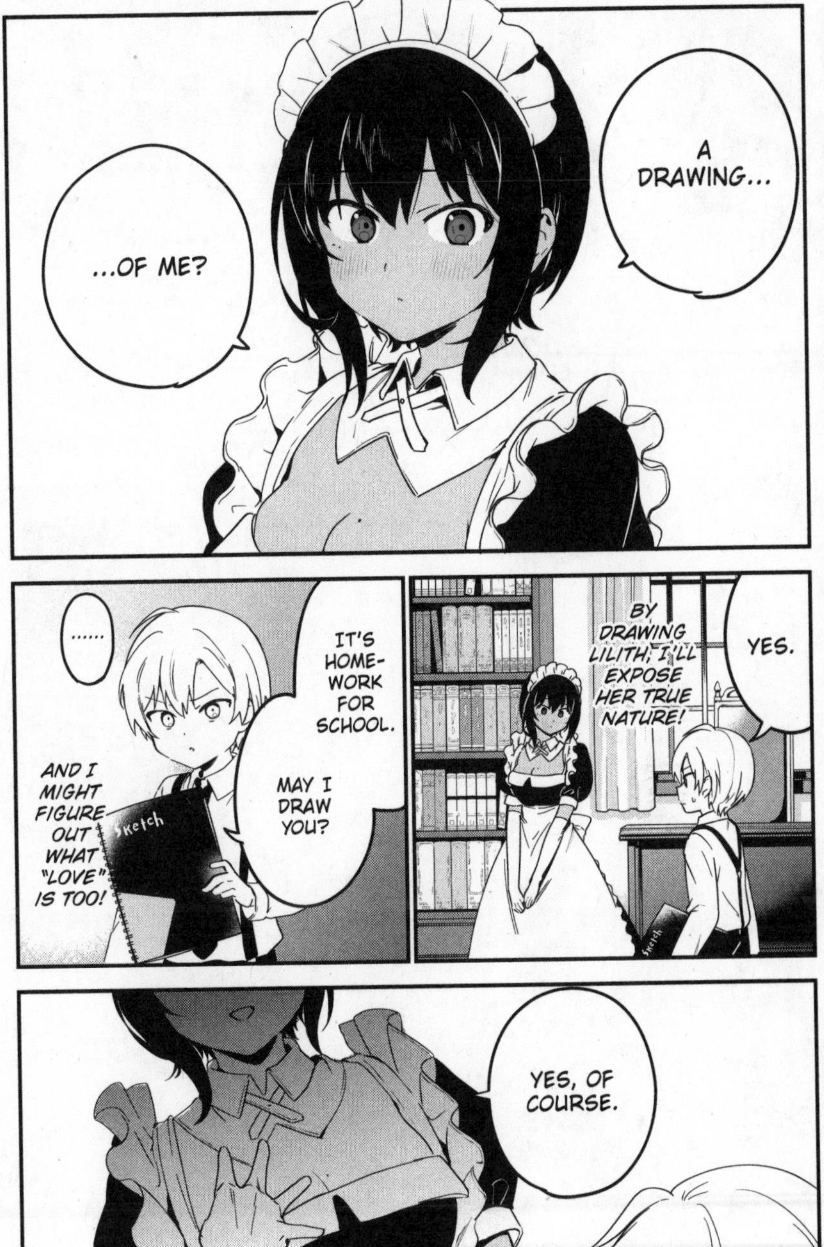
A DRAWING...
...OF ME?
YES.
BY DRAWING LILITH, I'LL EXPOSE HER TRUE NATURE!
IT'S HOME-WORK FOR SCHOOL.
MAY I DRAW YOU?
......
AND I MIGHT FIGURE OUT WHAT "LOVE" IS TOO!
Sketch
Sketch
YES, OF COURSE.

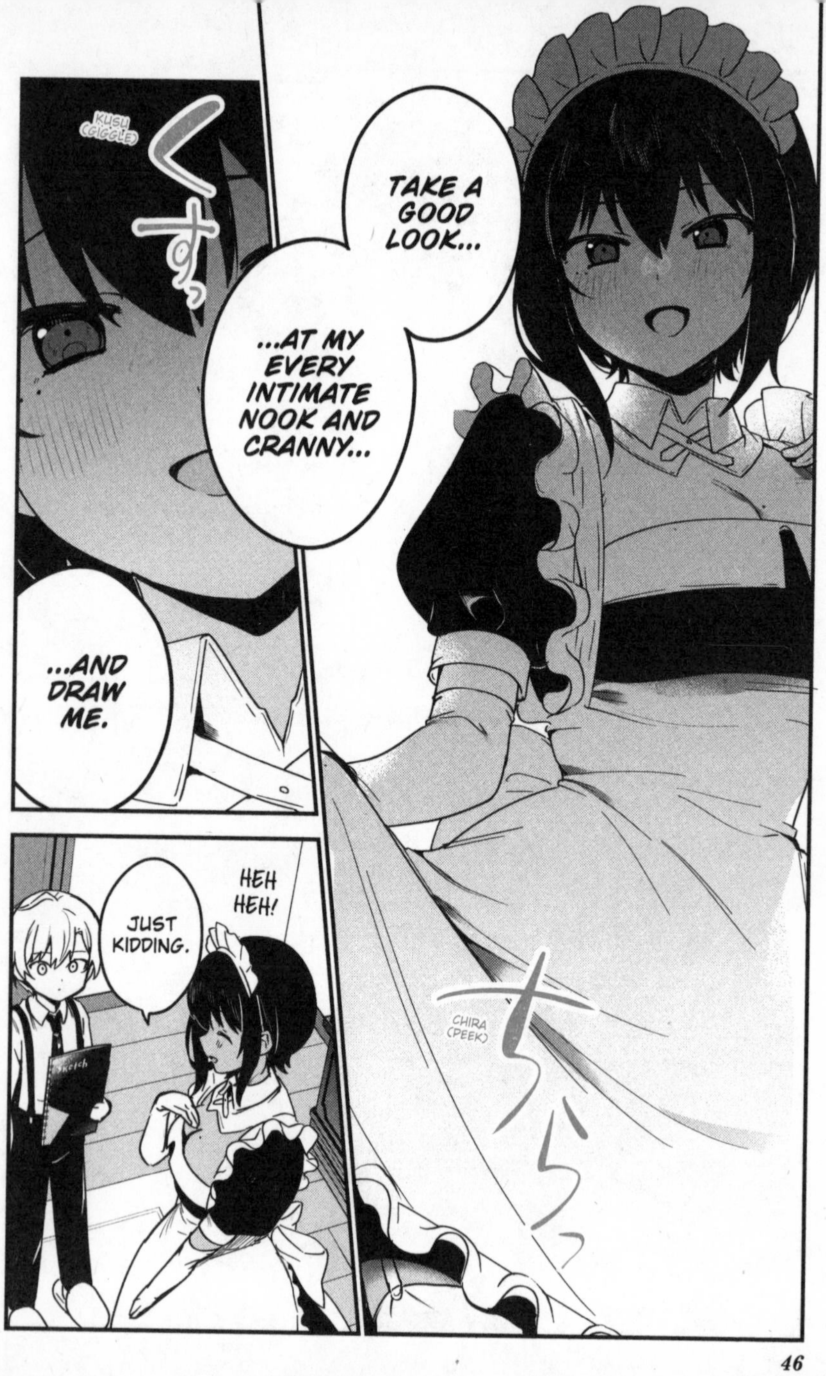
TAKE A GOOD LOOK...
...AT MY EVERY INTIMATE NOOK AND CRANNY...
CHIRA (PEEK)
KUSU (GIGGLE)
...AND DRAW ME.
HEH HEH!
JUST KIDDING.
Sketch

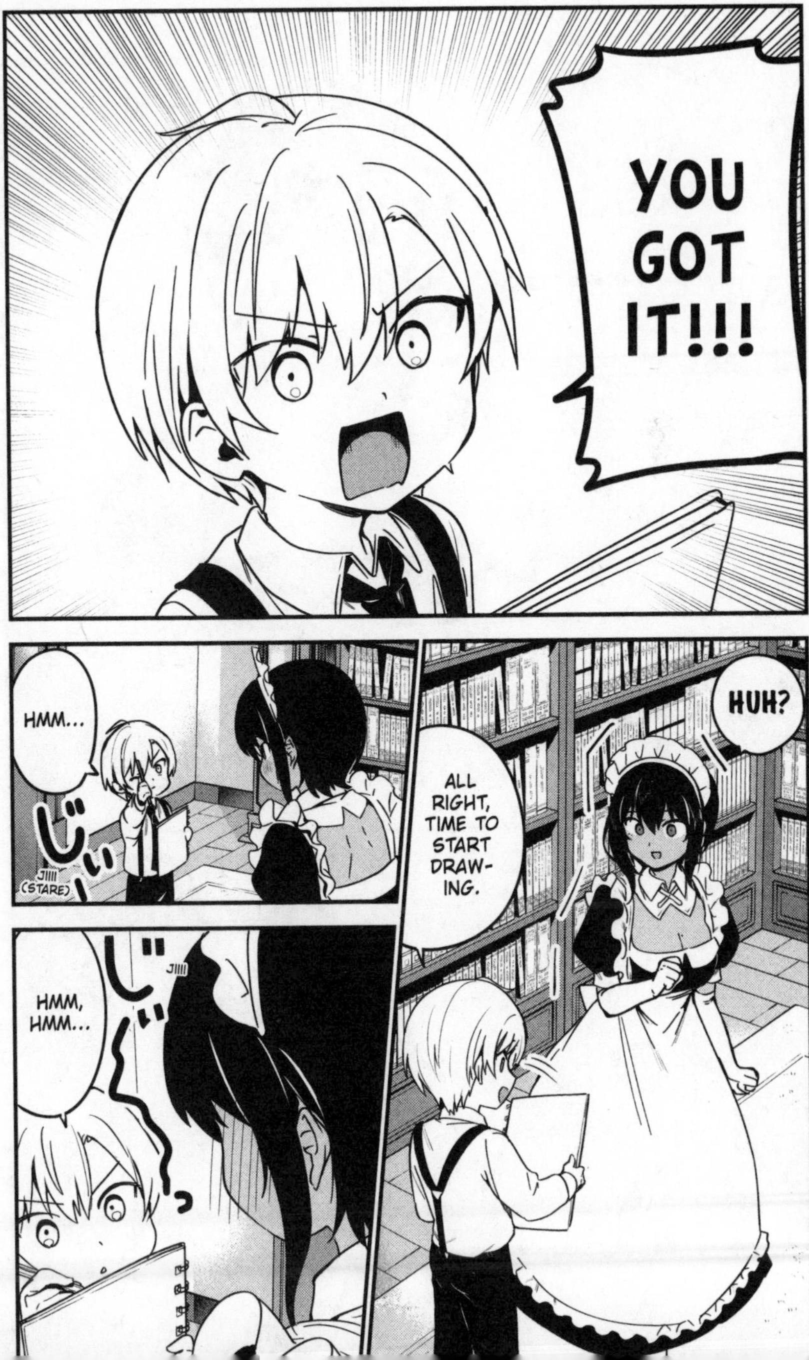

YOU GOT IT!!!
HUH?
ALL RIGHT, TIME TO START DRAWING.
HMM...
じぃ
JIIII (STARE)
HMM, HMM...
じぃ
JIIII

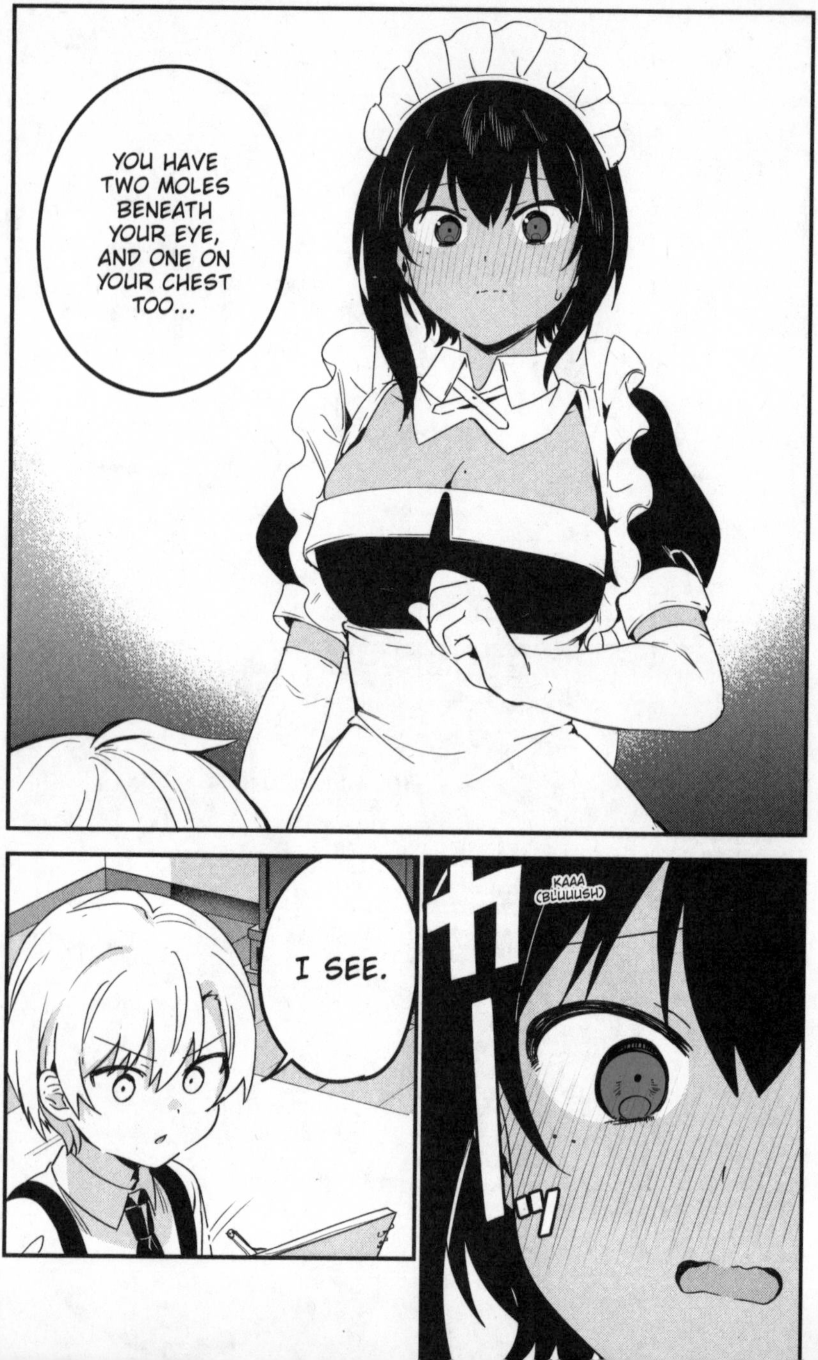
YOU HAVE TWO MOLES BENEATH YOUR EYE, AND ONE ON YOUR CHEST TOO...
KAAA (BLUUUUSH)
I SEE.

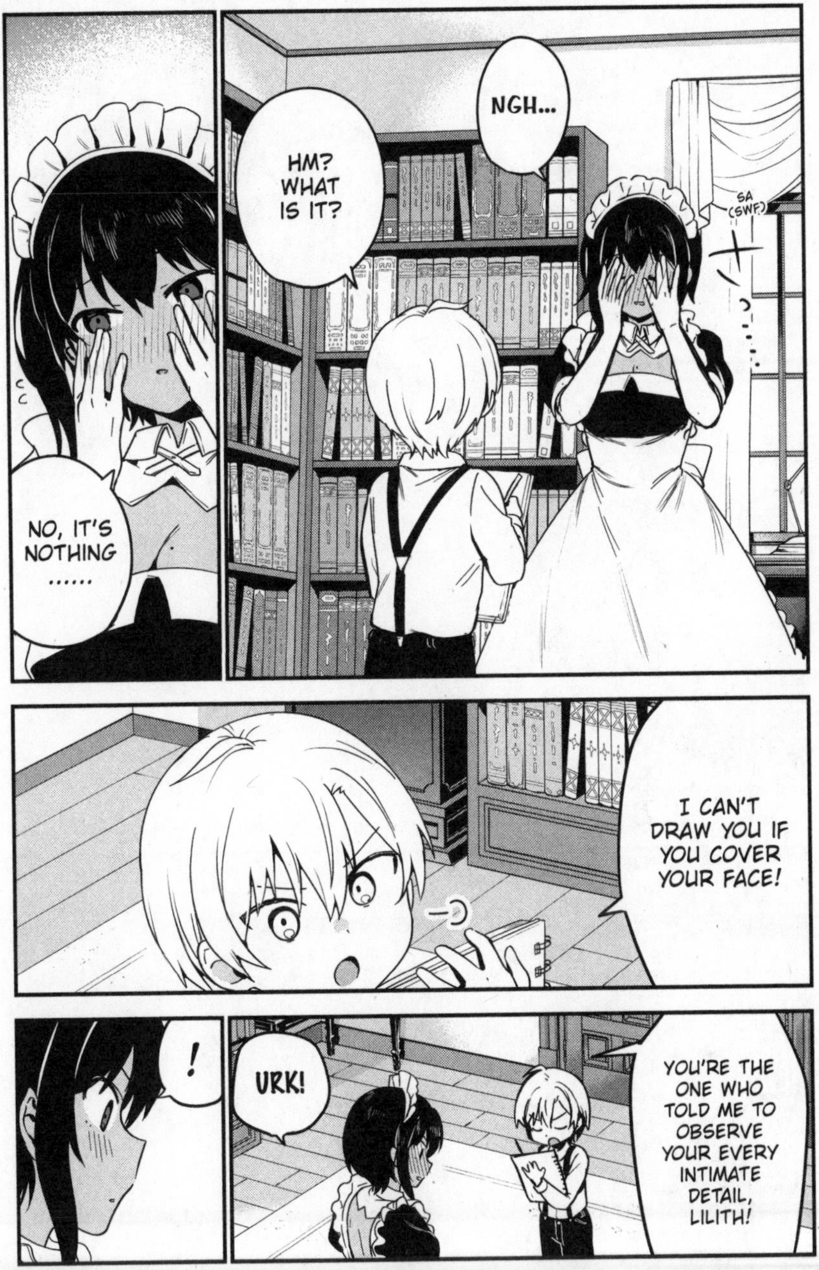
NGH...
SA (SWF)
HM? WHAT IS IT?
NO, IT'S NOTHING ......
I CAN'T DRAW YOU IF YOU COVER YOUR FACE!
YOU'RE THE ONE WHO TOLD ME TO OBSERVE YOUR EVERY INTIMATE DETAIL, LILITH!
URK!
!

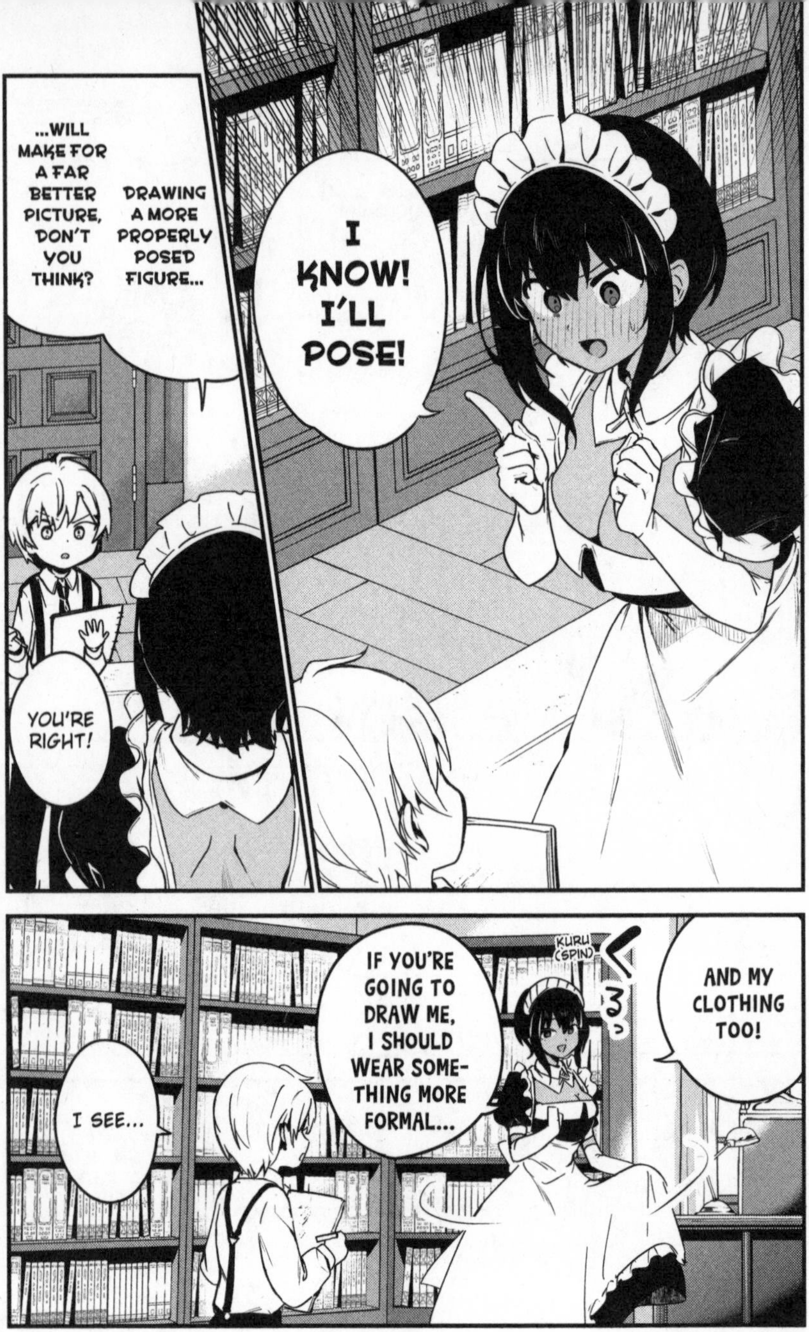
I KNOW! I'LL POSE!
DRAWING A MORE PROPERLY POSED FIGURE...
...WILL MAKE FOR A FAR BETTER PICTURE, DON'T YOU THINK?
YOU'RE RIGHT!
AND MY CLOTHING TOO!
KURU (SPIN)
IF YOU'RE GOING TO DRAW ME, I SHOULD WEAR SOME-THING MORE FORMAL...
I SEE...

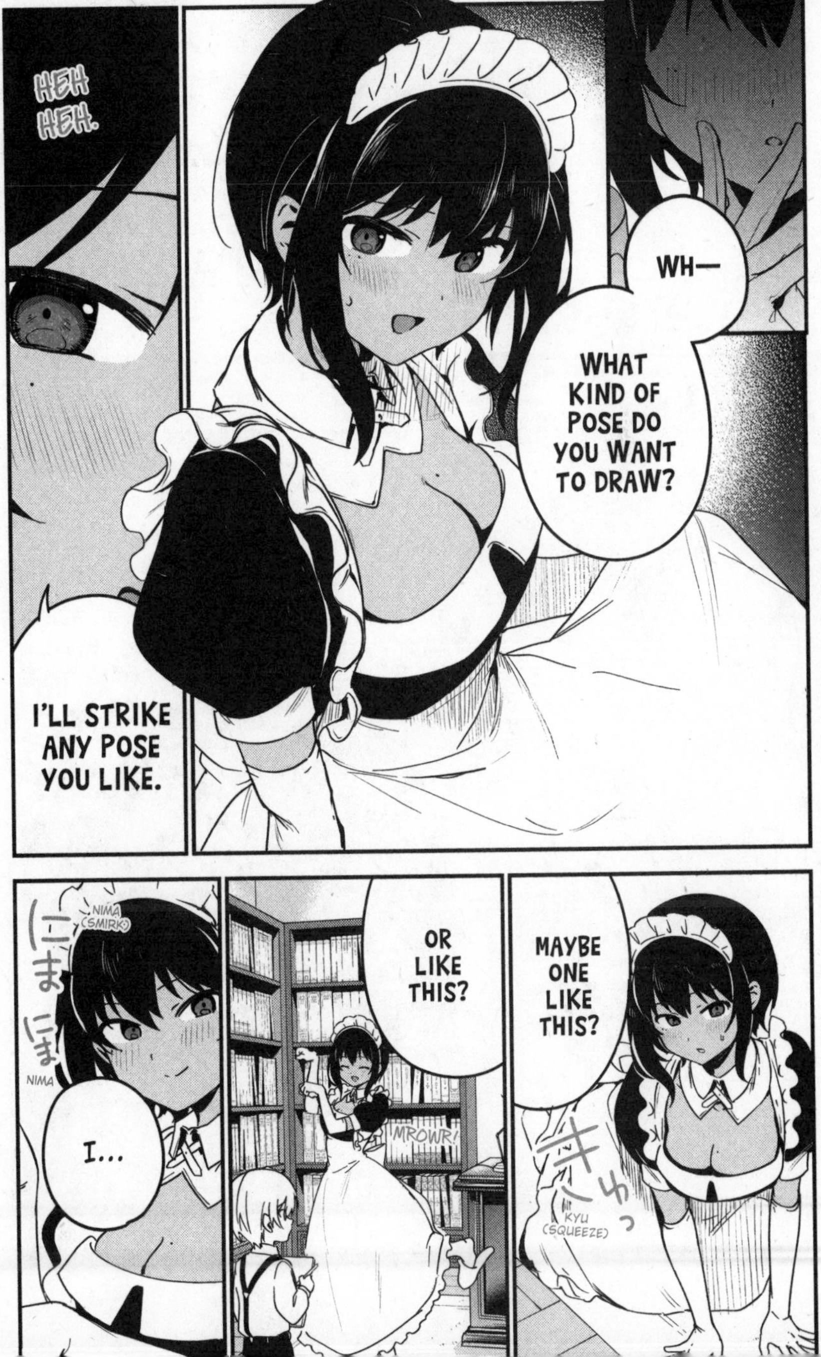
WH—
WHAT KIND OF POSE DO YOU WANT TO DRAW?
HEH HEH.
I'LL STRIKE ANY POSE YOU LIKE.
MAYBE ONE LIKE THIS?
キュッ
KYU (SQUEEZE)
OR LIKE THIS?
MROWR!
にまにま
NIMA (SMIRK)
NIMA
I...

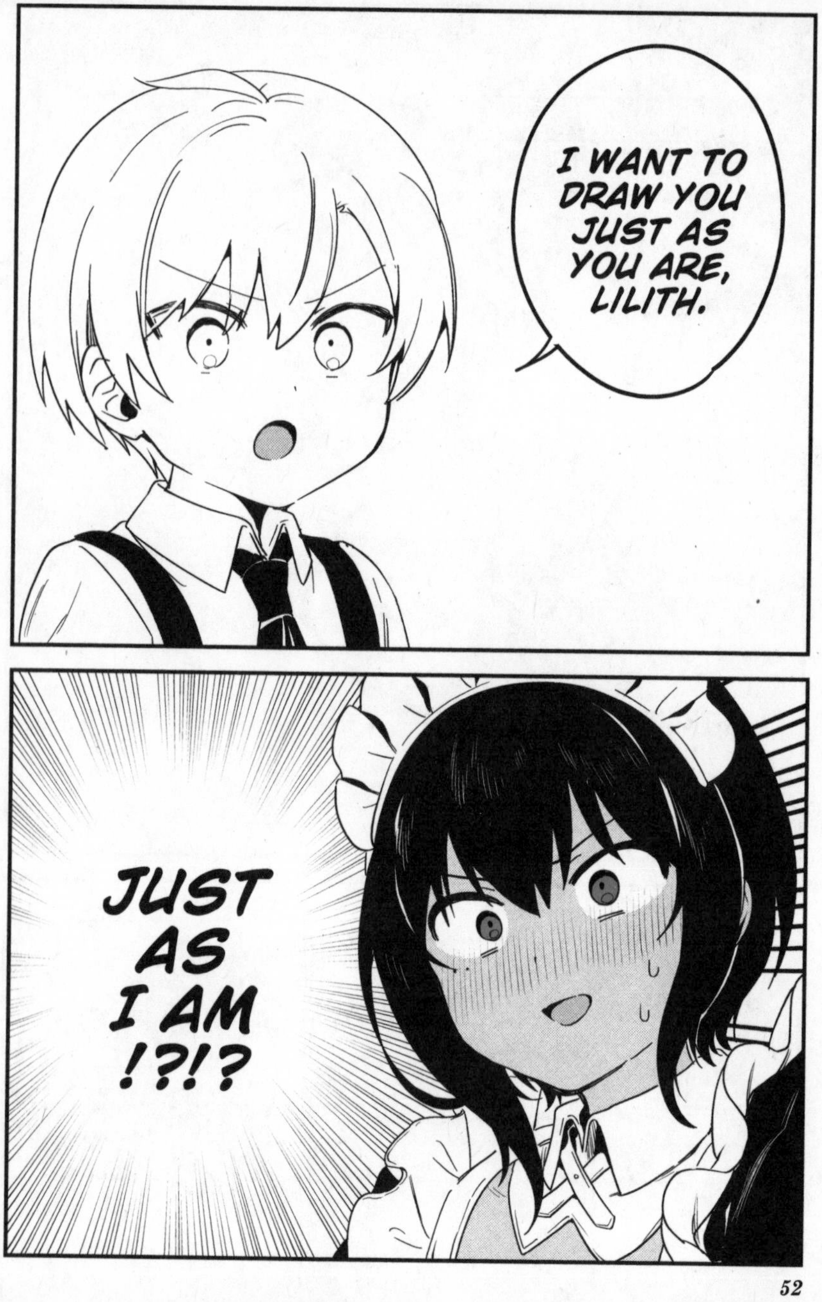
I WANT TO DRAW YOU JUST AS YOU ARE, LILITH.
JUST AS I AM !?!?

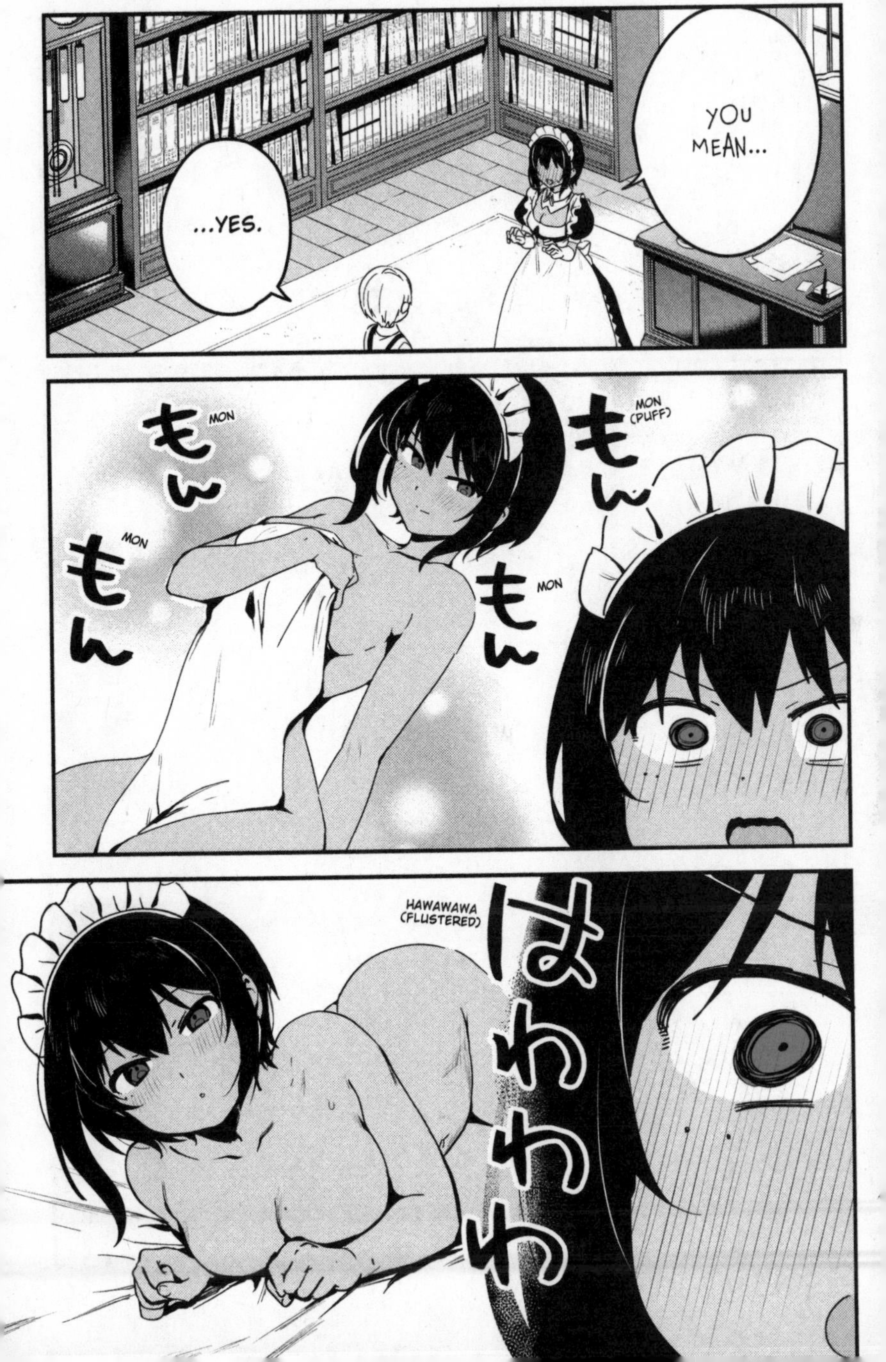
YOU MEAN...
...YES.
もん
MON (PUFF)
もん
MON
もん
MON
もん
MON
はわわわ
HAWAWAWA (FLUSTERED)

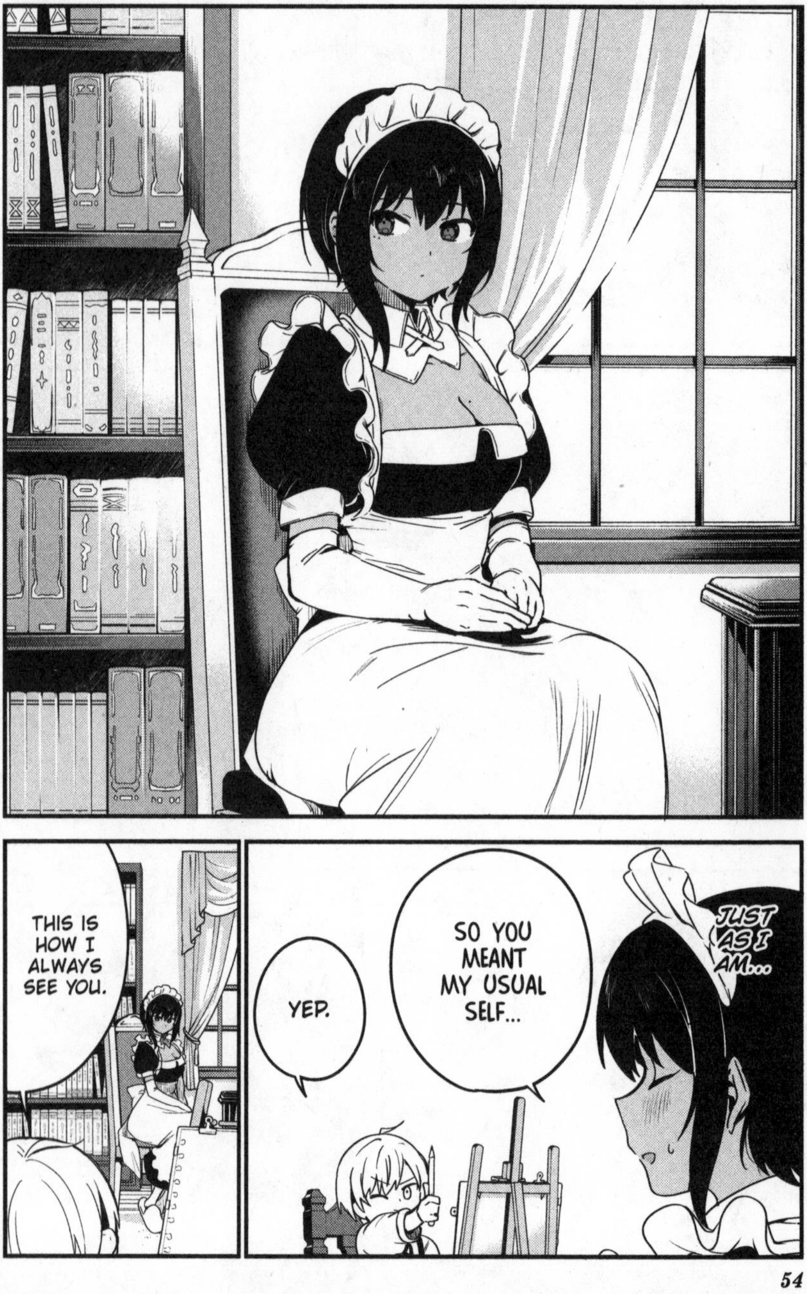
JUST AS I AM...
SO YOU MEANT MY USUAL SELF...
YEP.
THIS IS HOW I ALWAYS SEE YOU.

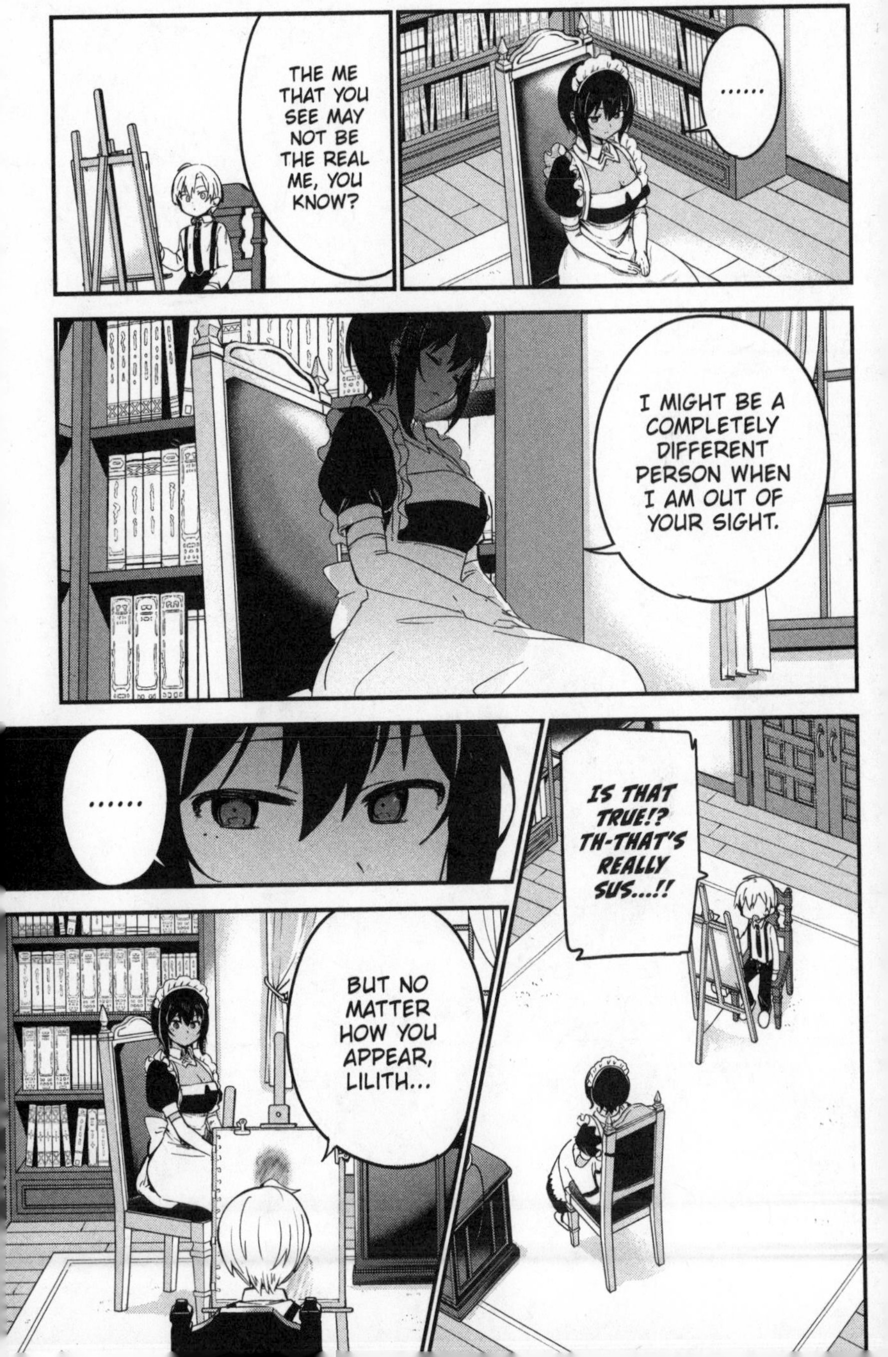
......
THE ME THAT YOU SEE MAY NOT BE THE REAL ME, YOU KNOW?
I MIGHT BE A COMPLETELY DIFFERENT PERSON WHEN I AM OUT OF YOUR SIGHT.
IS THAT TRUE!? TH-THAT'S REALLY SUS...!!
......
BUT NO MATTER HOW YOU APPEAR, LILITH...

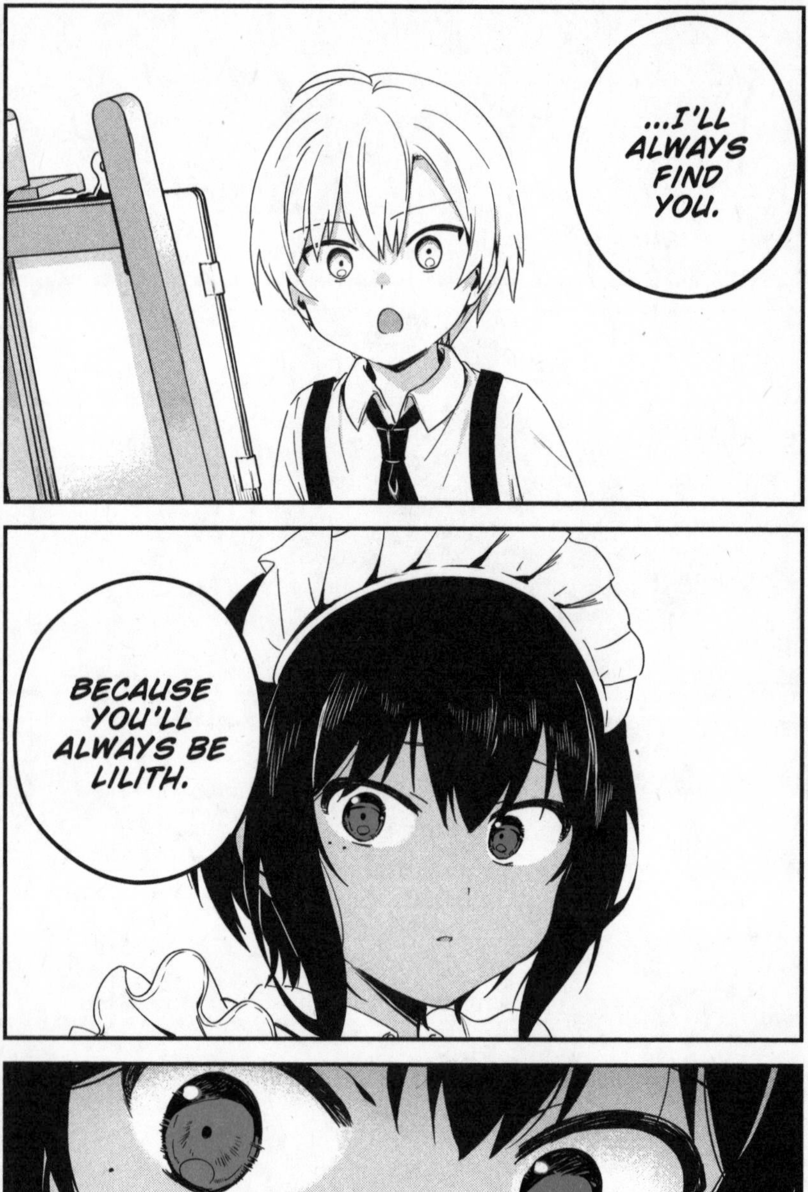
...I'LL ALWAYS FIND YOU.
BECAUSE YOU'LL ALWAYS BE LILITH.

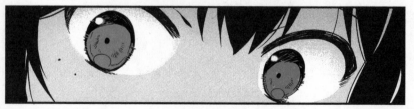

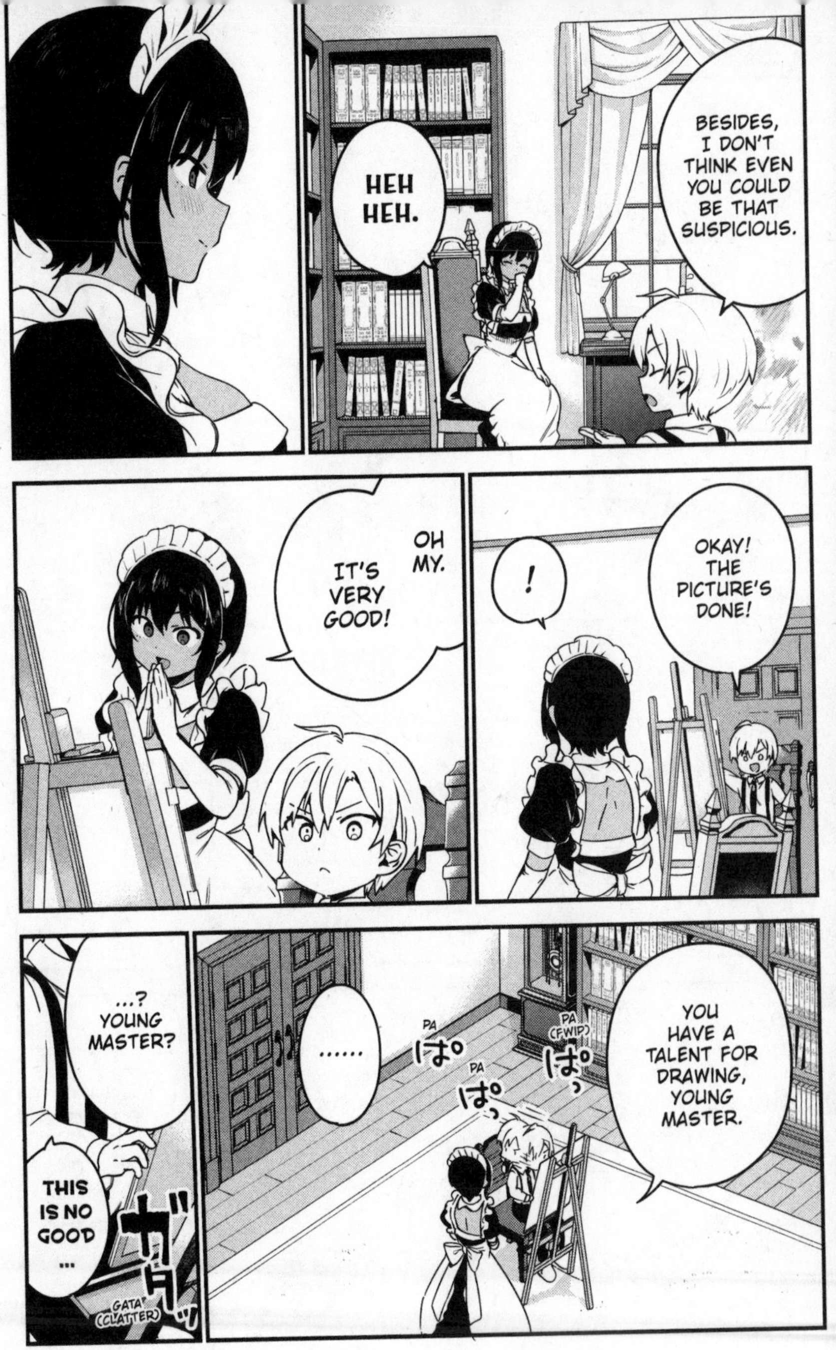
BESIDES, I DON'T THINK EVEN YOU COULD BE THAT SUSPICIOUS.
HEH HEH.
OKAY! THE PICTURE'S DONE!
!
OH MY.
IT'S VERY GOOD!
YOU HAVE A TALENT FOR DRAWING, YOUNG MASTER.
PA (FWIP) ぱっ
PA ぱっ
PA ぱっ
......
...? YOUNG MASTER?
THIS IS NO GOOD ...
GATA (CLATTER) ガタッ

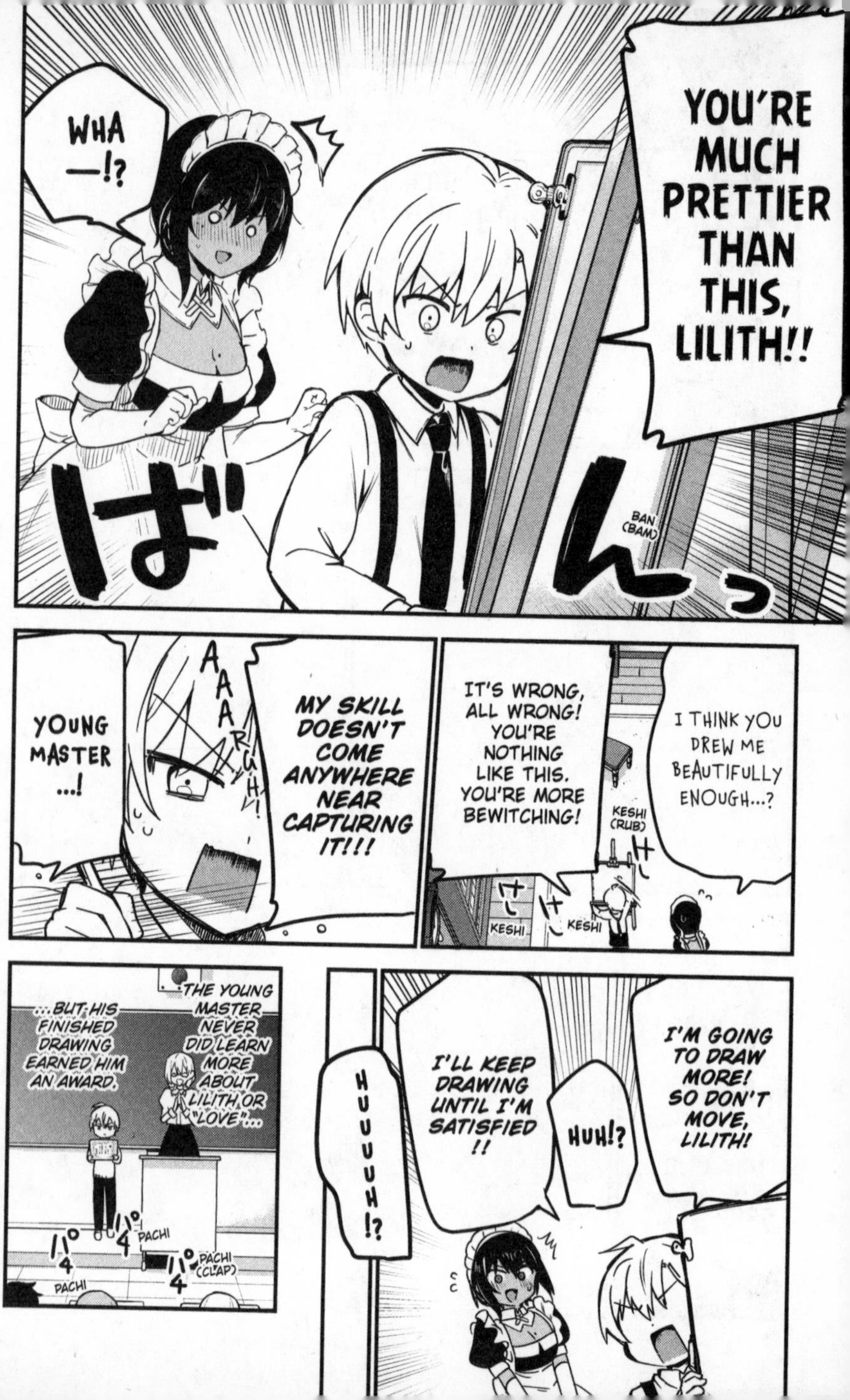
YOU'RE MUCH PRETTIER THAN THIS, LILITH!!
WHA—!?
BAN (BAM)
I THINK YOU DREW ME BEAUTIFULLY ENOUGH...?
IT'S WRONG, ALL WRONG! YOU'RE NOTHING LIKE THIS. YOU'RE MORE BEWITCHING!
KESHI (RUB)
KESHI
KESHI
MY SKILL DOESN'T COME ANYWHERE NEAR CAPTURING IT!!!
AAARGH!
YOUNG MASTER...!
I'M GOING TO DRAW MORE! SO DON'T MOVE, LILITH!
HUH!?
I'LL KEEP DRAWING UNTIL I'M SATISFIED!!
HUUUUH!?
THE YOUNG MASTER NEVER DID LEARN MORE ABOUT LILITH OR "LOVE"...
...BUT HIS FINISHED DRAWING EARNED HIM AN AWARD.
PACHI
PACHI (CLAP)
PACHI

The Maid I Hired Recently Is Mysterious

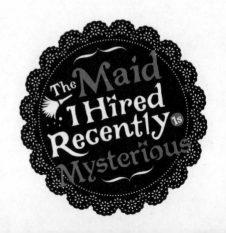

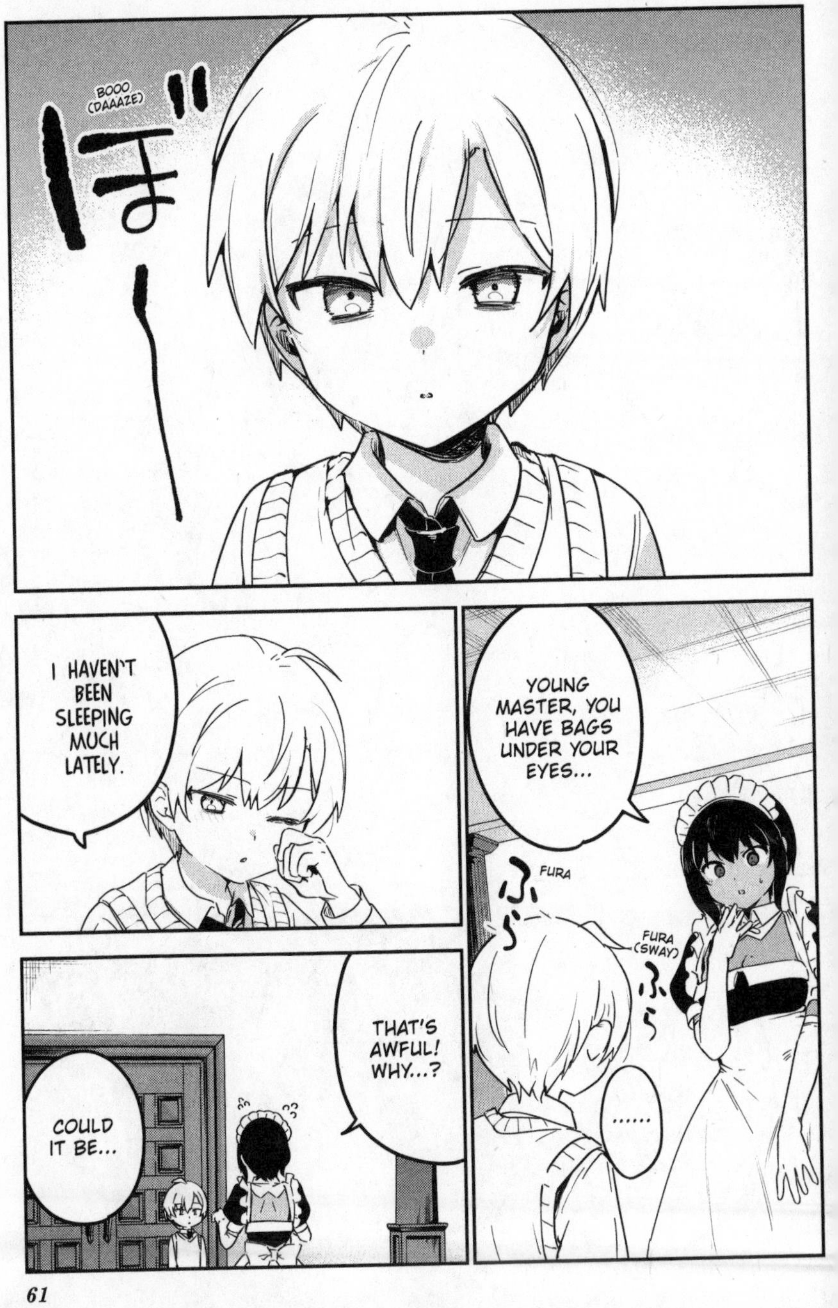
BOOO (DAAAZE)
ぼー
YOUNG MASTER, YOU HAVE BAGS UNDER YOUR EYES...
FURA
ふら
FURA (SWAY)
ふら
......
I HAVEN'T BEEN SLEEPING MUCH LATELY.
THAT'S AWFUL! WHY...?
COULD IT BE...

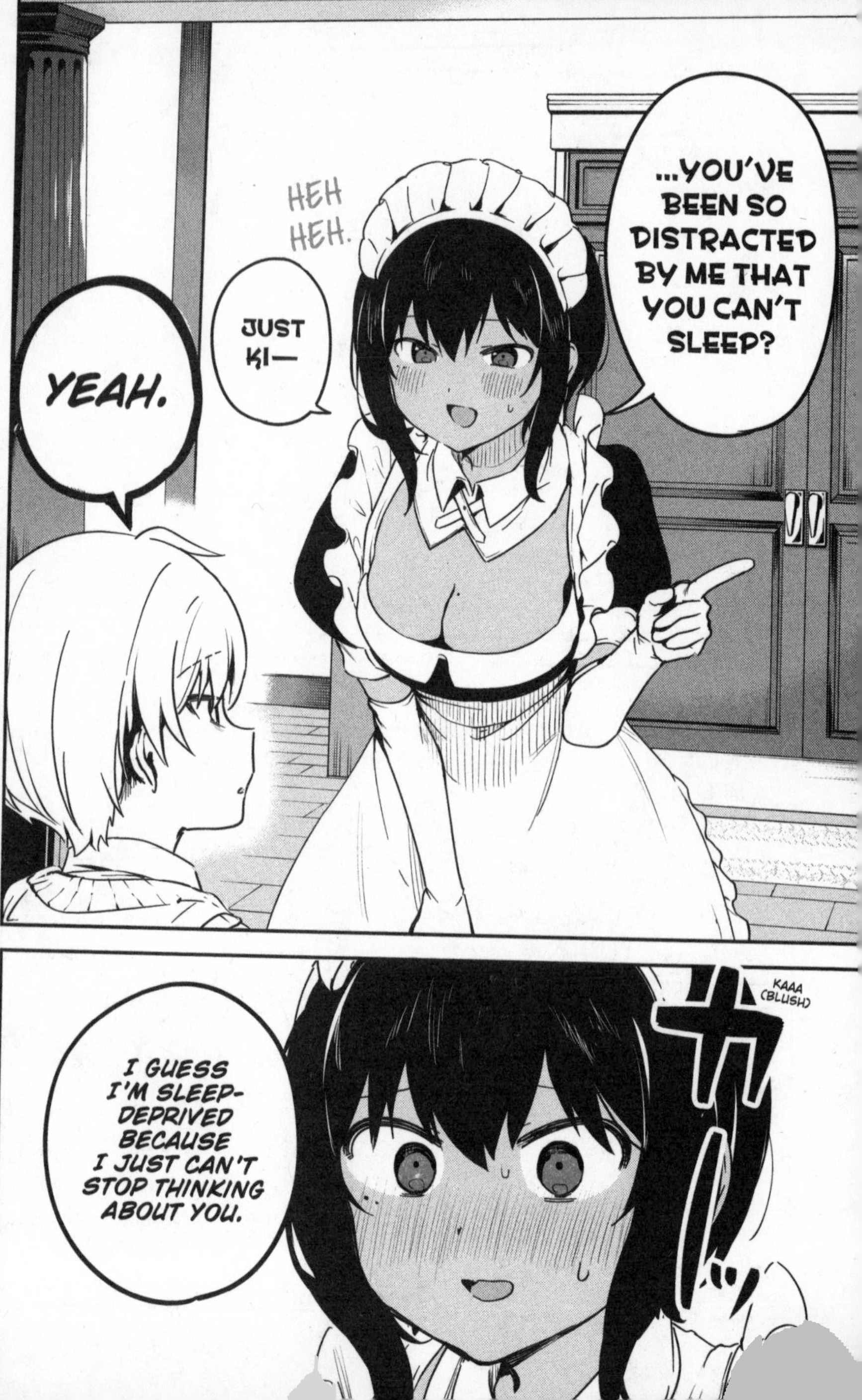
...YOU'VE BEEN SO DISTRACTED BY ME THAT YOU CAN'T SLEEP?
HEH HEH.
JUST KI—
YEAH.
KAAA (BLUSH)
I GUESS I'M SLEEP-DEPRIVED BECAUSE I JUST CAN'T STOP THINKING ABOUT YOU.

# CHAPTER 39

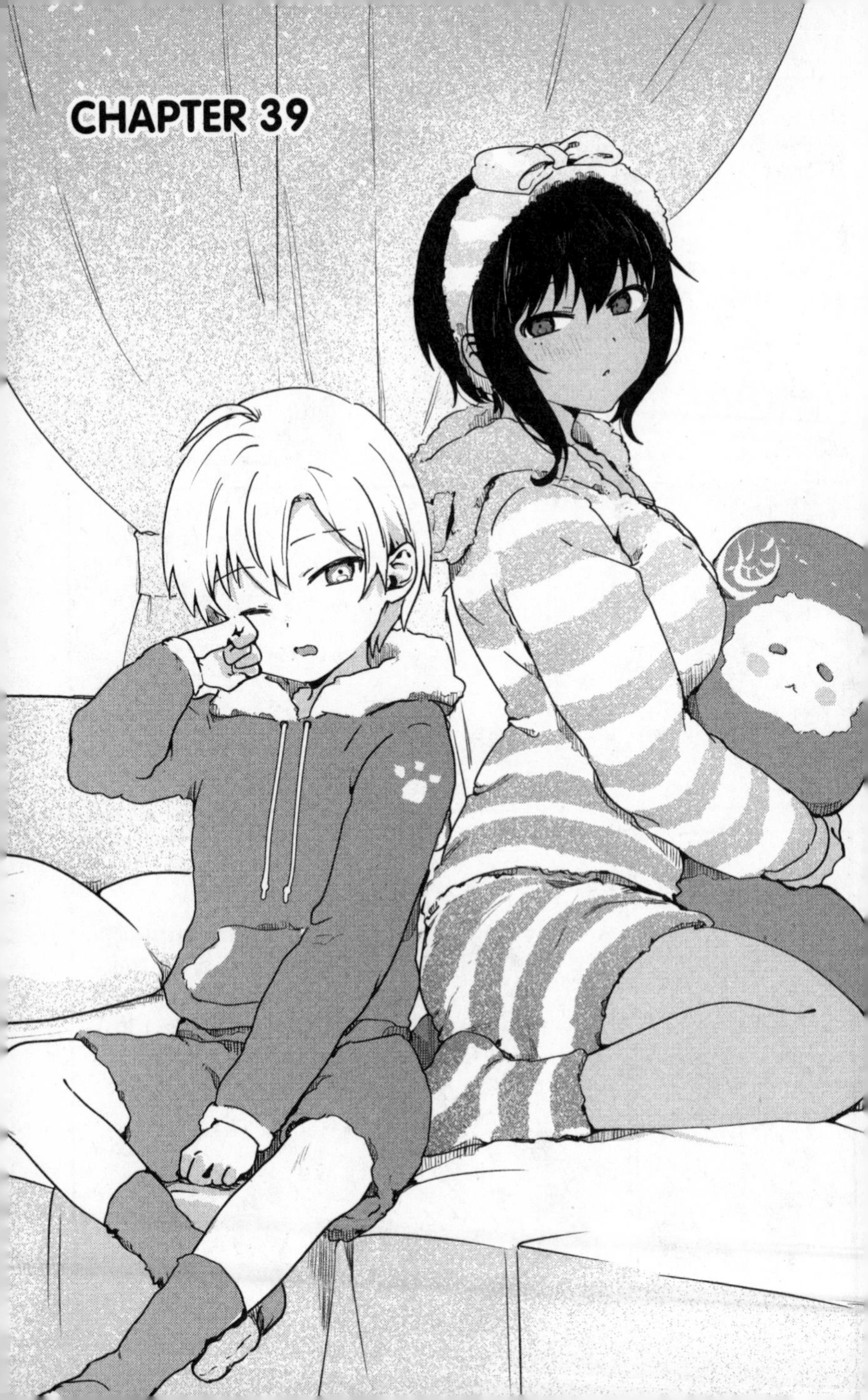

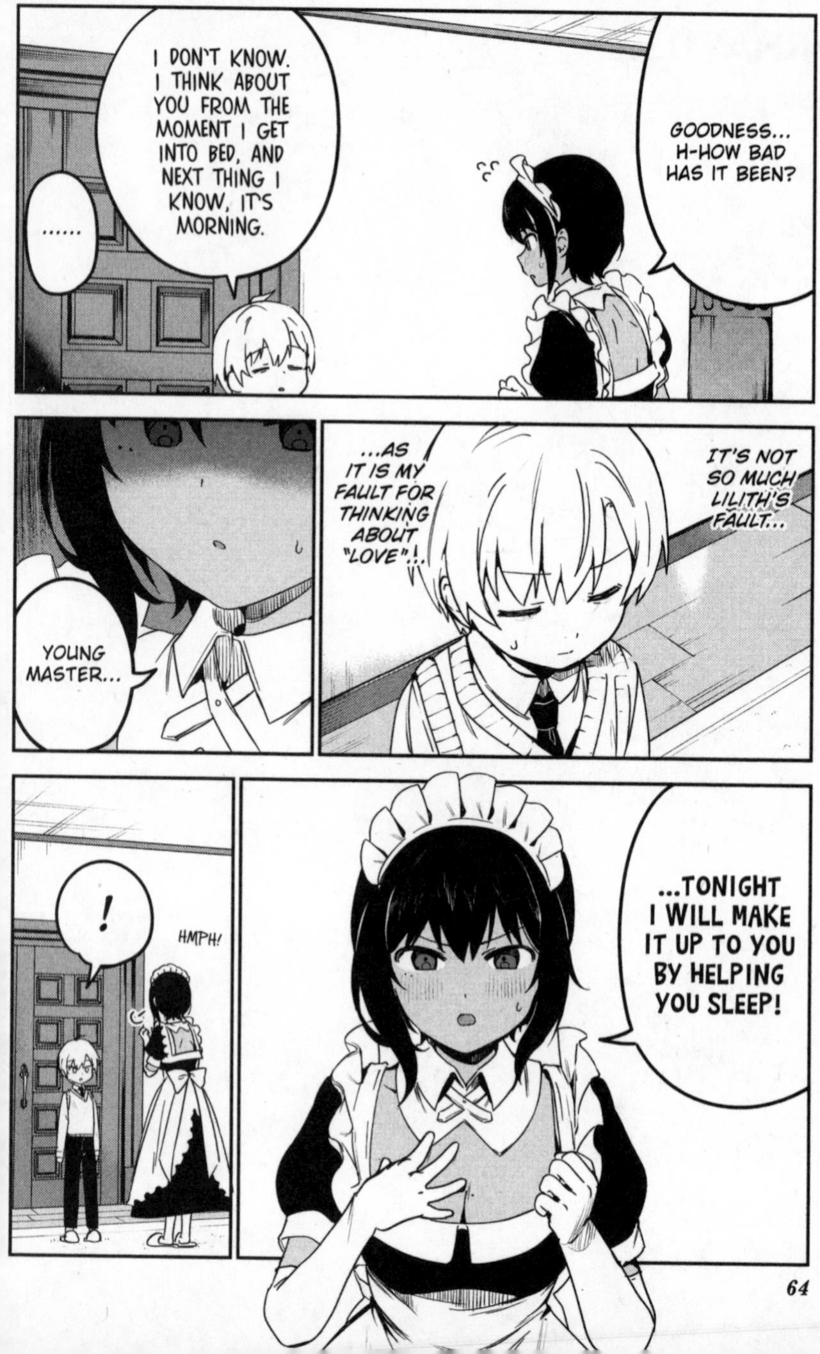
GOODNESS... H-HOW BAD HAS IT BEEN?
I DON'T KNOW. I THINK ABOUT YOU FROM THE MOMENT I GET INTO BED, AND NEXT THING I KNOW, IT'S MORNING.
......
IT'S NOT SO MUCH LILITH'S FAULT...
...AS IT IS MY FAULT FOR THINKING ABOUT "LOVE"...
YOUNG MASTER...
...TONIGHT I WILL MAKE IT UP TO YOU BY HELPING YOU SLEEP!
HMPH!
!

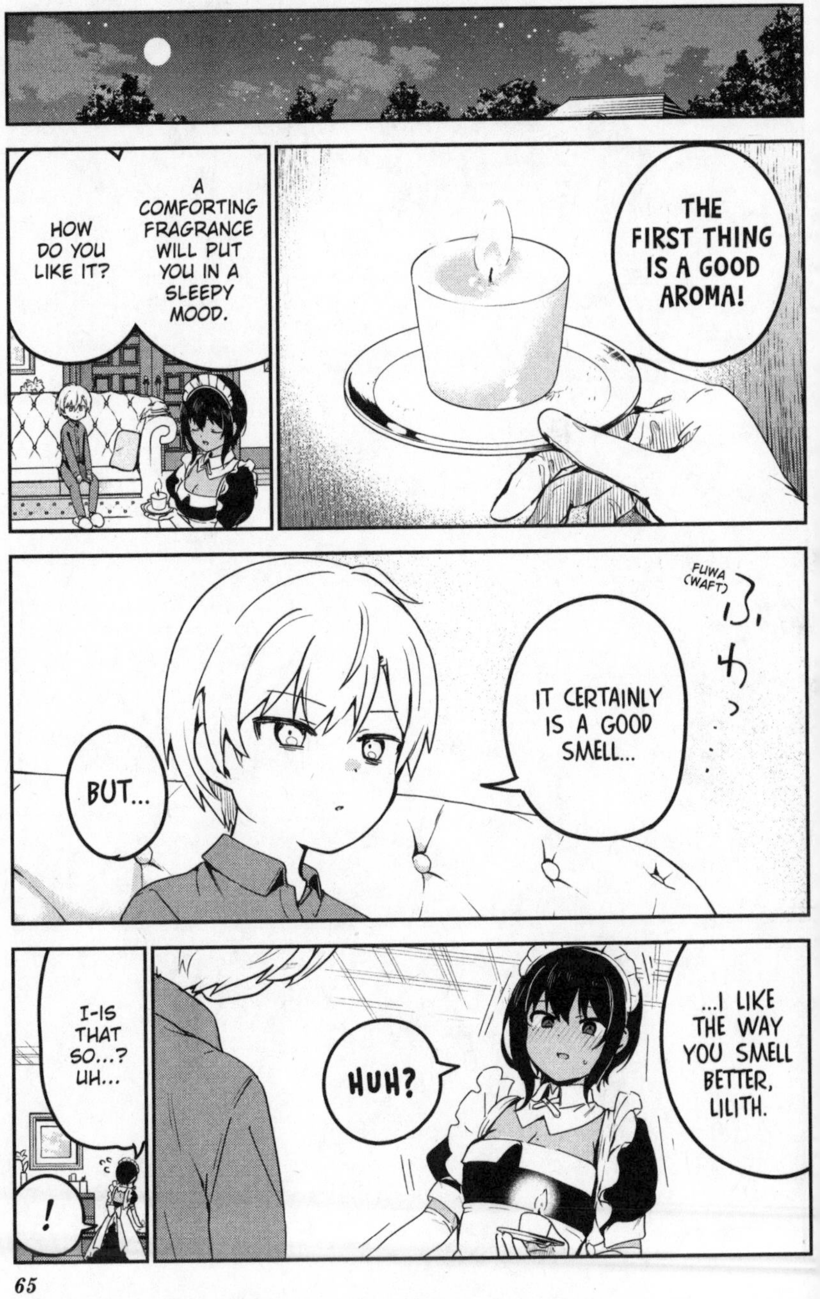
THE FIRST THING IS A GOOD AROMA!
A COMFORTING FRAGRANCE WILL PUT YOU IN A SLEEPY MOOD.
HOW DO YOU LIKE IT?
FUWA (WAFT)
ふわっ
IT CERTAINLY IS A GOOD SMELL...
BUT...
...I LIKE THE WAY YOU SMELL BETTER, LILITH.
HUH?
I-IS THAT SO...? UH...
!

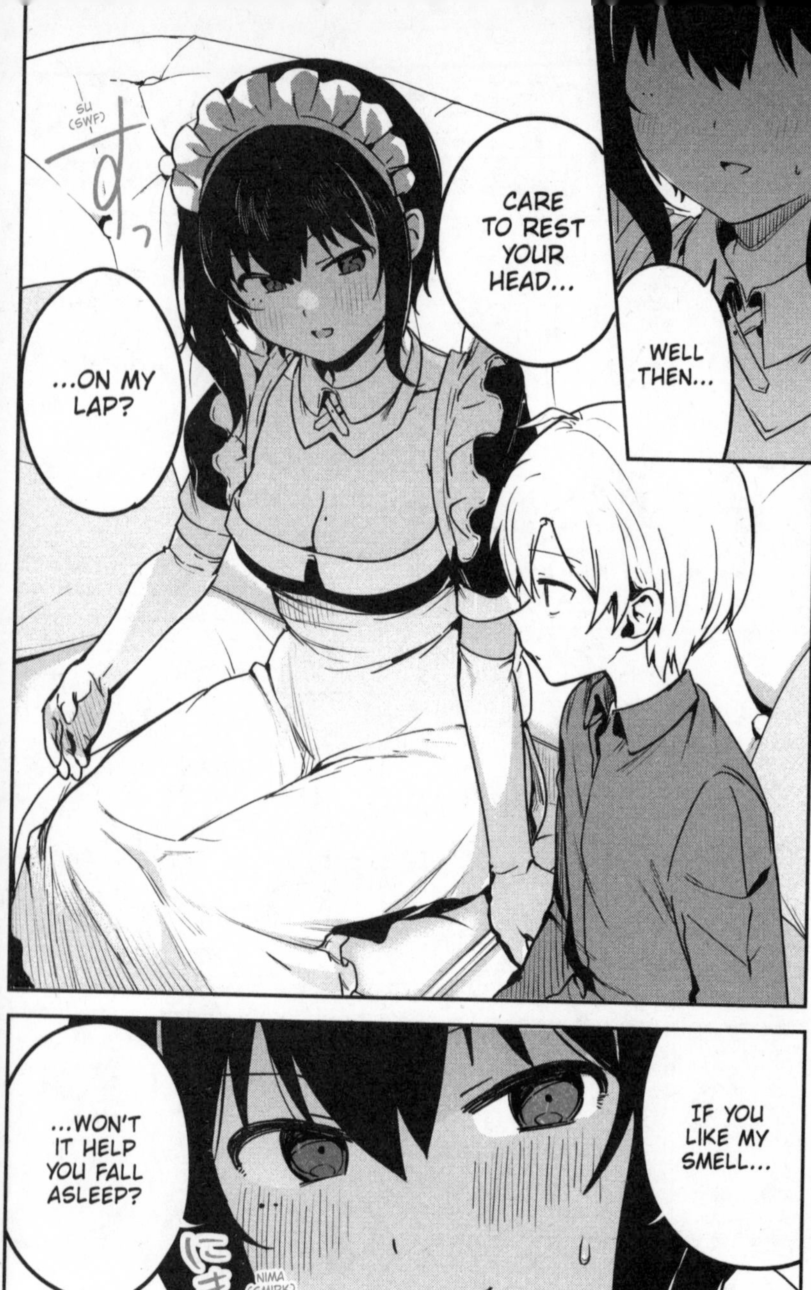
WELL THEN...
CARE TO REST YOUR HEAD...
...ON MY LAP?
すっ
SU (SWF)
IF YOU LIKE MY SMELL...
...WON'T IT HELP YOU FALL ASLEEP?
にまっ
NIMA (SMIRK)

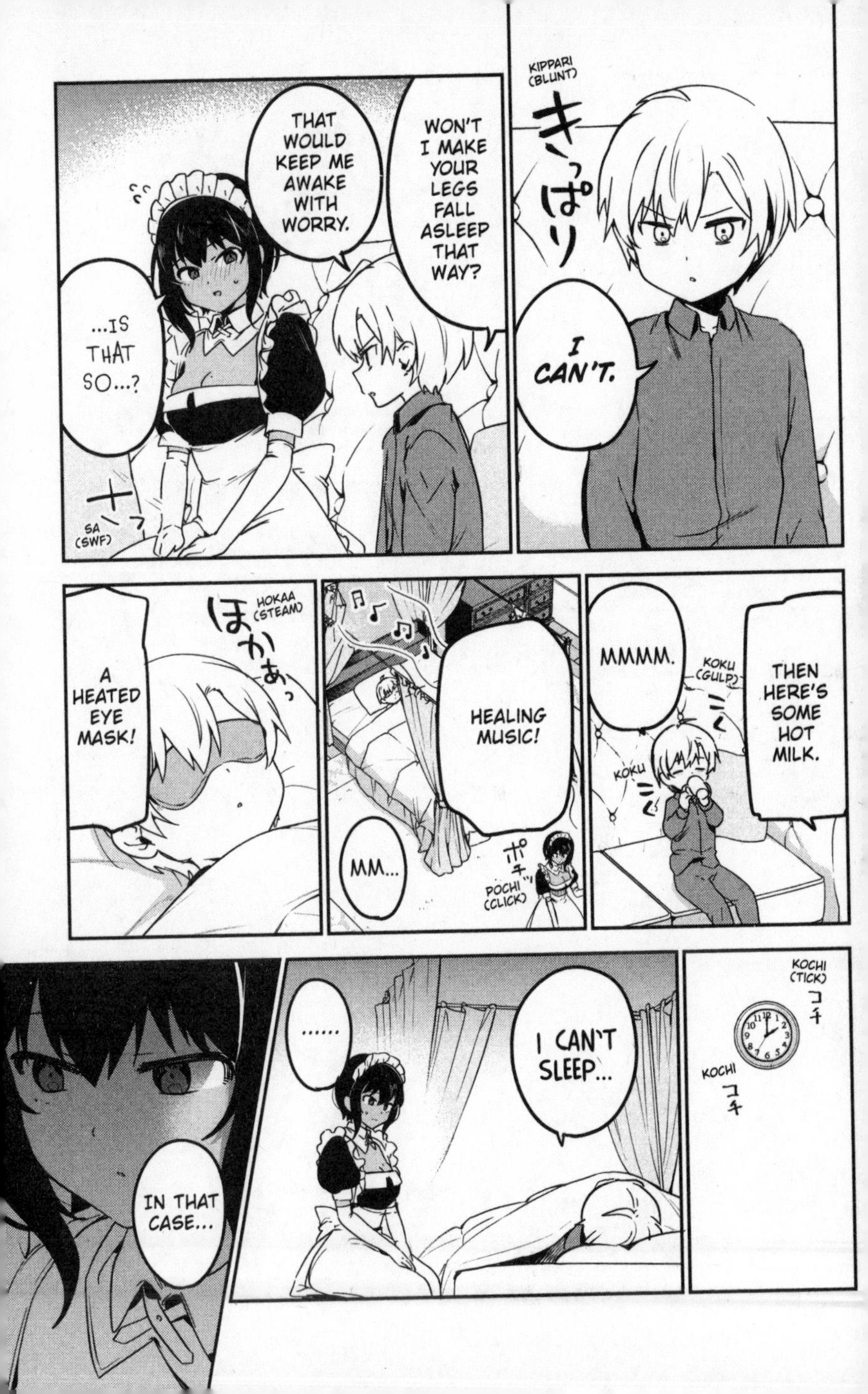
KIPPARI (BLUNT)
きっぱり
I CAN'T.
WON'T I MAKE YOUR LEGS FALL ASLEEP THAT WAY?
THAT WOULD KEEP ME AWAKE WITH WORRY.
...IS THAT SO...?
SA (SWF)
THEN HERE'S SOME HOT MILK.
KOKU (GULP)
KOKU
MMMM.
HEALING MUSIC!
MM...
POCHI (CLICK)
HOKAA (STEAM)
ほかぁっ
A HEATED EYE MASK!
KOCHI (TICK)
コチ
KOCHI
コチ
I CAN'T SLEEP...
......
IN THAT CASE...

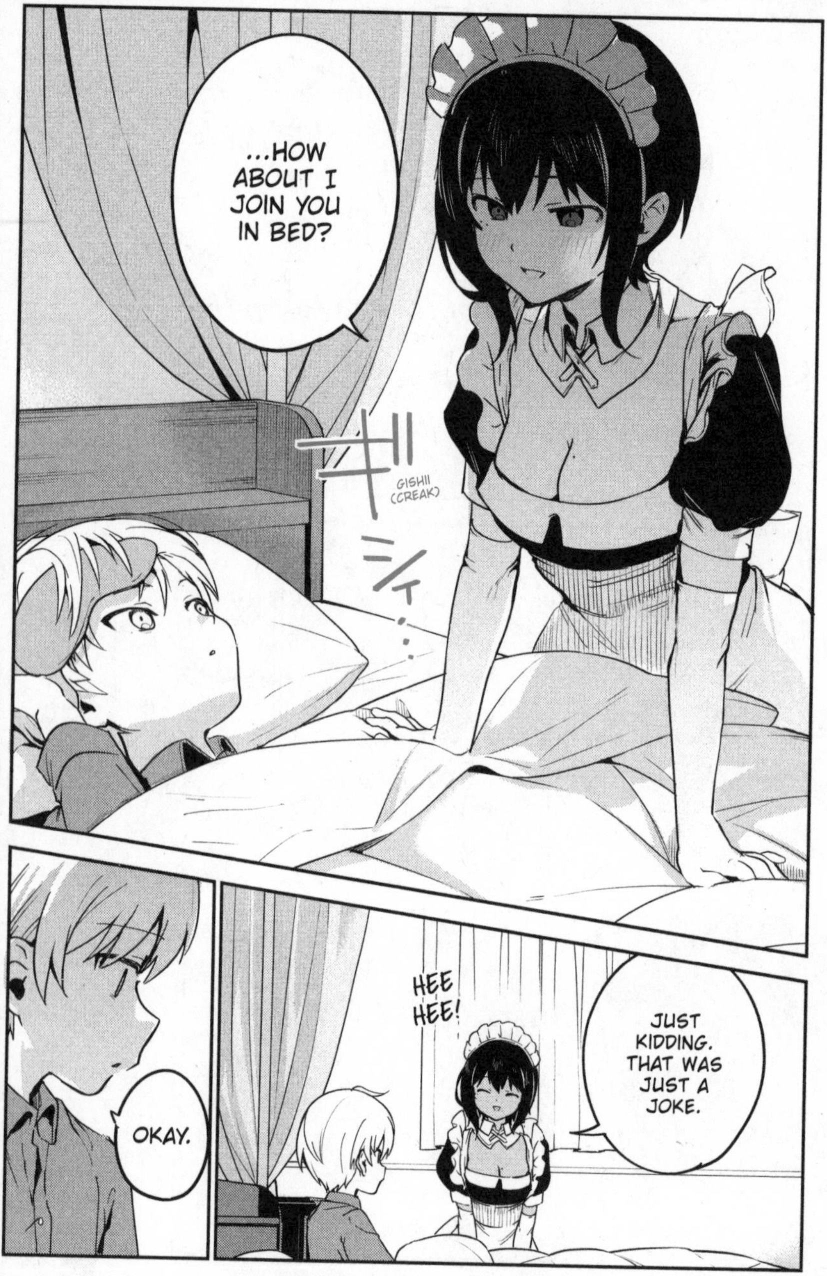
...HOW ABOUT I JOIN YOU IN BED?
ギシィ…
GISHII (CREAK)
HEE HEE!
JUST KIDDING. THAT WAS JUST A JOKE.
OKAY.

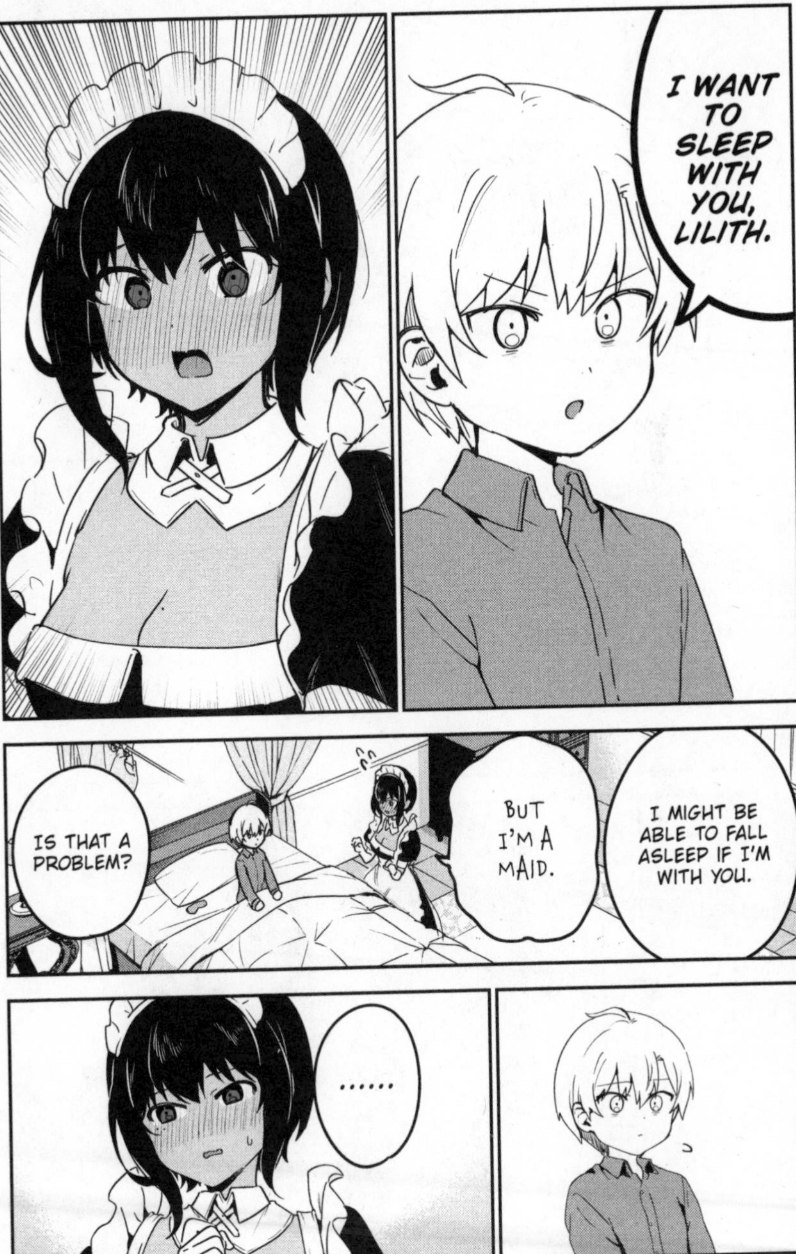
I WANT TO SLEEP WITH YOU, LILITH.
I MIGHT BE ABLE TO FALL ASLEEP IF I'M WITH YOU.
BUT I'M A MAID.
IS THAT A PROBLEM?
......

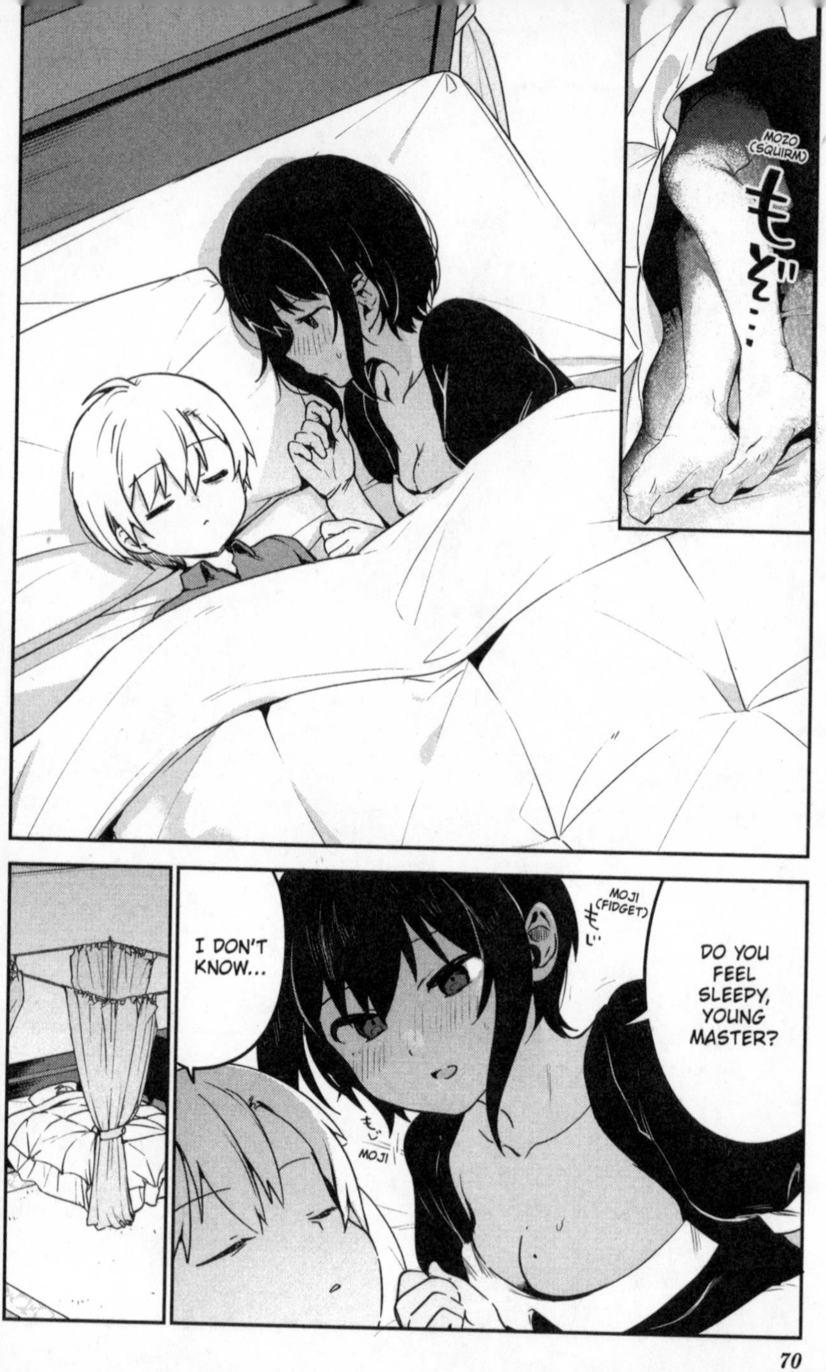
MOZO (SQUIRM)
もぞ…
DO YOU FEEL SLEEPY, YOUNG MASTER?
MOJI (FIDGET)
もじ
I DON'T KNOW…
もじ
MOJI

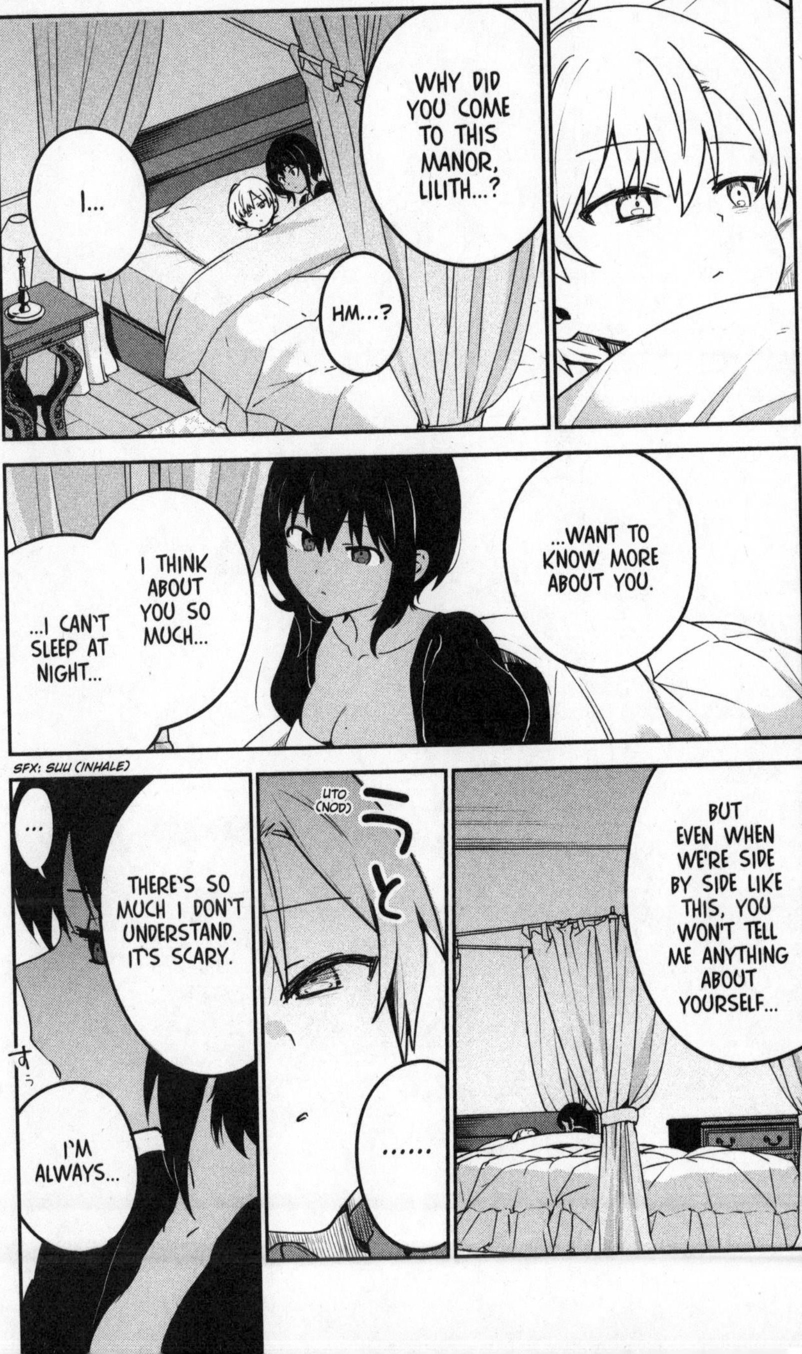
WHY DID YOU COME TO THIS MANOR, LILITH...?
HM...?
I...
...WANT TO KNOW MORE ABOUT YOU.
I THINK ABOUT YOU SO MUCH...
...I CAN'T SLEEP AT NIGHT...
SFX: SUU (INHALE)
BUT EVEN WHEN WE'RE SIDE BY SIDE LIKE THIS, YOU WON'T TELL ME ANYTHING ABOUT YOURSELF...
UTO (NOD)
うと
......
...
THERE'S SO MUCH I DON'T UNDERSTAND. IT'S SCARY.
すぅ
I'M ALWAYS...

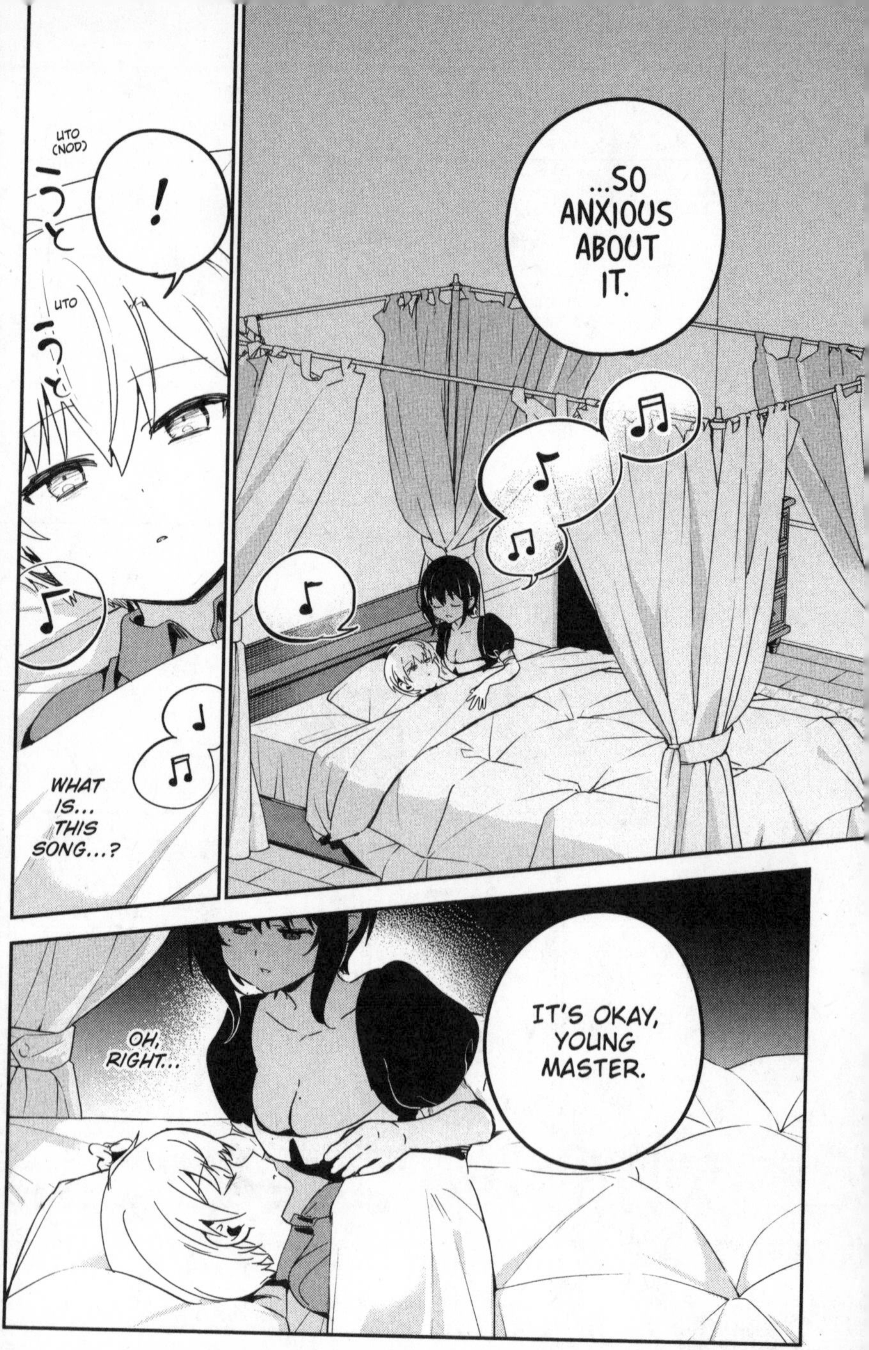
...SO ANXIOUS ABOUT IT.
!
UTO (NOD)
うと
UTO
うと
WHAT IS... THIS SONG...?
IT'S OKAY, YOUNG MASTER.
OH, RIGHT...

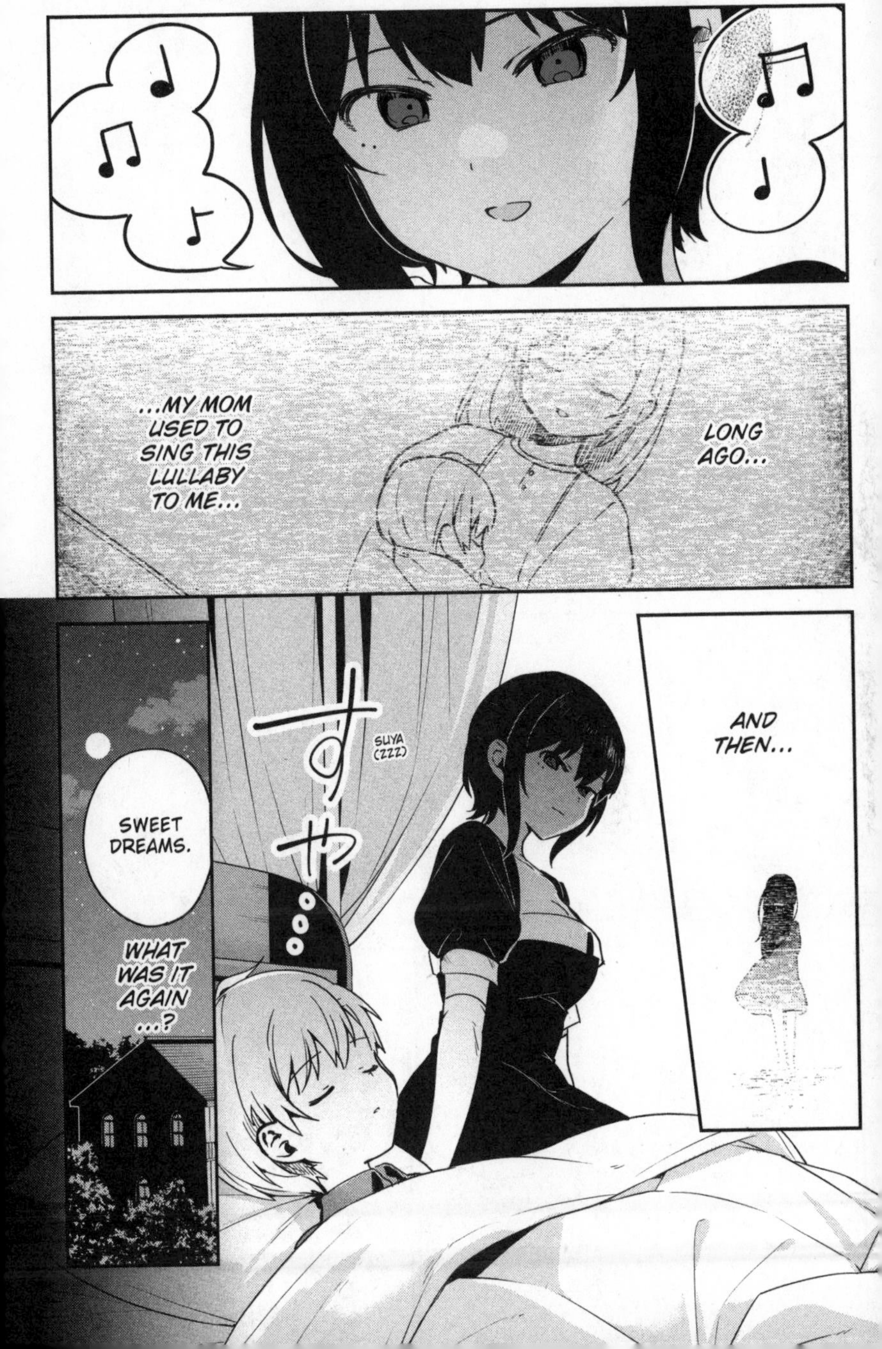
LONG AGO...
...MY MOM USED TO SING THIS LULLABY TO ME...
AND THEN...
すや
SUYA (ZZZ)
SWEET DREAMS.
WHAT WAS IT AGAIN ...?

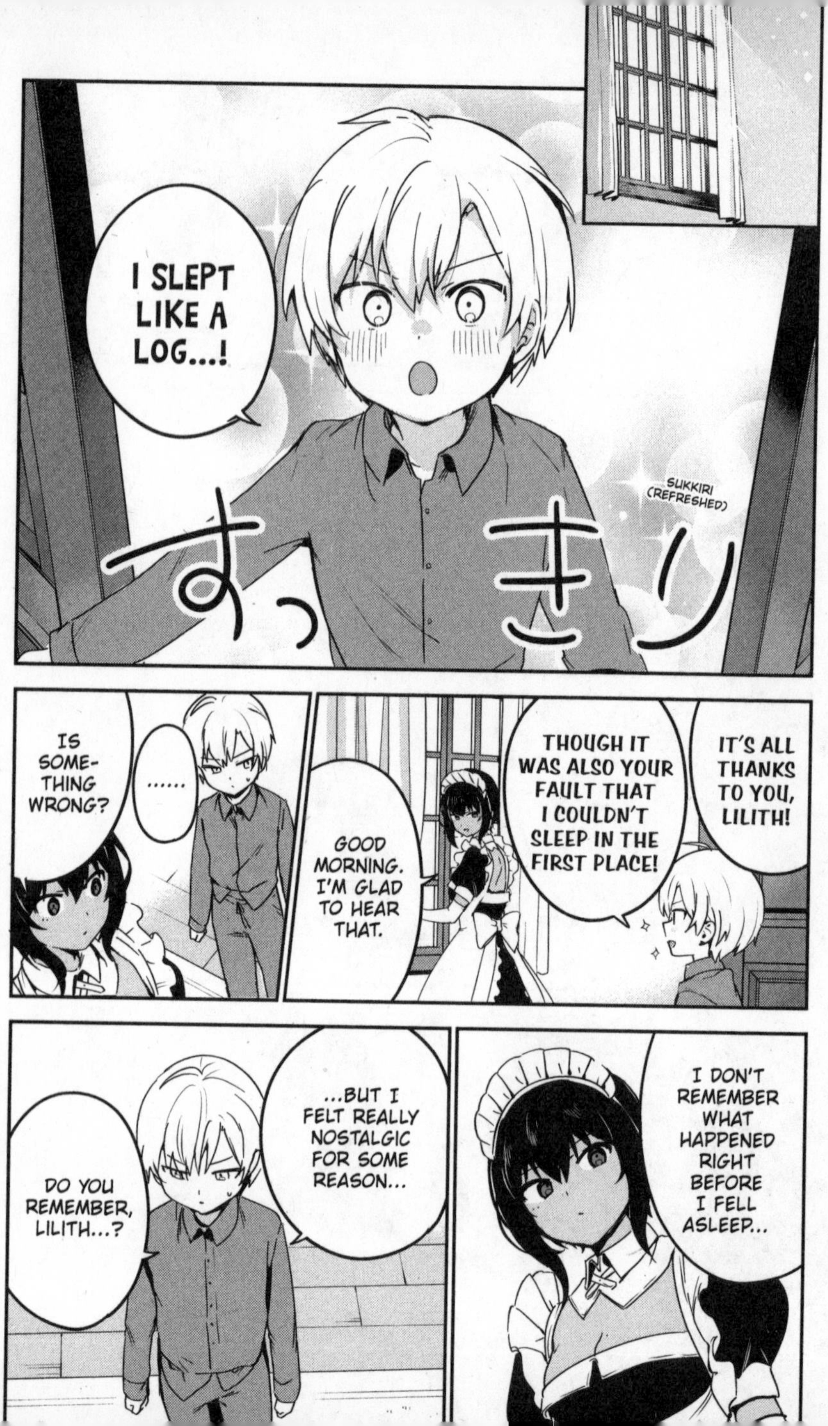
I SLEPT LIKE A LOG...!
すっきり
SUKKIRI (REFRESHED)
IT'S ALL THANKS TO YOU, LILITH!
THOUGH IT WAS ALSO YOUR FAULT THAT I COULDN'T SLEEP IN THE FIRST PLACE!
GOOD MORNING. I'M GLAD TO HEAR THAT.
......
IS SOMETHING WRONG?
I DON'T REMEMBER WHAT HAPPENED RIGHT BEFORE I FELL ASLEEP...
...BUT I FELT REALLY NOSTALGIC FOR SOME REASON...
DO YOU REMEMBER, LILITH...?

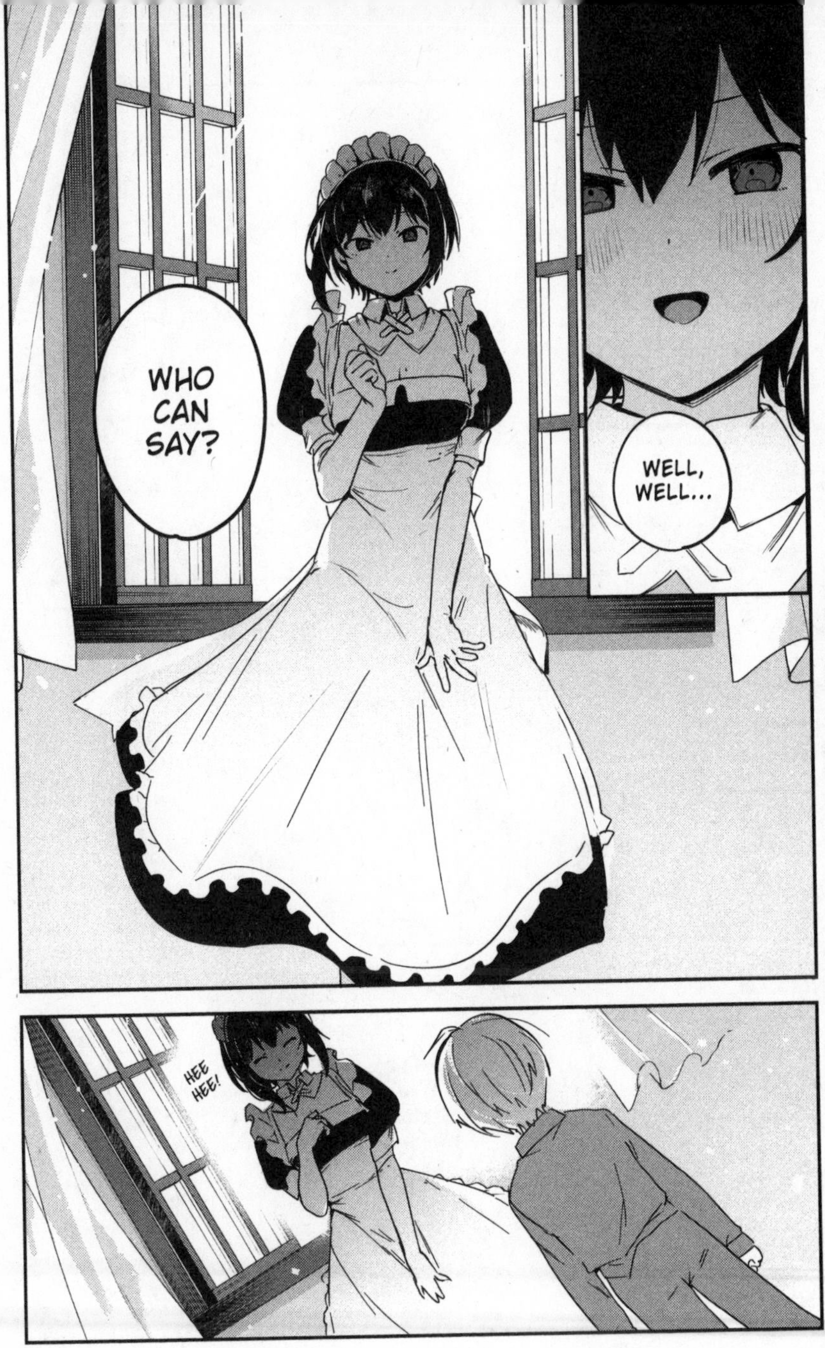
WELL, WELL...
WHO CAN SAY?
HEE HEE!

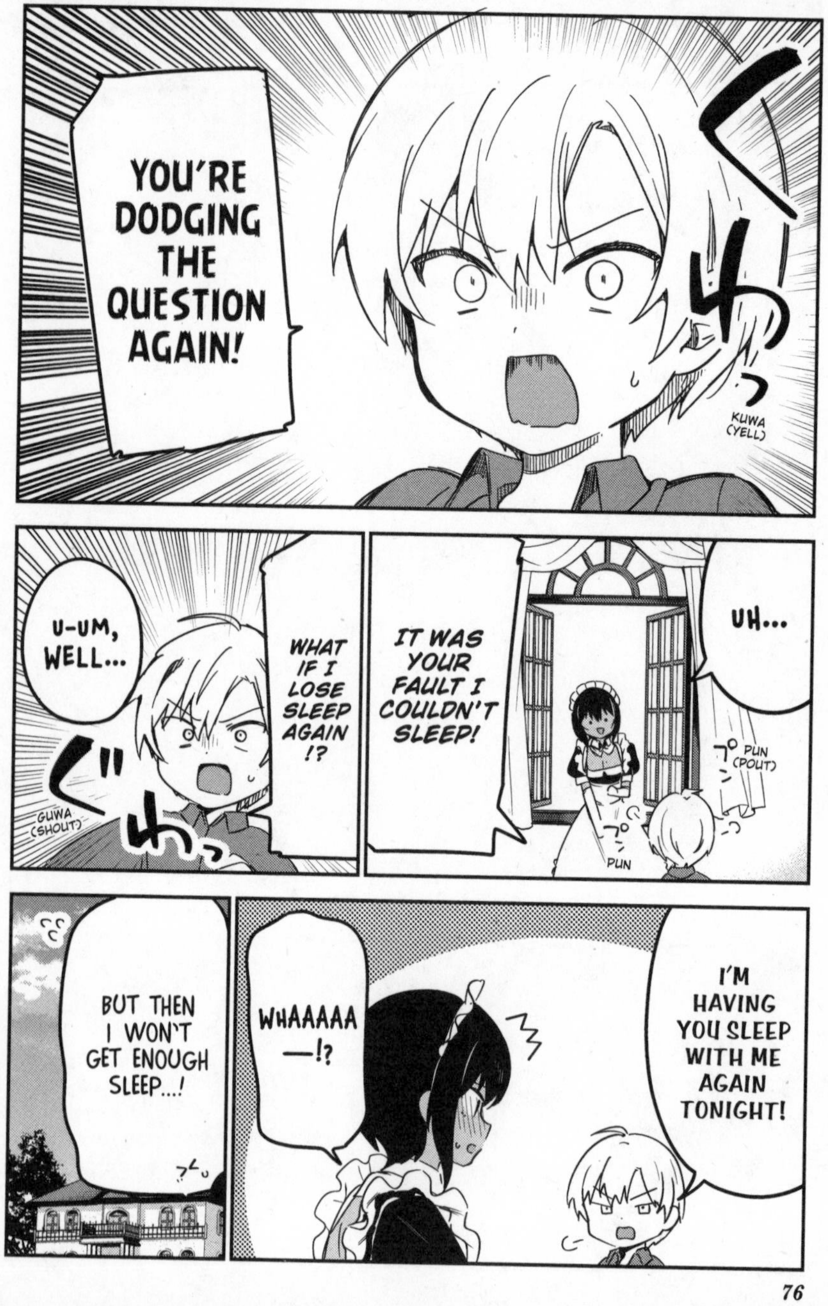
YOU'RE DODGING THE QUESTION AGAIN!
KUWA (YELL)
UH...
IT WAS YOUR FAULT I COULDN'T SLEEP!
PUN (POUT)
PUN
WHAT IF I LOSE SLEEP AGAIN!?
U-UM, WELL...
GUWA (SHOUT)
I'M HAVING YOU SLEEP WITH ME AGAIN TONIGHT!
WHAAAAA—!?
BUT THEN I WON'T GET ENOUGH SLEEP...!

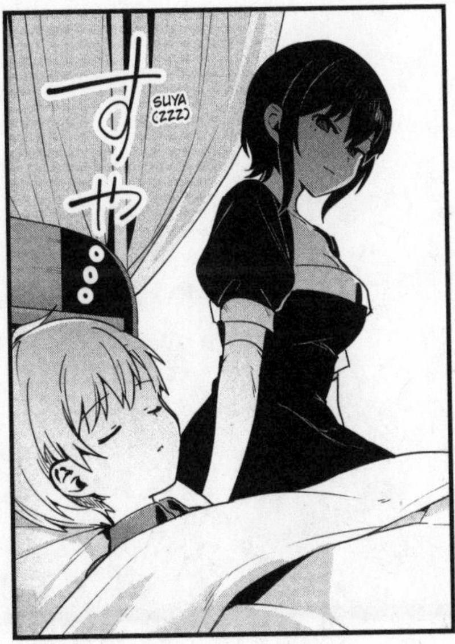
すや…
SUYA (ZZZ)

The Maid I Hired Recently Is Mysterious

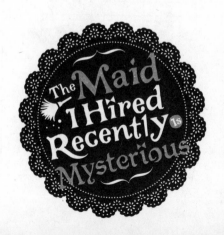

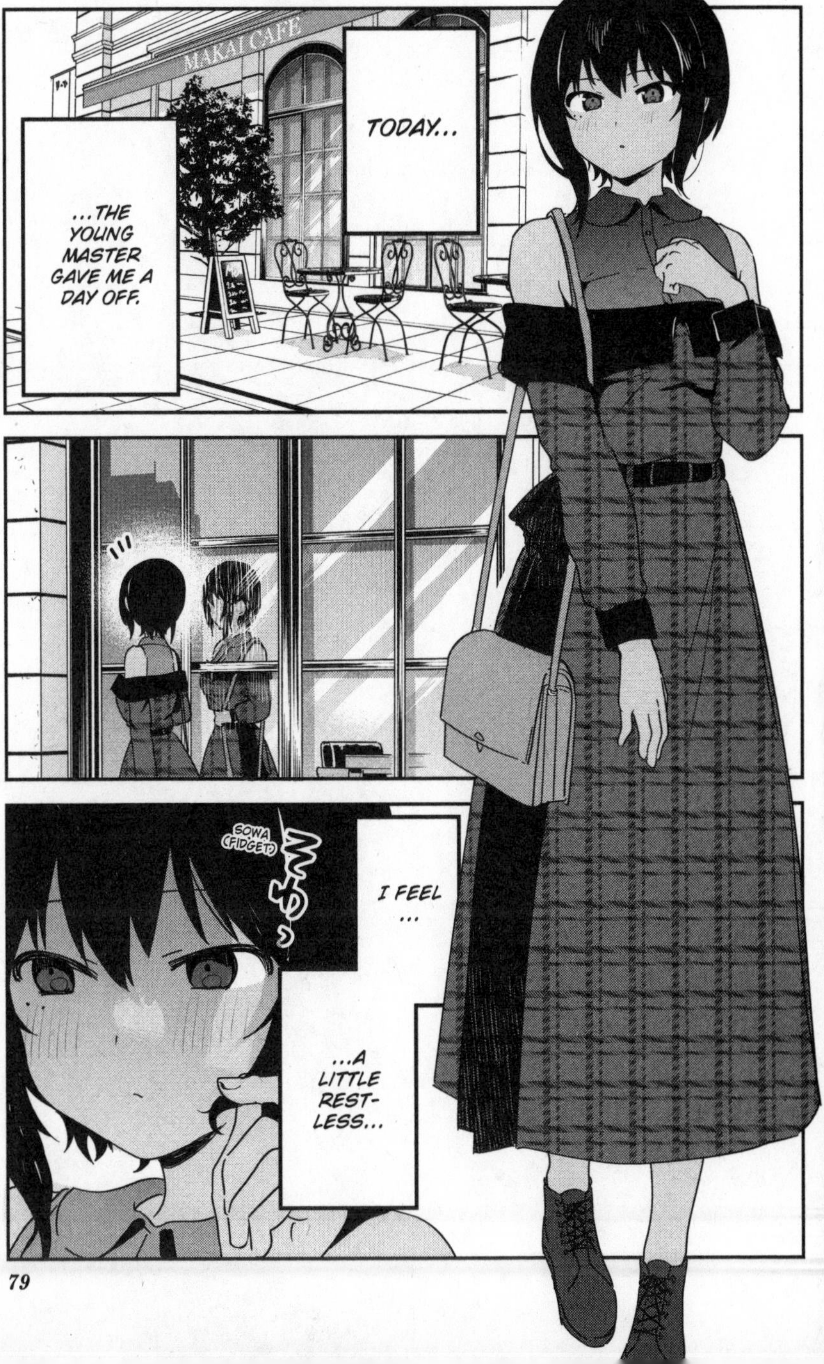
TODAY...
...THE YOUNG MASTER GAVE ME A DAY OFF.
MAKAI CAFE
SOWA (FIDGET)
I FEEL ...
...A LITTLE REST-LESS...

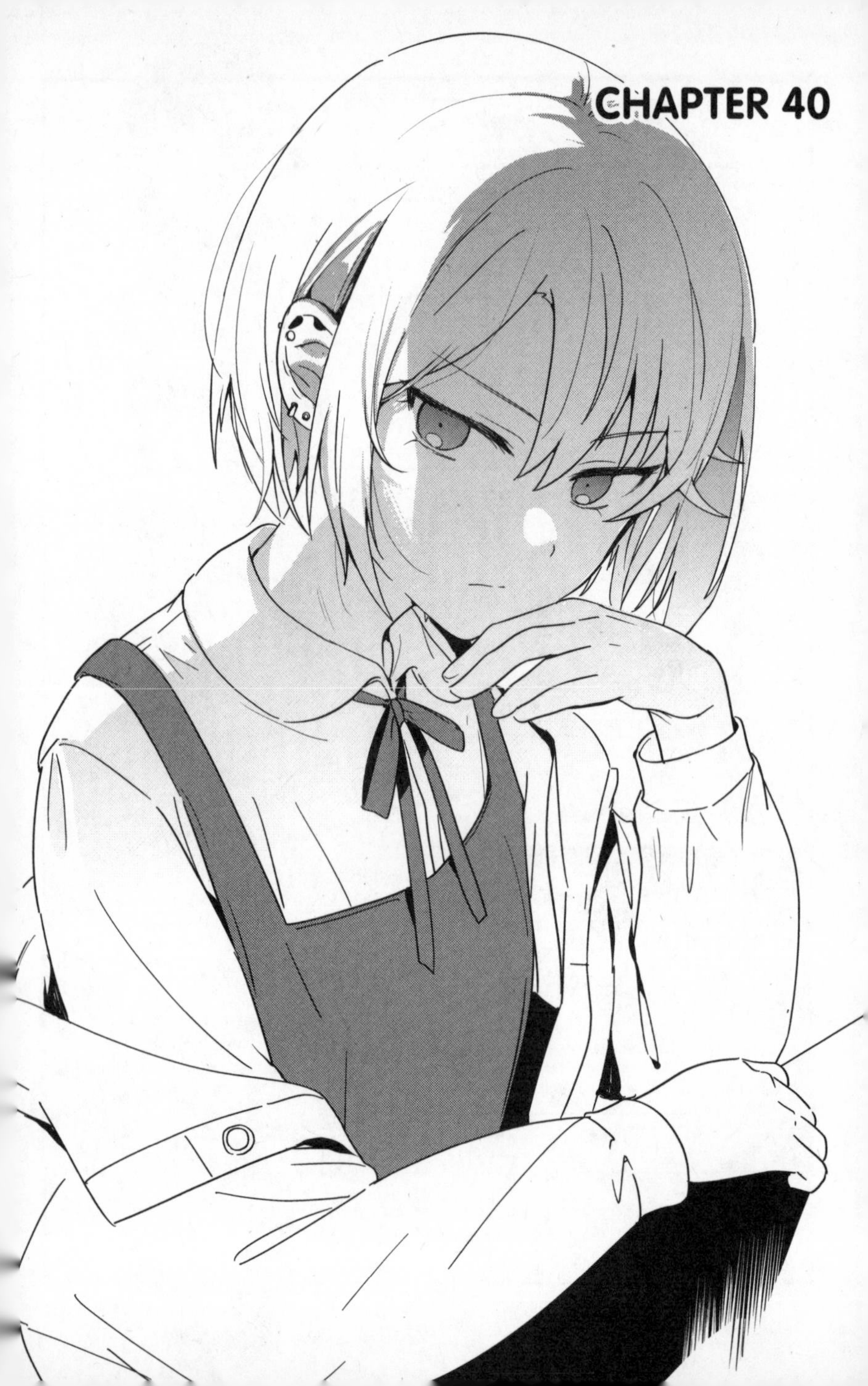
CHAPTER 40

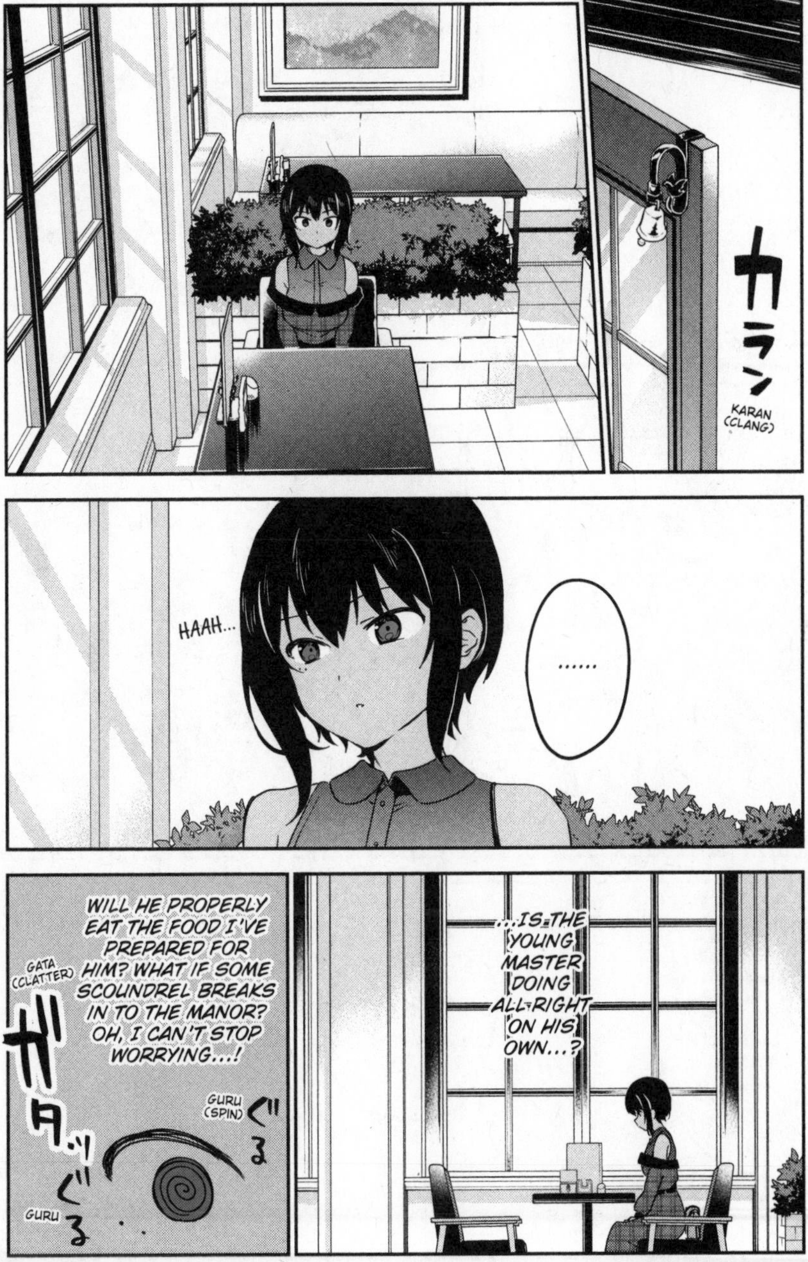
カラン
KARAN (CLANG)
......
HAAH...
...IS THE YOUNG MASTER DOING ALL RIGHT ON HIS OWN...?
WILL HE PROPERLY EAT THE FOOD I'VE PREPARED FOR HIM? WHAT IF SOME SCOUNDREL BREAKS IN TO THE MANOR? OH, I CAN'T STOP WORRYING...!
GATA (CLATTER)
ガタッ
GURU (SPIN)
ぐる
ぐる
GURU

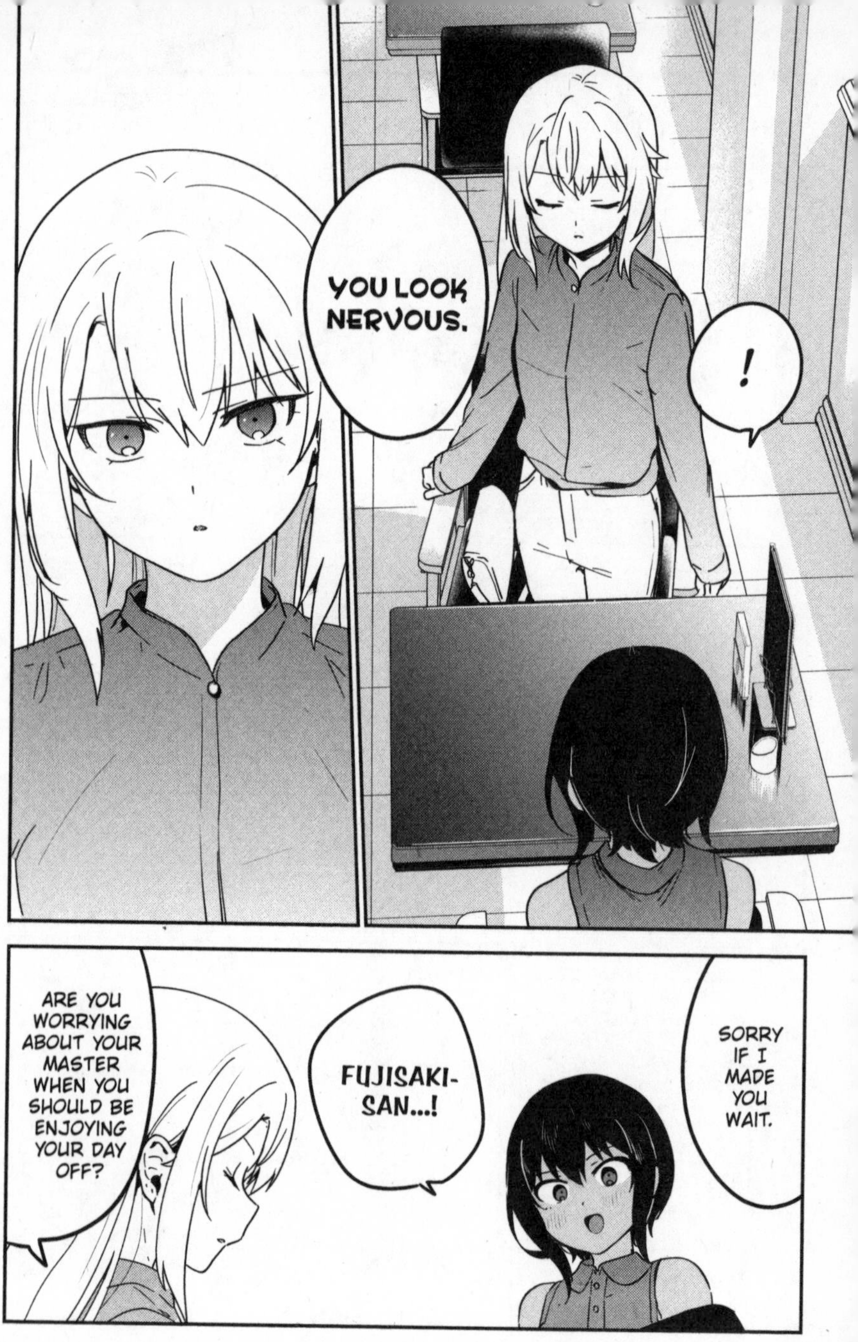
YOU LOOK NERVOUS.
!
SORRY IF I MADE YOU WAIT.
FUJISAKI-SAN...!
ARE YOU WORRYING ABOUT YOUR MASTER WHEN YOU SHOULD BE ENJOYING YOUR DAY OFF?

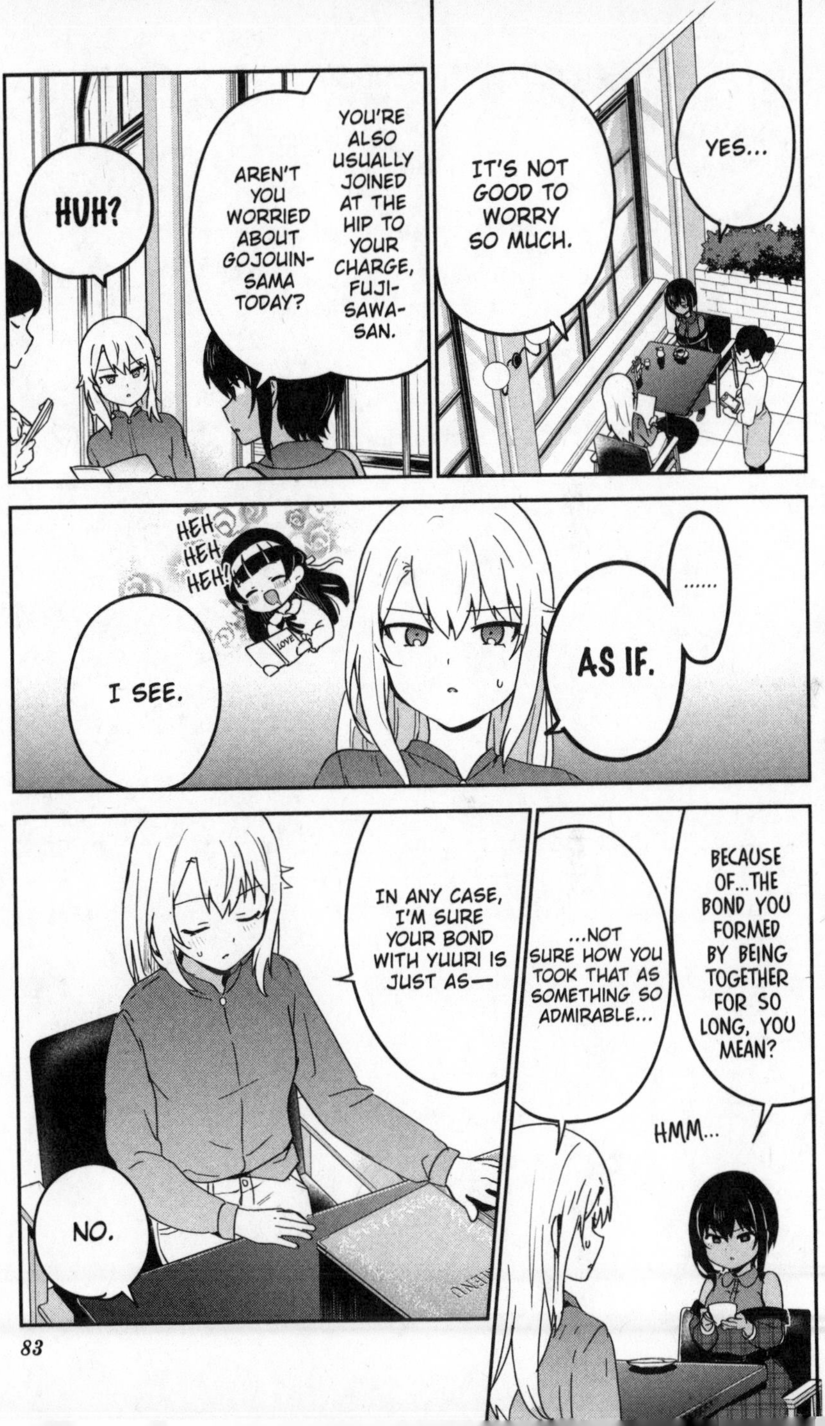

YES...
IT'S NOT GOOD TO WORRY SO MUCH.
YOU'RE ALSO USUALLY JOINED AT THE HIP TO YOUR CHARGE, FUJISAWA-SAN.
AREN'T YOU WORRIED ABOUT GOJOUIN-SAMA TODAY?
HUH?
......
AS IF.
HEH HEH HEH!
LOVE
I SEE.
BECAUSE OF...THE BOND YOU FORMED BY BEING TOGETHER FOR SO LONG, YOU MEAN?
...NOT SURE HOW YOU TOOK THAT AS SOMETHING SO ADMIRABLE...
HMM...
IN ANY CASE, I'M SURE YOUR BOND WITH YUURI IS JUST AS—
NO.

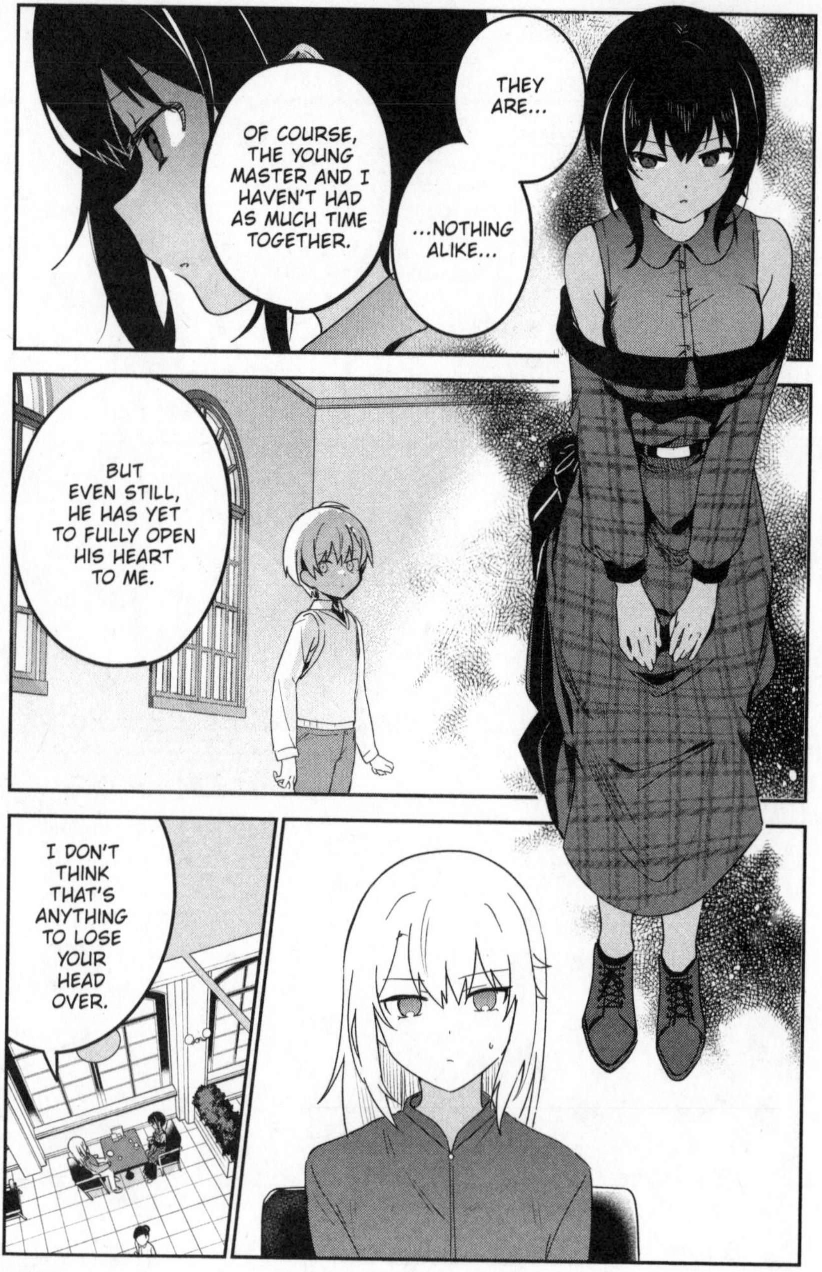
THEY ARE...
...NOTHING ALIKE...
OF COURSE, THE YOUNG MASTER AND I HAVEN'T HAD AS MUCH TIME TOGETHER.
BUT EVEN STILL, HE HAS YET TO FULLY OPEN HIS HEART TO ME.
I DON'T THINK THAT'S ANYTHING TO LOSE YOUR HEAD OVER.

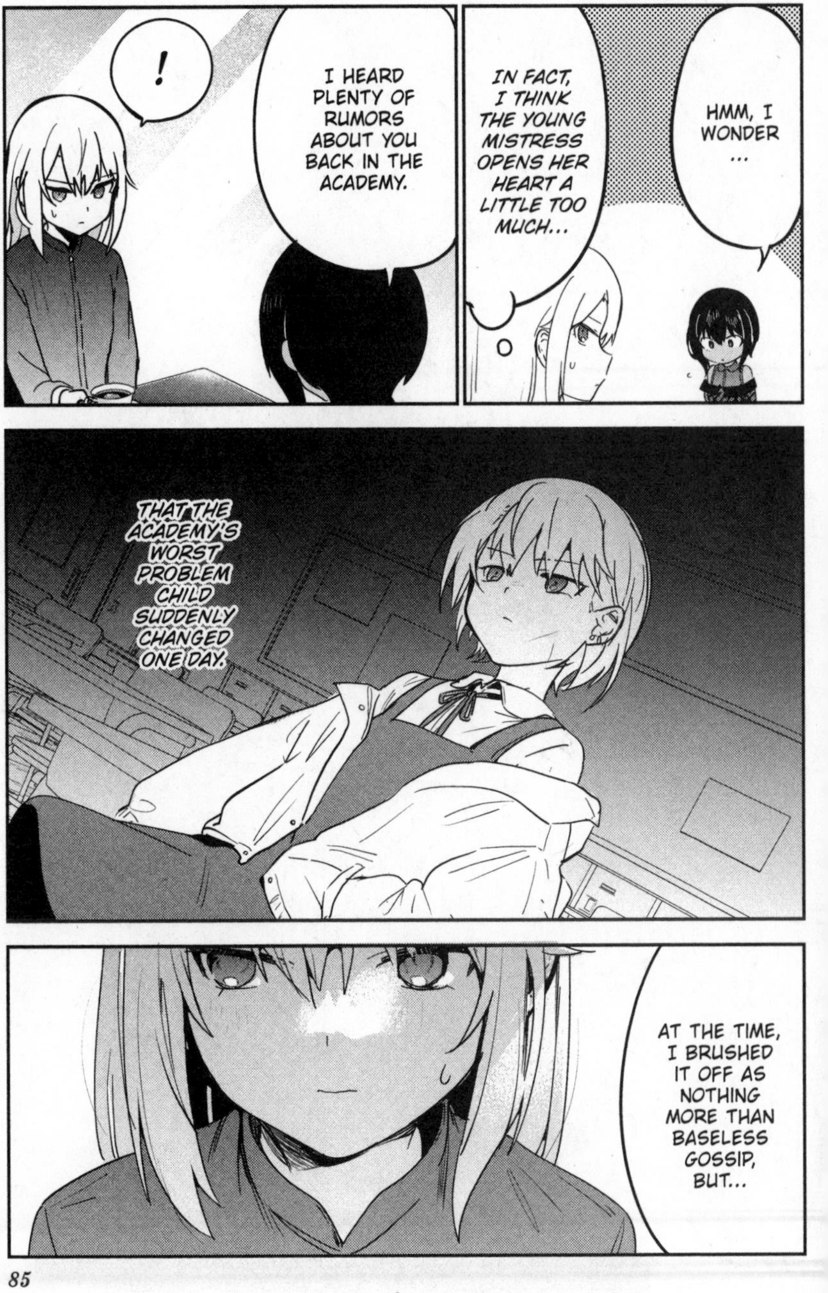
HMM, I WONDER ...
IN FACT, I THINK THE YOUNG MISTRESS OPENS HER HEART A LITTLE TOO MUCH...
I HEARD PLENTY OF RUMORS ABOUT YOU BACK IN THE ACADEMY.
!
THAT THE ACADEMY'S WORST PROBLEM CHILD SUDDENLY CHANGED ONE DAY.
AT THE TIME, I BRUSHED IT OFF AS NOTHING MORE THAN BASELESS GOSSIP, BUT...

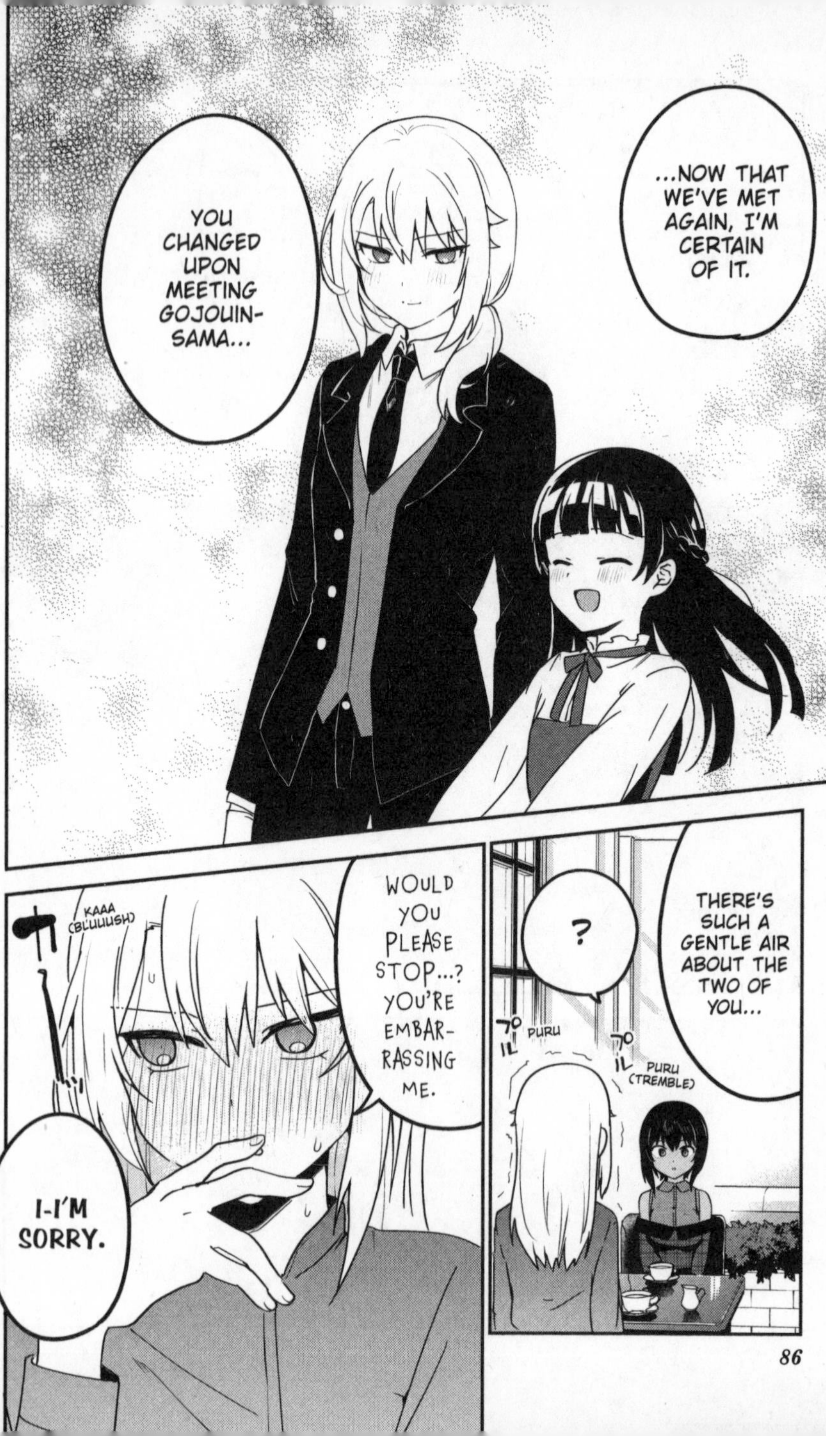
...NOW THAT WE'VE MET AGAIN, I'M CERTAIN OF IT.
YOU CHANGED UPON MEETING GOJOUIN-SAMA...
THERE'S SUCH A GENTLE AIR ABOUT THE TWO OF YOU...
?
PURU
PURU (TREMBLE)
WOULD YOU PLEASE STOP...? YOU'RE EMBARRASSING ME.
KAAA (BLUUUSH)
I-I'M SORRY.

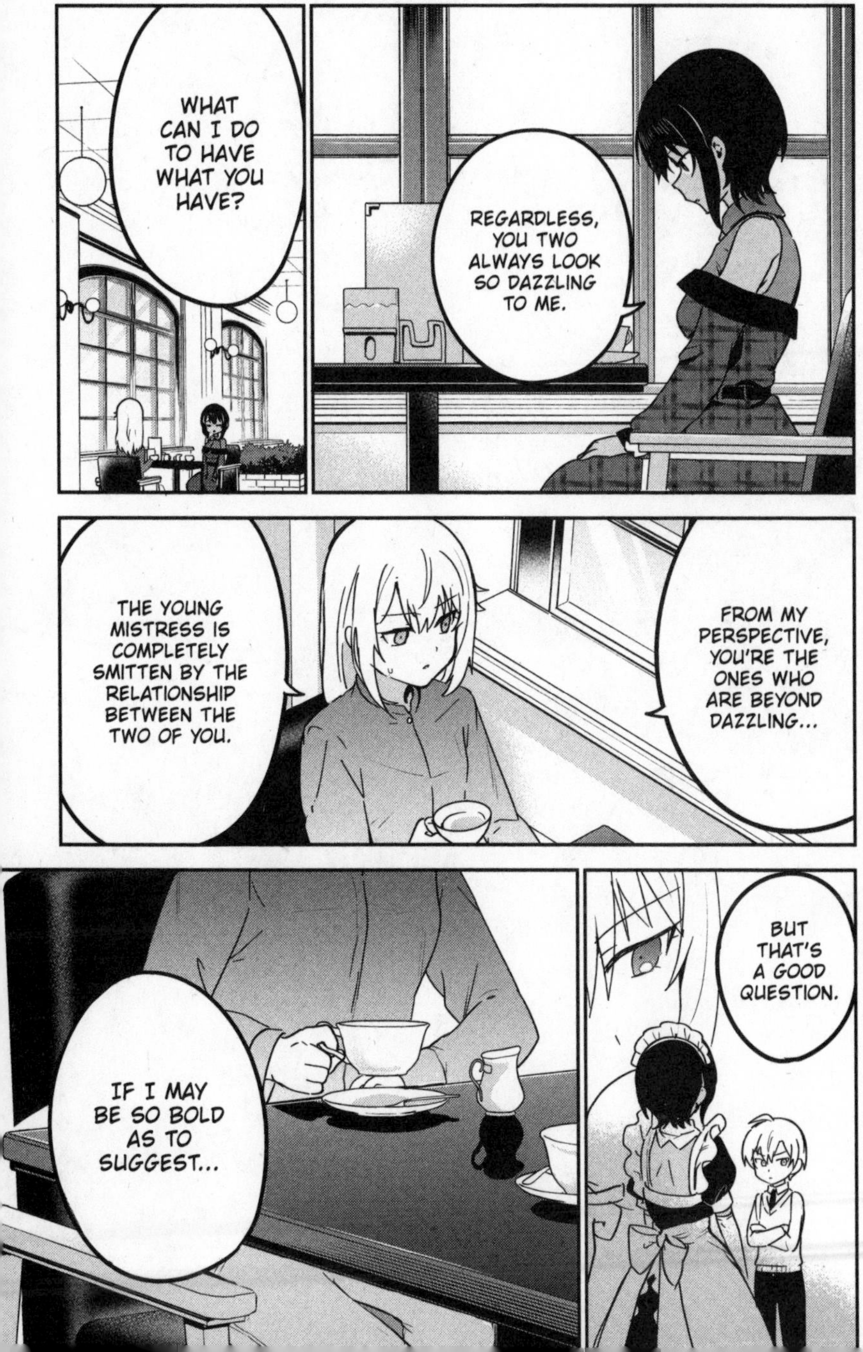
REGARDLESS, YOU TWO ALWAYS LOOK SO DAZZLING TO ME.
WHAT CAN I DO TO HAVE WHAT YOU HAVE?
FROM MY PERSPECTIVE, YOU'RE THE ONES WHO ARE BEYOND DAZZLING...
THE YOUNG MISTRESS IS COMPLETELY SMITTEN BY THE RELATIONSHIP BETWEEN THE TWO OF YOU.
BUT THAT'S A GOOD QUESTION.
IF I MAY BE SO BOLD AS TO SUGGEST...

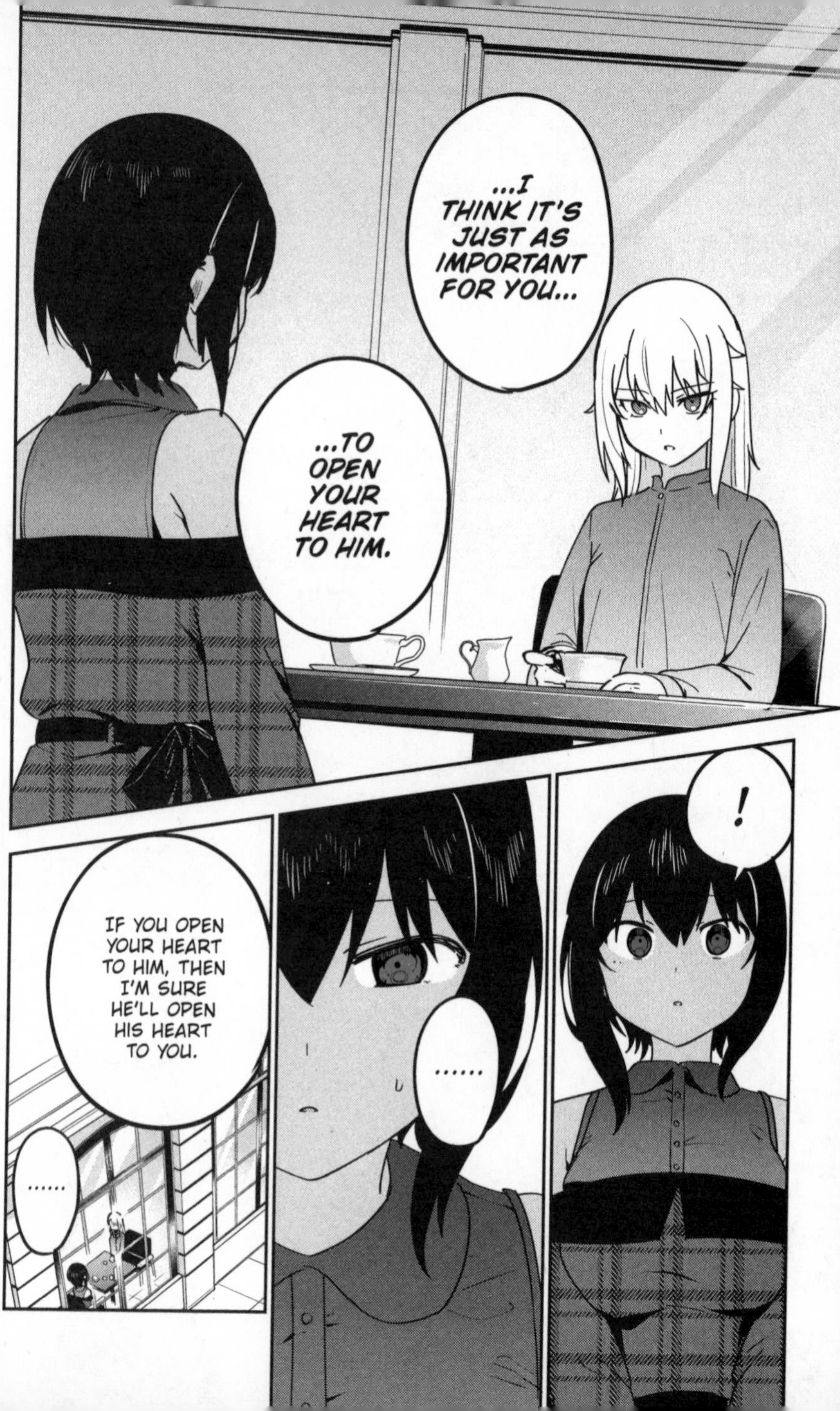
...I THINK IT'S JUST AS IMPORTANT FOR YOU...
...TO OPEN YOUR HEART TO HIM.
!
......
IF YOU OPEN YOUR HEART TO HIM, THEN I'M SURE HE'LL OPEN HIS HEART TO YOU.
......

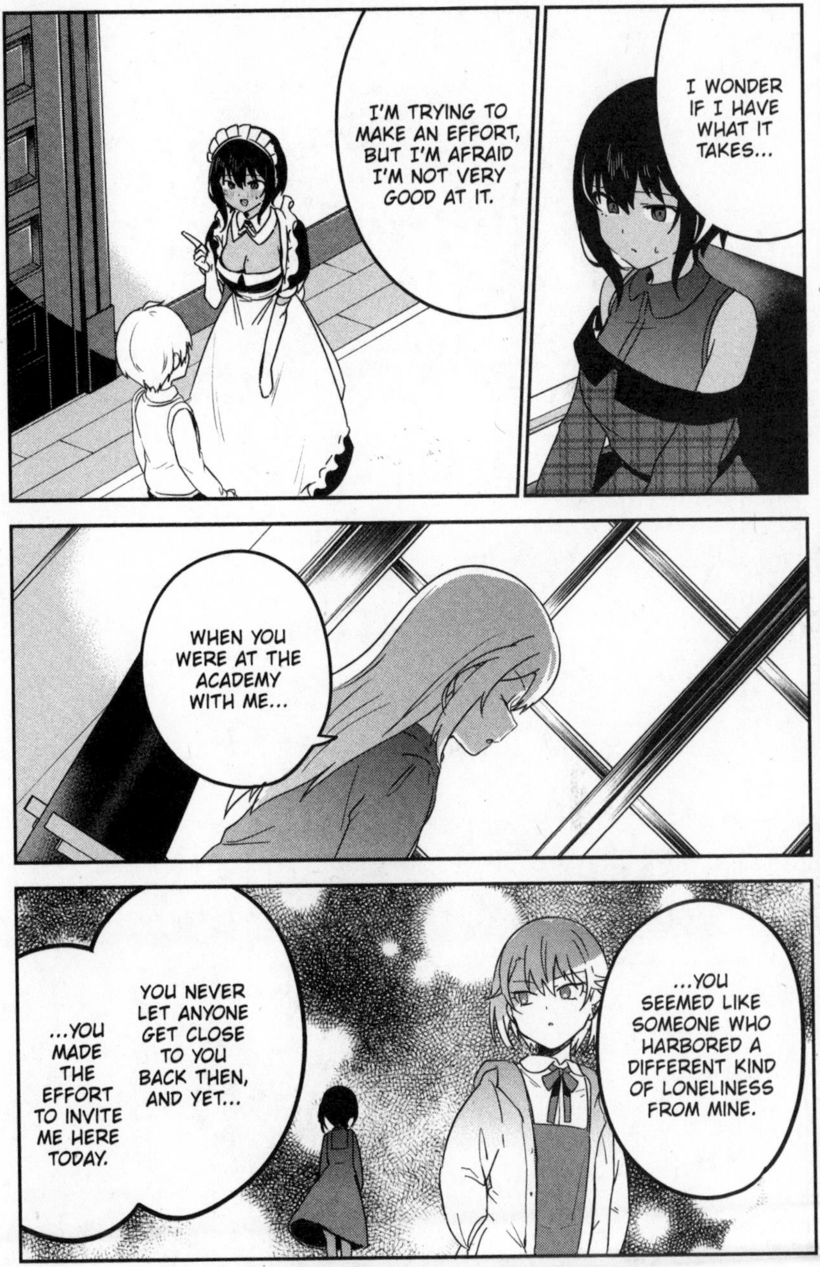
I WONDER IF I HAVE WHAT IT TAKES...
I'M TRYING TO MAKE AN EFFORT, BUT I'M AFRAID I'M NOT VERY GOOD AT IT.
WHEN YOU WERE AT THE ACADEMY WITH ME...
...YOU SEEMED LIKE SOMEONE WHO HARBORED A DIFFERENT KIND OF LONELINESS FROM MINE.
YOU NEVER LET ANYONE GET CLOSE TO YOU BACK THEN, AND YET...
...YOU MADE THE EFFORT TO INVITE ME HERE TODAY.

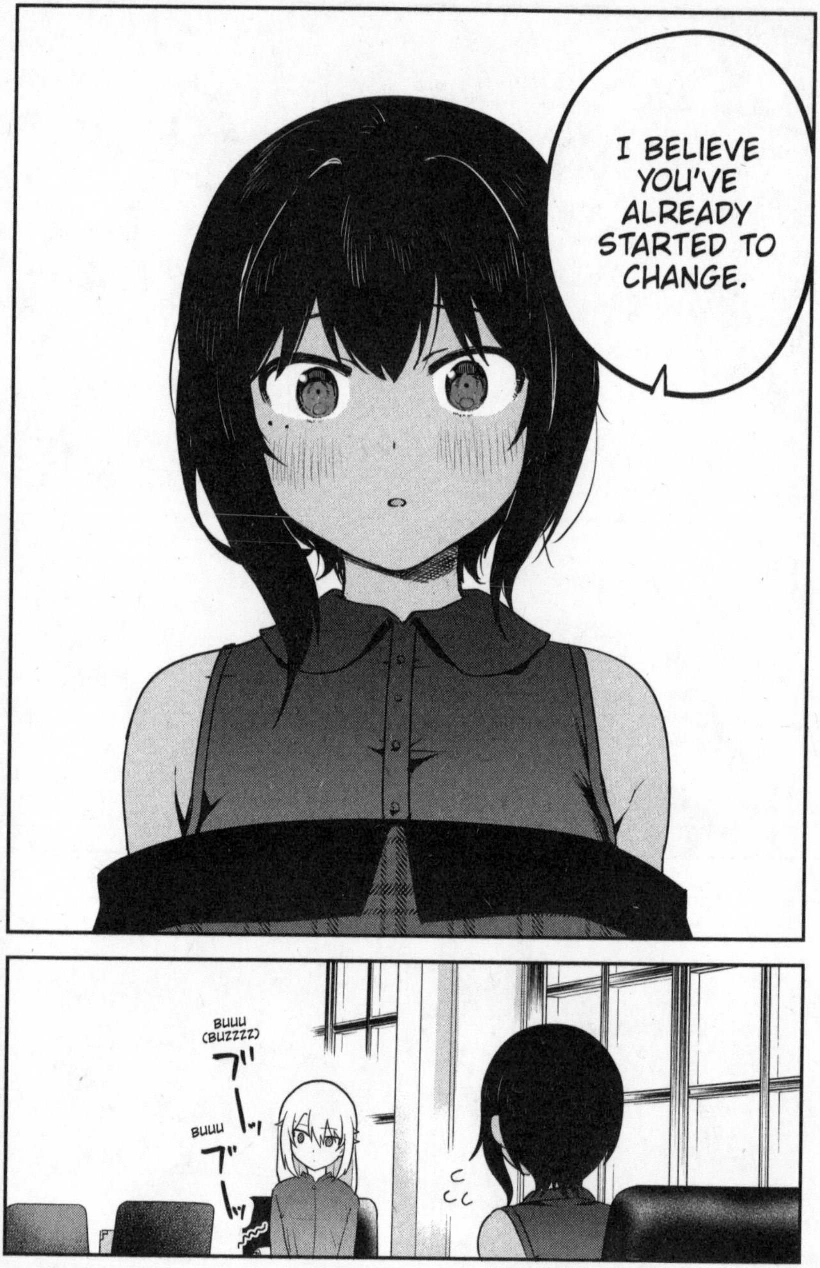
I BELIEVE YOU'VE ALREADY STARTED TO CHANGE.
BUUU (BUZZZZ)
ブーッ
BUUU
ブーッ

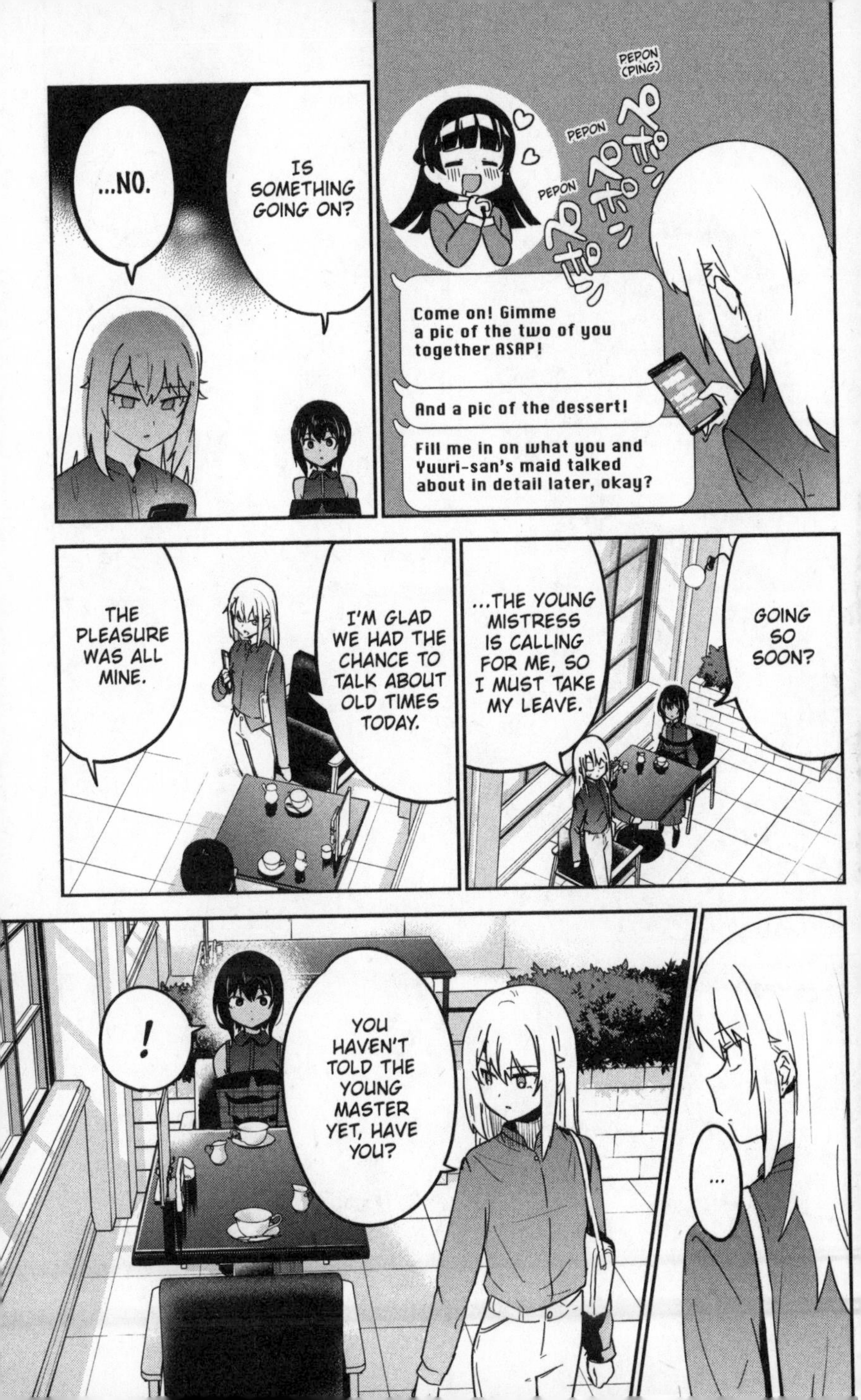
PEPON (PING)
PEPON
PEPON
Come on! Gimme a pic of the two of you together ASAP!
And a pic of the dessert!
Fill me in on what you and Yuuri-san's maid talked about in detail later, okay?
IS SOMETHING GOING ON?
...NO.
GOING SO SOON?
...THE YOUNG MISTRESS IS CALLING FOR ME, SO I MUST TAKE MY LEAVE.
I'M GLAD WE HAD THE CHANCE TO TALK ABOUT OLD TIMES TODAY.
THE PLEASURE WAS ALL MINE.
...
YOU HAVEN'T TOLD THE YOUNG MASTER YET, HAVE YOU?
!

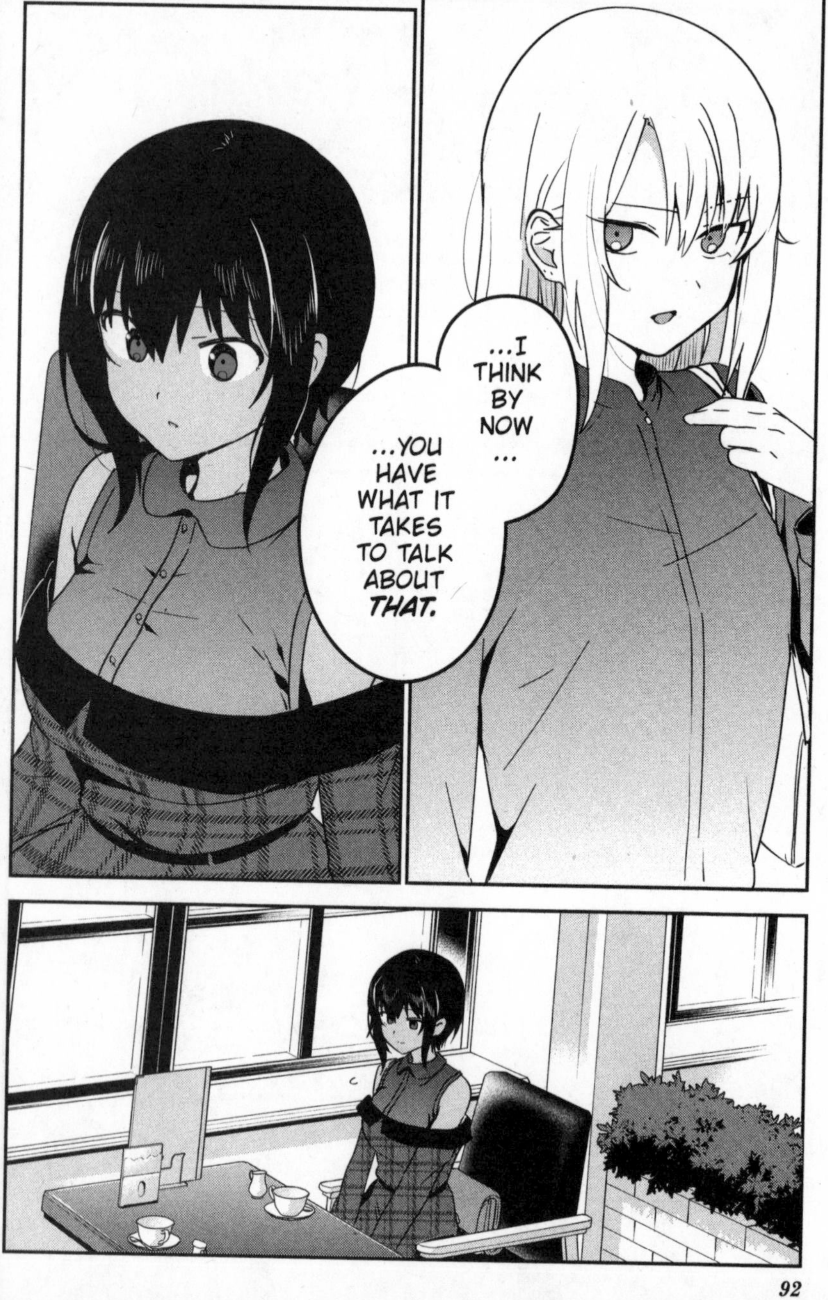
...I THINK BY NOW...
...YOU HAVE WHAT IT TAKES TO TALK ABOUT *THAT.*

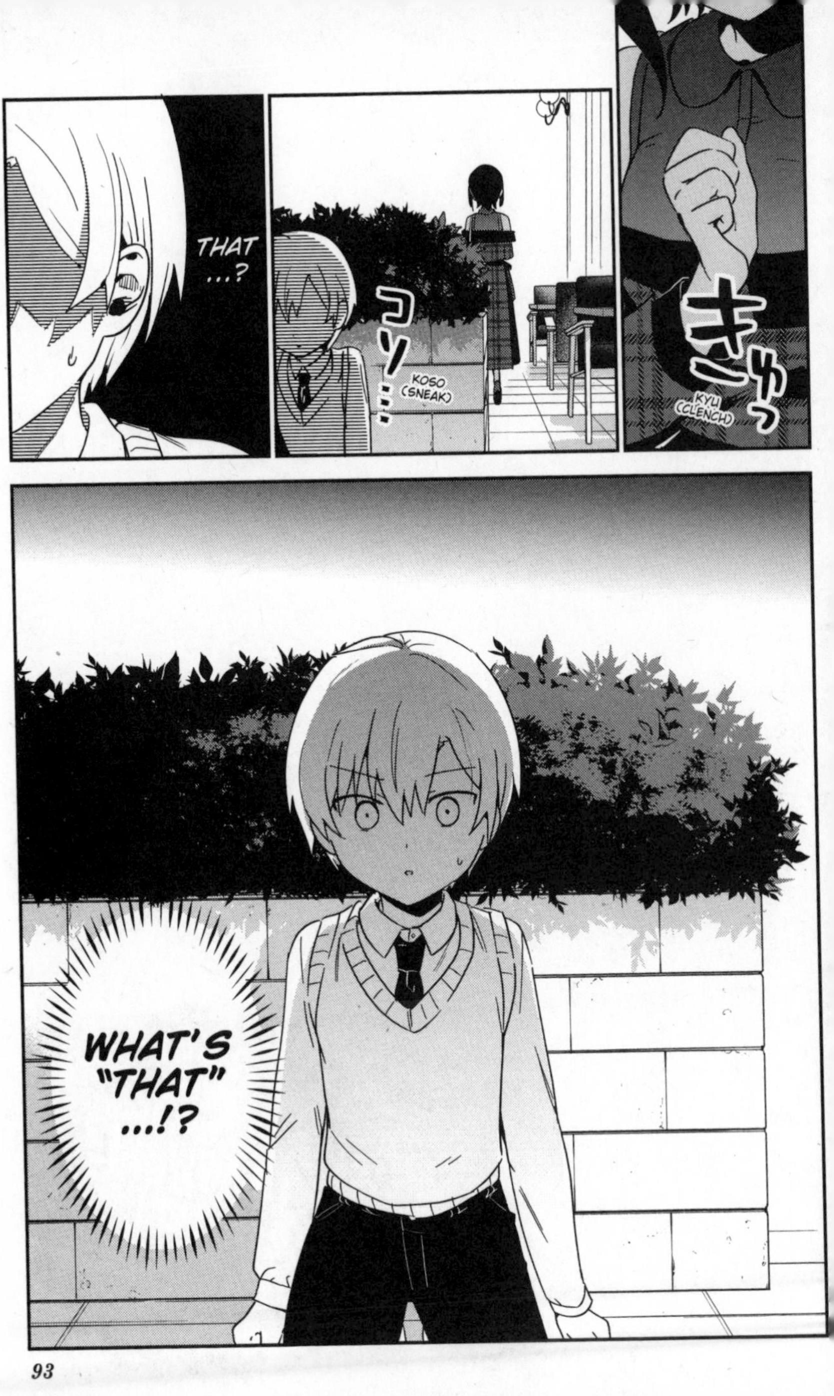
キュッ
KYU (CLENCH)
コソ…
KOSO (SNEAK)
THAT …?
WHAT'S "THAT" …!?

The Maid I Hired Recently Is Mysterious

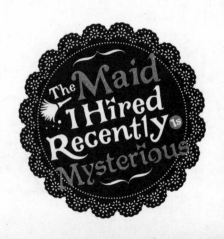

# CHAPTER 41

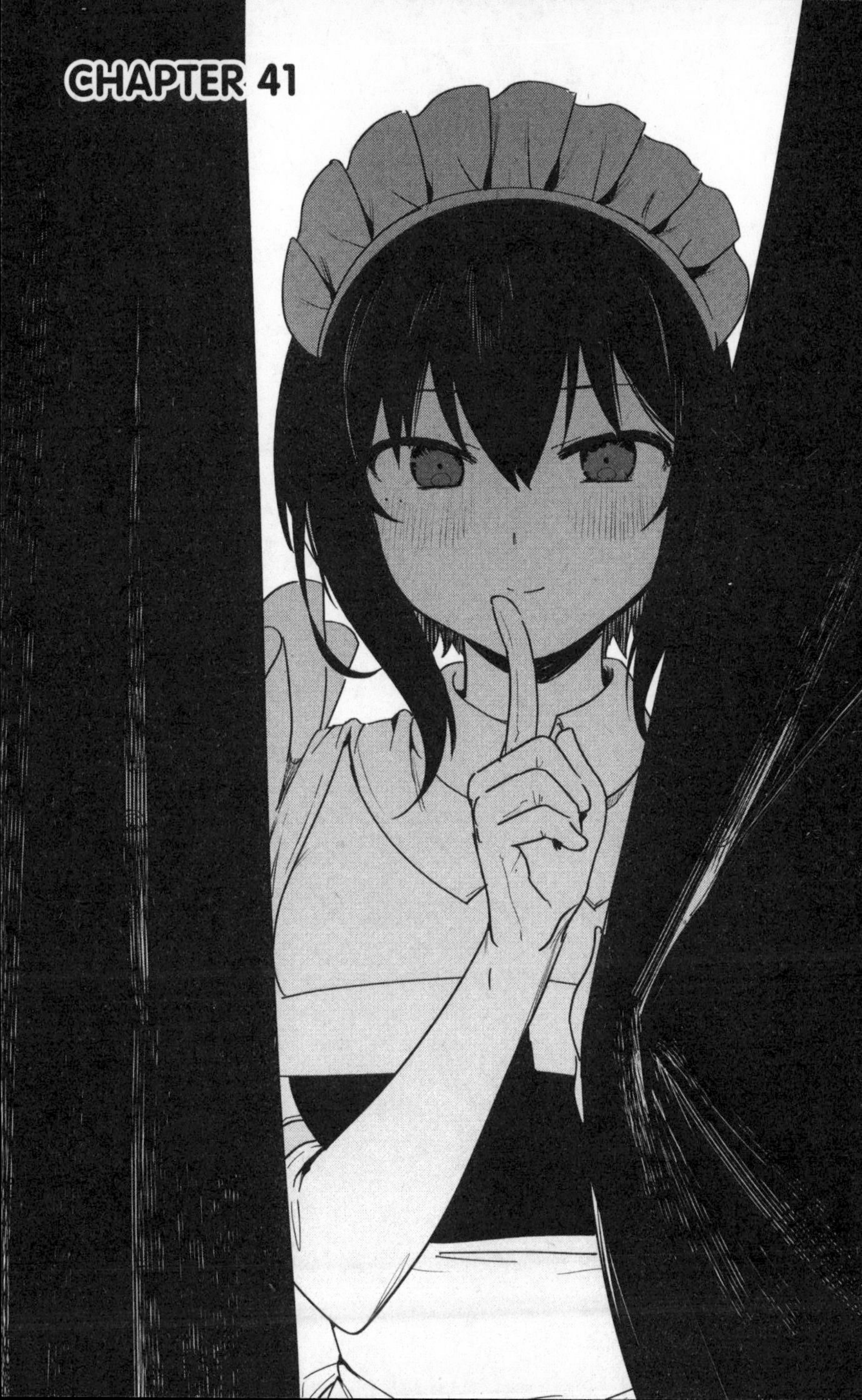

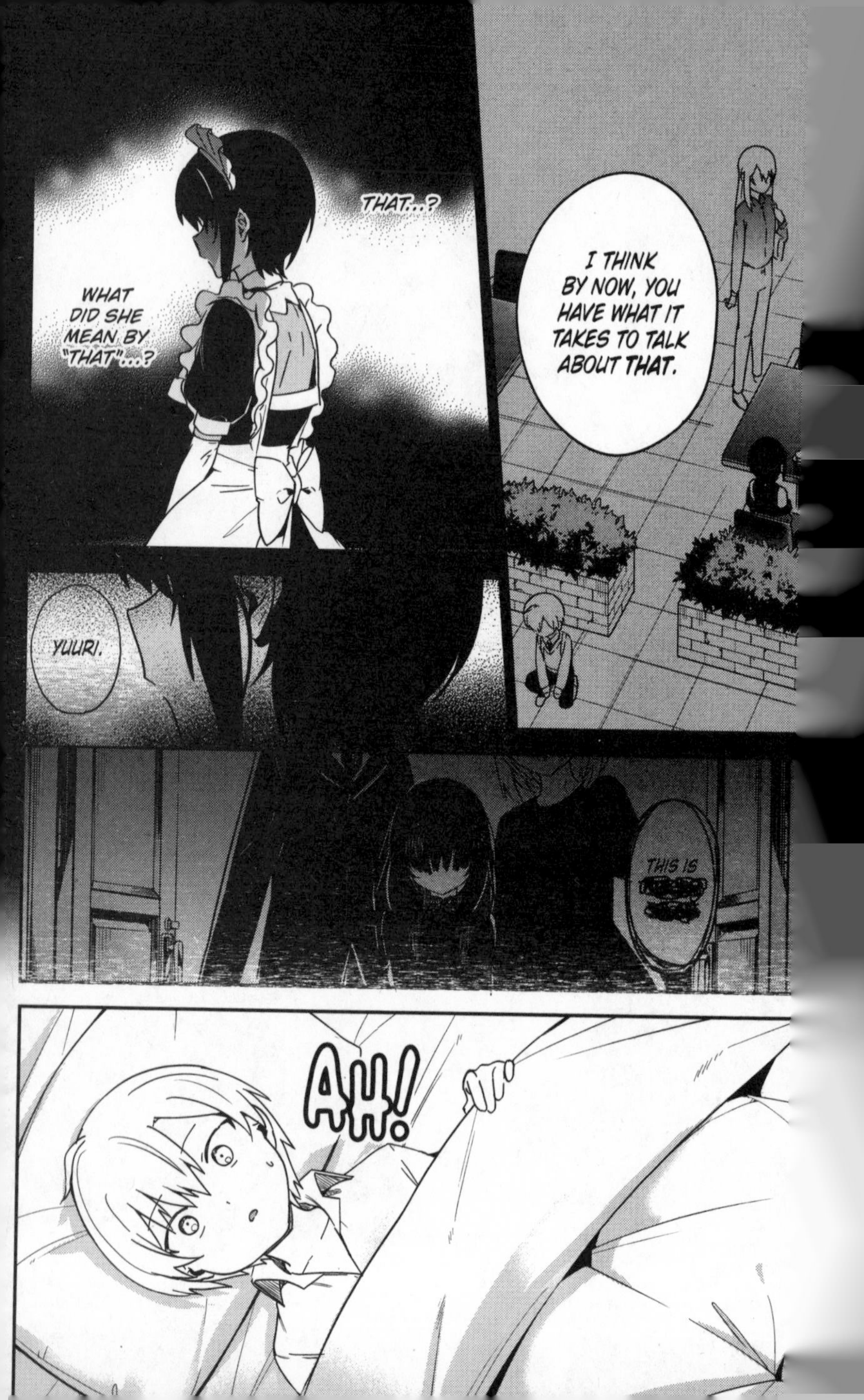
I THINK BY NOW, YOU HAVE WHAT IT TAKES TO TALK ABOUT THAT.
THAT...?
WHAT DID SHE MEAN BY "THAT"...?
YUURI.
THIS IS [redacted]
AH!

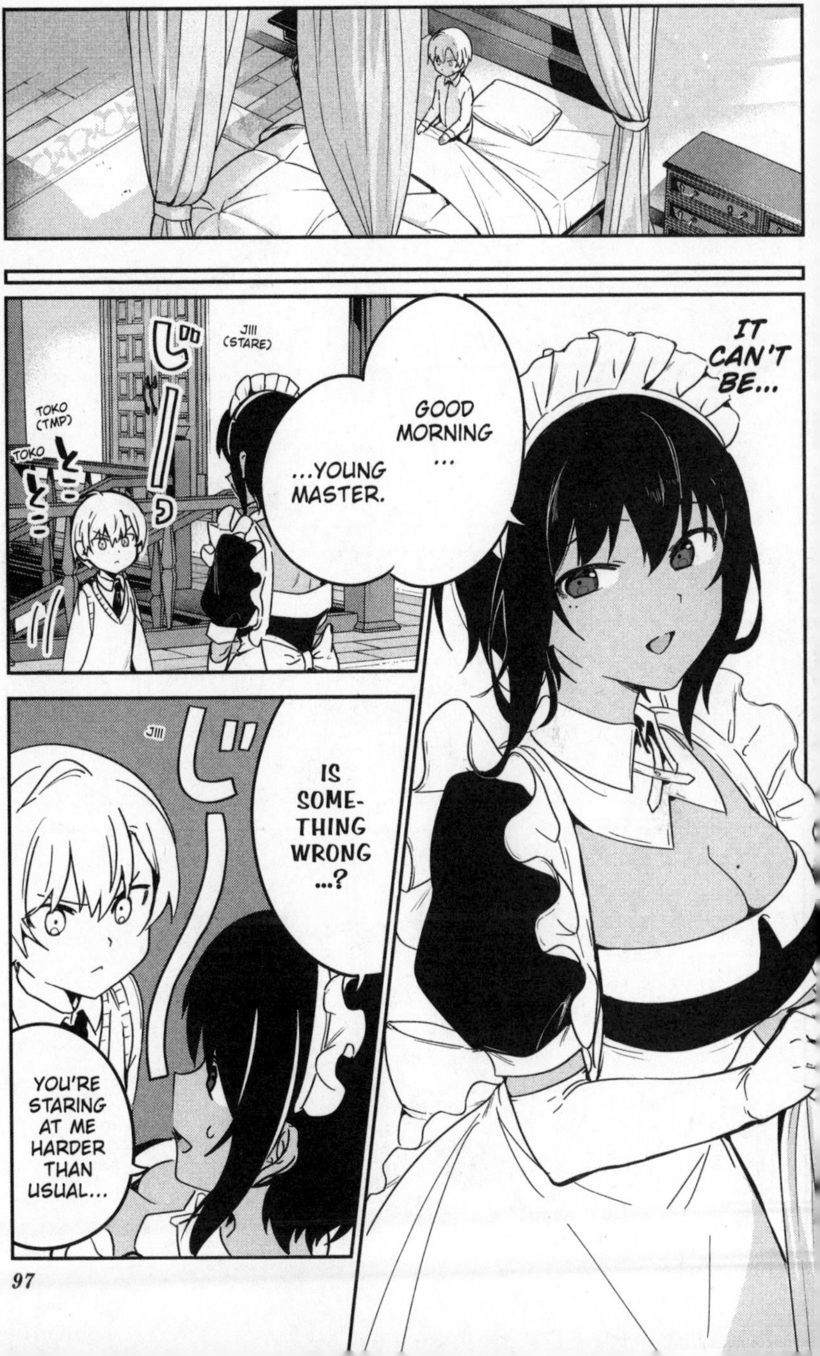
IT CAN'T BE...
GOOD MORNING ... ...YOUNG MASTER.
JIII (STARE)
TOKO (TMP)
TOKO
JIII
IS SOMETHING WRONG ...?
YOU'RE STARING AT ME HARDER THAN USUAL...

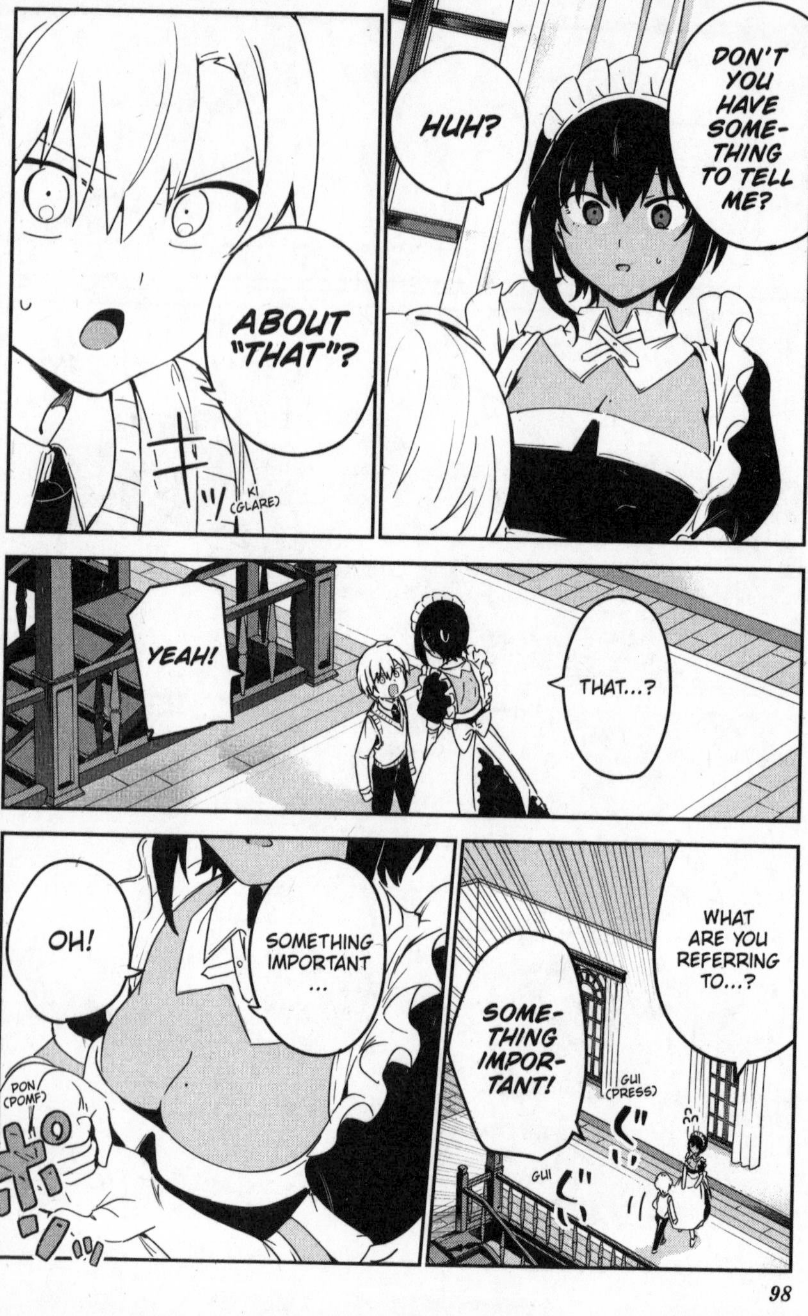
DON'T YOU HAVE SOME-THING TO TELL ME?
HUH?
ABOUT "THAT"?
KI (GLARE)
THAT...?
YEAH!
WHAT ARE YOU REFERRING TO...?
SOME-THING IMPOR-TANT!
GUI (PRESS)
GUI
SOMETHING IMPORTANT ...
OH!
PON (POMF)

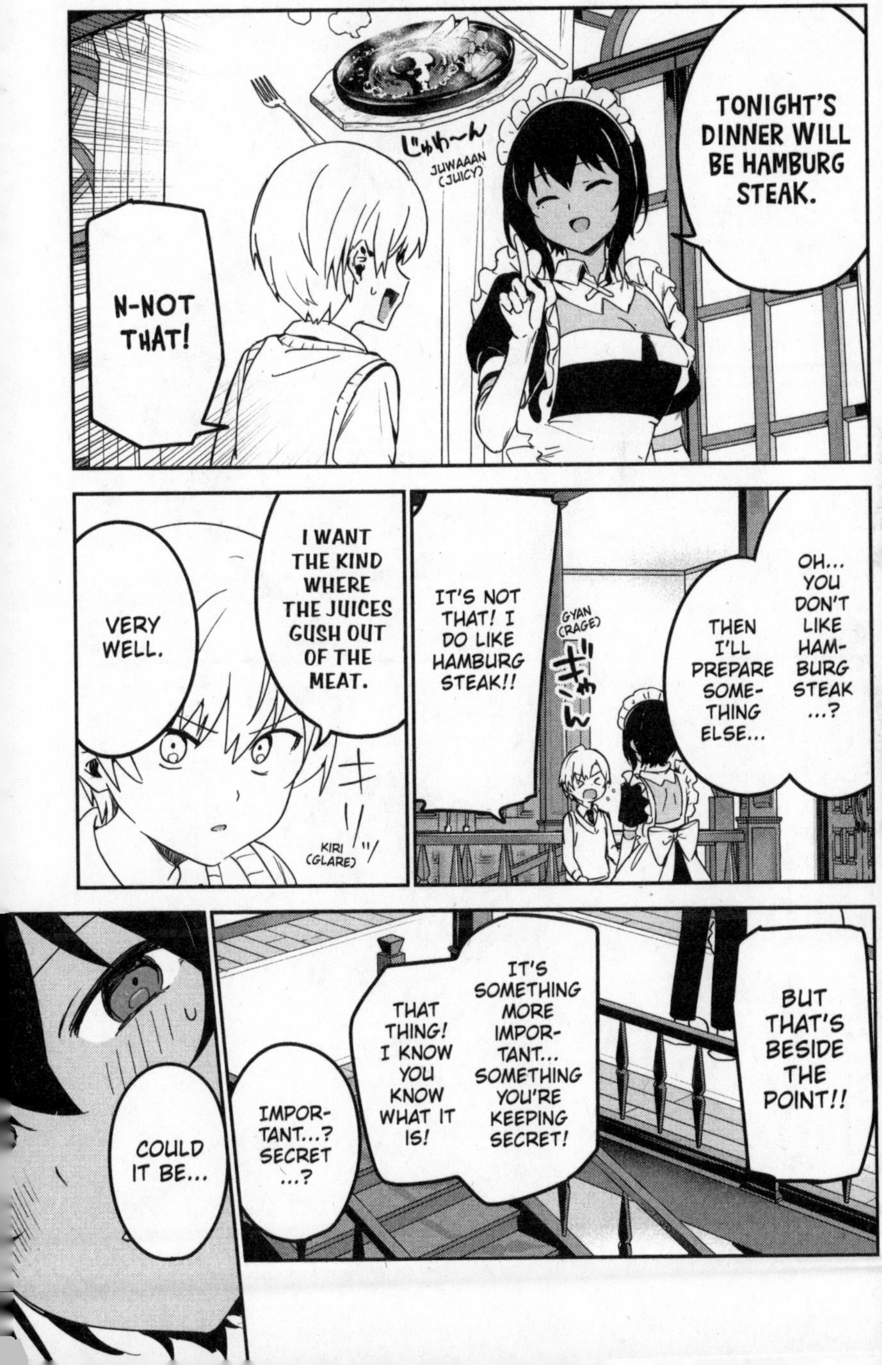
TONIGHT'S DINNER WILL BE HAMBURG STEAK.
じゅわ~ん
JUWAAAN (JUICY)
N-NOT THAT!
OH... YOU DON'T LIKE HAM-BURG STEAK ...?
THEN I'LL PREPARE SOME-THING ELSE...
GYAN (RAGE)
ぎゃん
IT'S NOT THAT! I DO LIKE HAMBURG STEAK!!
I WANT THE KIND WHERE THE JUICES GUSH OUT OF THE MEAT.
KIRI (GLARE)
VERY WELL.
BUT THAT'S BESIDE THE POINT!!
IT'S SOMETHING MORE IMPOR-TANT... SOMETHING YOU'RE KEEPING SECRET!
THAT THING! I KNOW YOU KNOW WHAT IT IS!
IMPOR-TANT...? SECRET ...?
COULD IT BE...

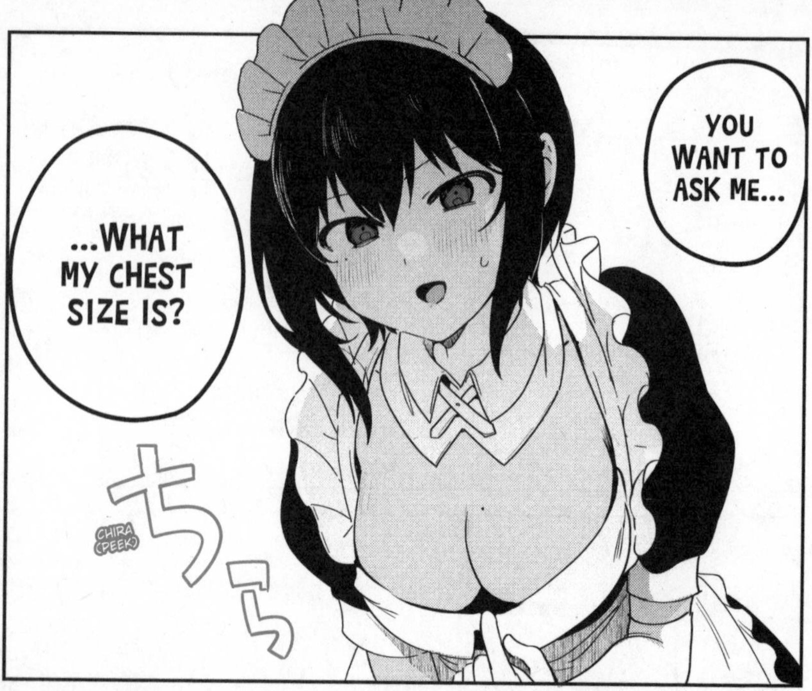
YOU WANT TO ASK ME...
...WHAT MY CHEST SIZE IS?
ちら
CHIRA (PEEK)

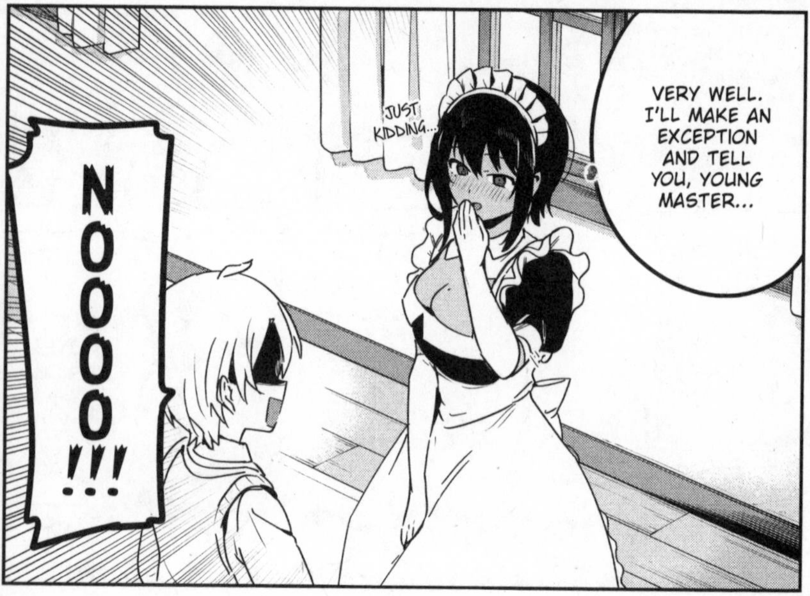
VERY WELL. I'LL MAKE AN EXCEPTION AND TELL YOU, YOUNG MASTER...
JUST KIDDING...
NOOOOO!!!

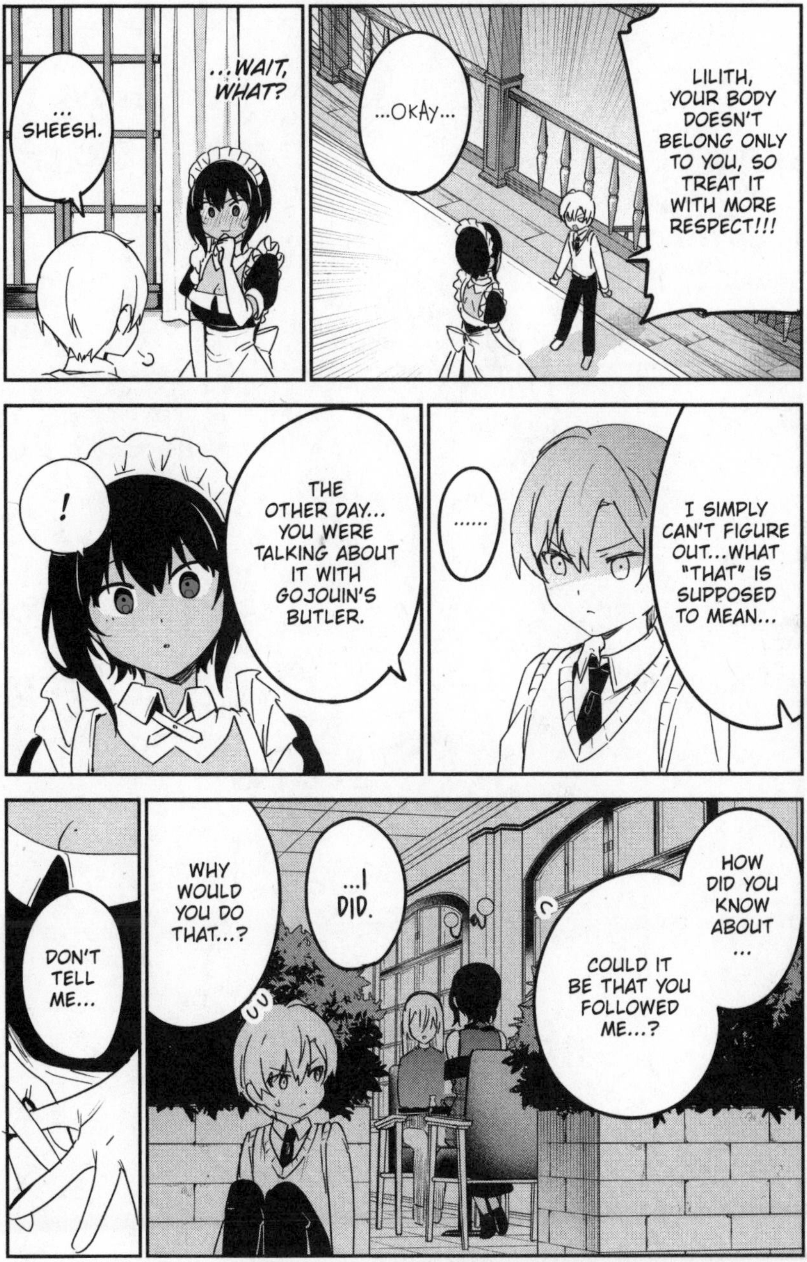
LILITH, YOUR BODY DOESN'T BELONG ONLY TO YOU, SO TREAT IT WITH MORE RESPECT!!!
...OKAY...
...WAIT, WHAT?
... SHEESH.
I SIMPLY CAN'T FIGURE OUT...WHAT "THAT" IS SUPPOSED TO MEAN...
......
THE OTHER DAY... YOU WERE TALKING ABOUT IT WITH GOJOUIN'S BUTLER.
!
HOW DID YOU KNOW ABOUT ...
COULD IT BE THAT YOU FOLLOWED ME...?
...I DID.
WHY WOULD YOU DO THAT...?
DON'T TELL ME...

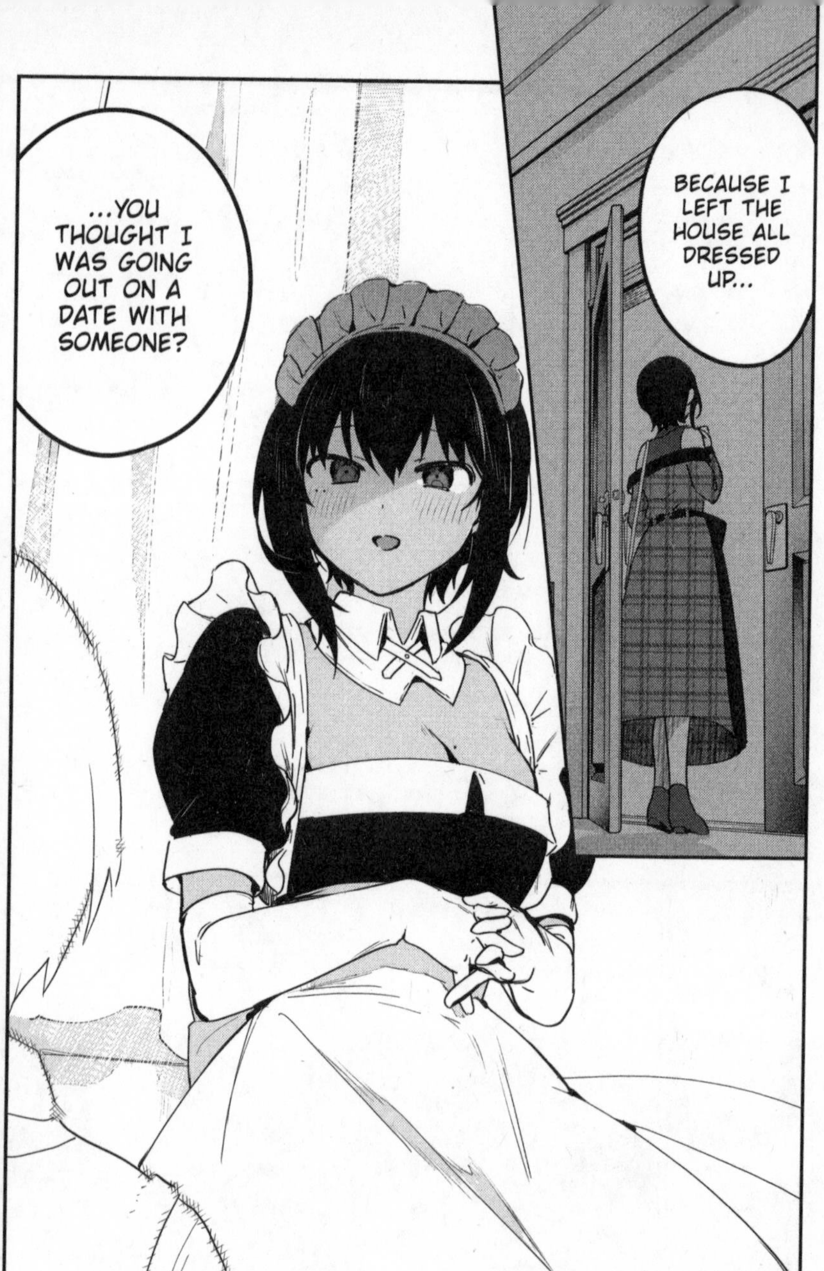
BECAUSE I LEFT THE HOUSE ALL DRESSED UP...
...YOU THOUGHT I WAS GOING OUT ON A DATE WITH SOMEONE?

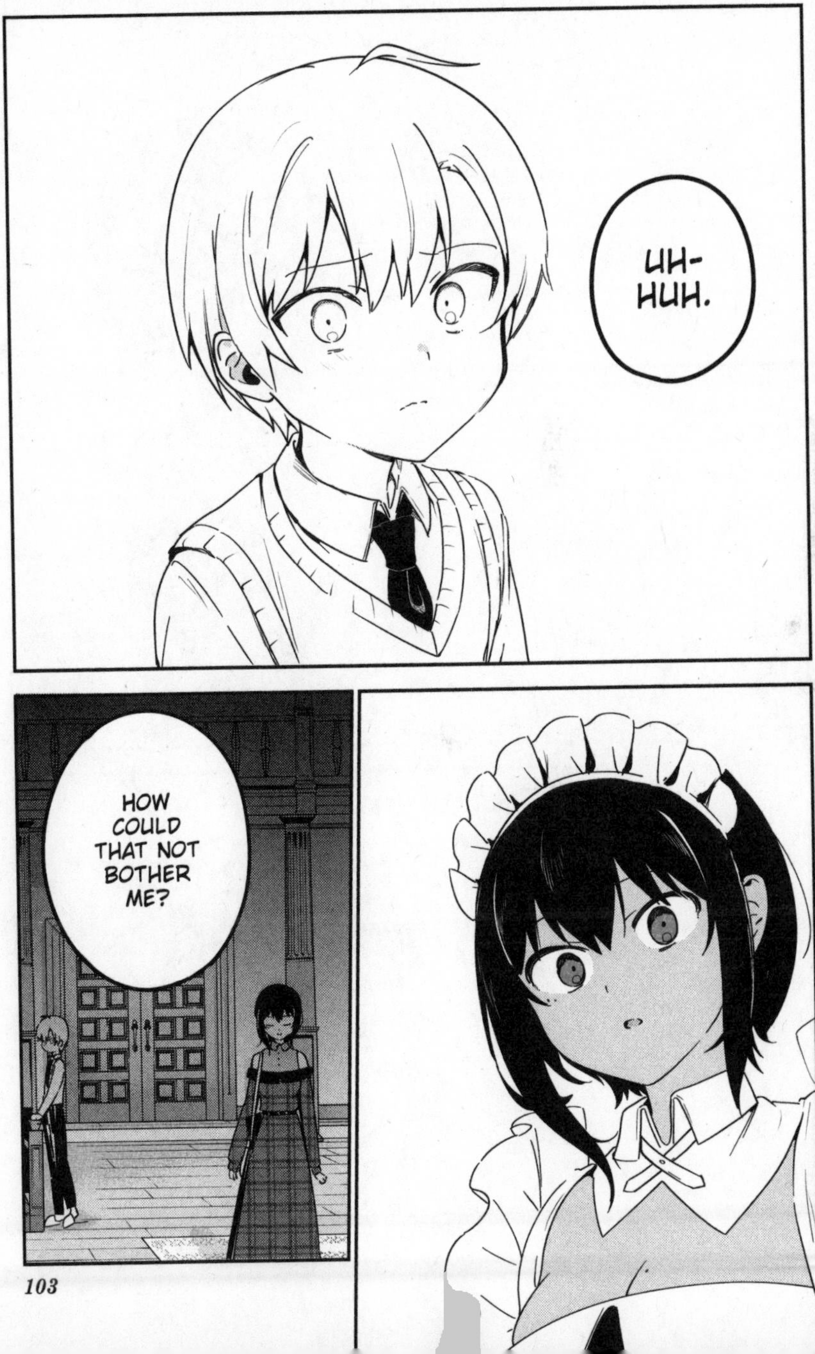
UH-HUH.
HOW COULD THAT NOT BOTHER ME?

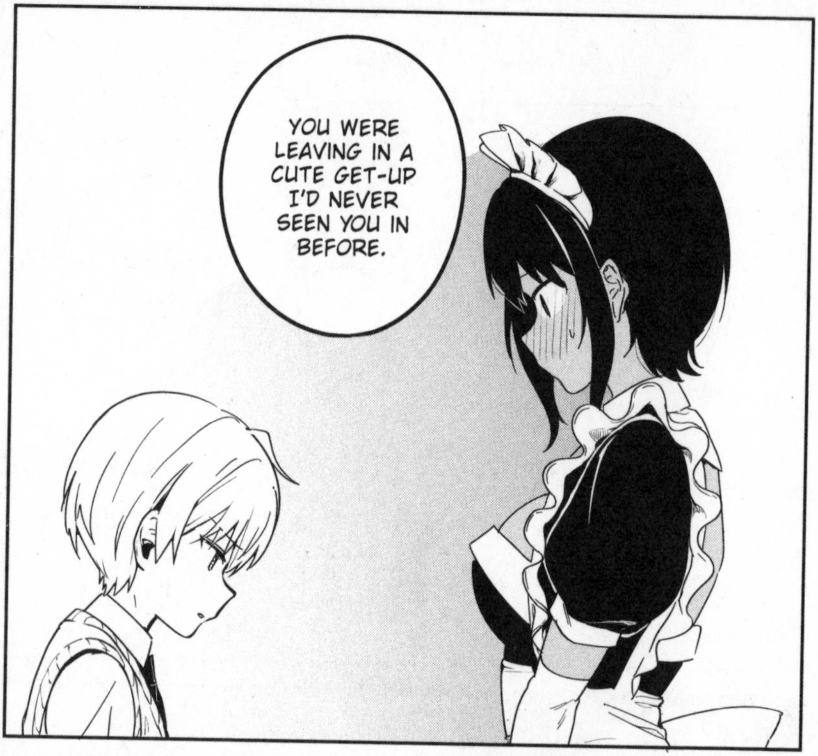
YOU WERE LEAVING IN A CUTE GET-UP I'D NEVER SEEN YOU IN BEFORE.

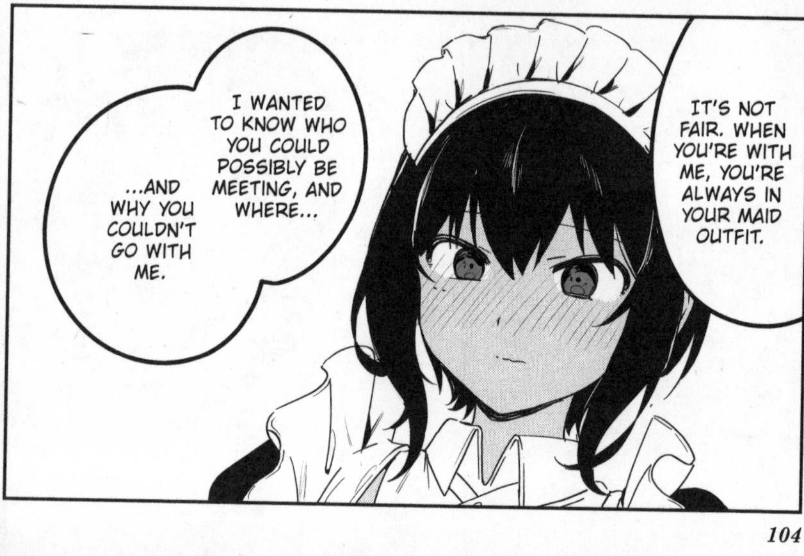
IT'S NOT FAIR. WHEN YOU'RE WITH ME, YOU'RE ALWAYS IN YOUR MAID OUTFIT.
I WANTED TO KNOW WHO YOU COULD POSSIBLY BE MEETING, AND WHERE...
...AND WHY YOU COULDN'T GO WITH ME.

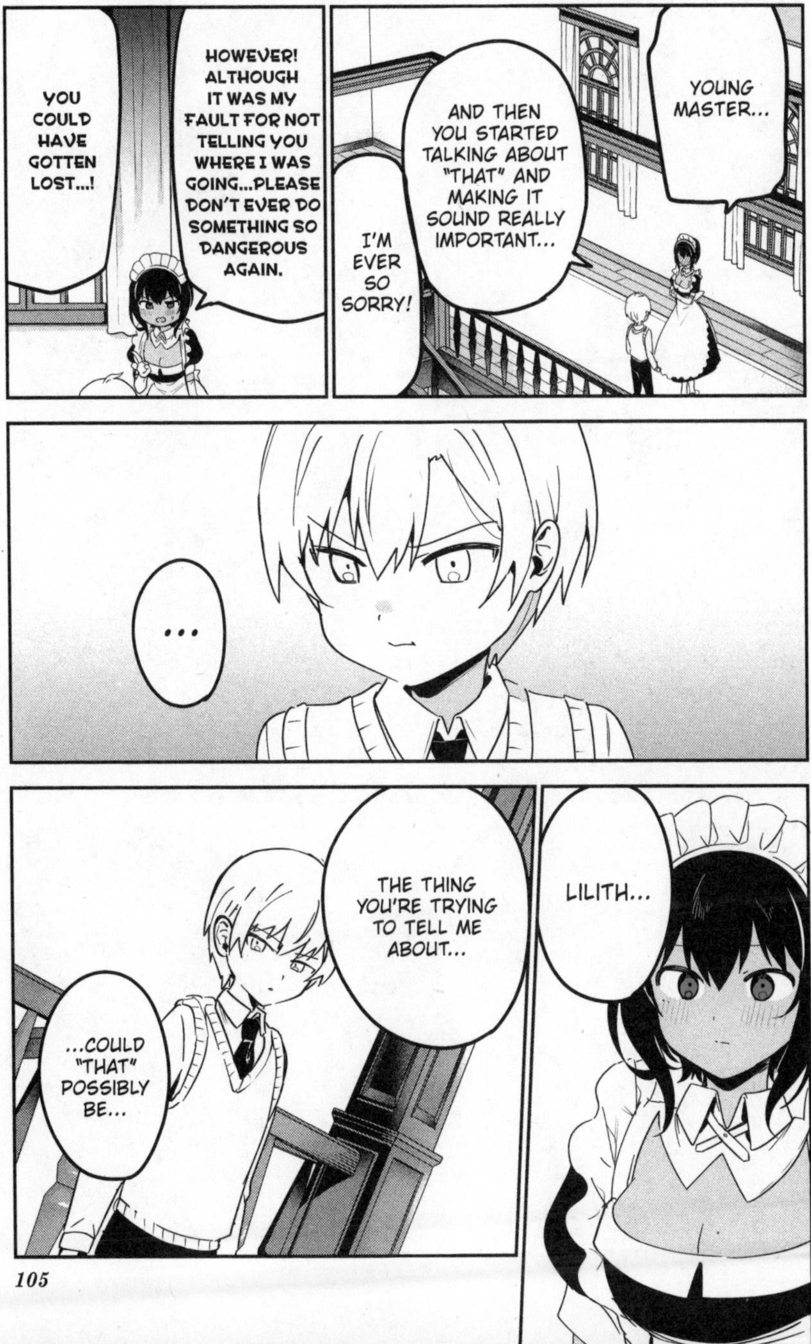
YOUNG MASTER...
AND THEN YOU STARTED TALKING ABOUT "THAT" AND MAKING IT SOUND REALLY IMPORTANT...
I'M EVER SO SORRY!
HOWEVER! ALTHOUGH IT WAS MY FAULT FOR NOT TELLING YOU WHERE I WAS GOING...PLEASE DON'T EVER DO SOMETHING SO DANGEROUS AGAIN.
YOU COULD HAVE GOTTEN LOST...!
...
LILITH...
THE THING YOU'RE TRYING TO TELL ME ABOUT...
...COULD "THAT" POSSIBLY BE...

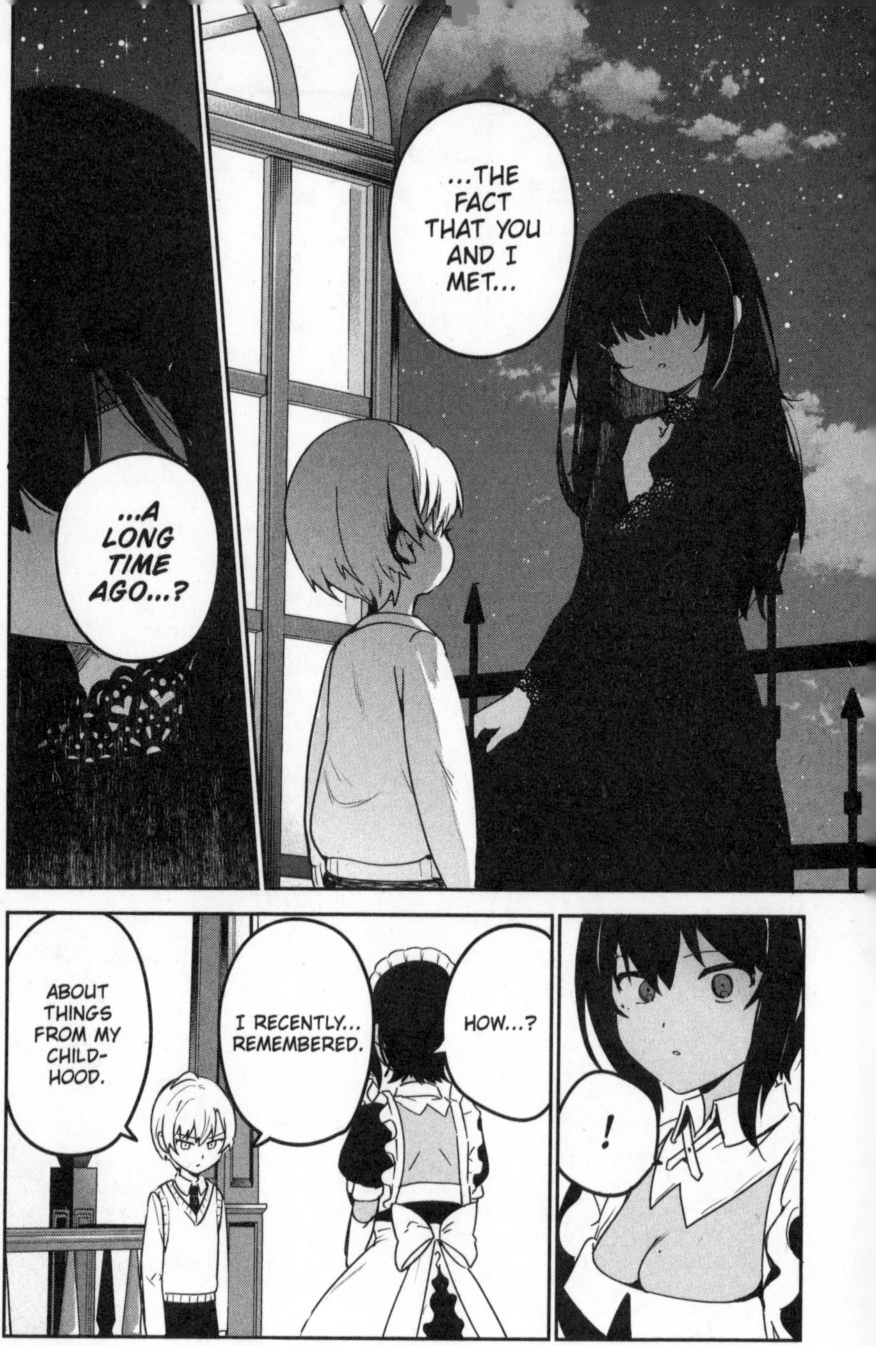
...THE FACT THAT YOU AND I MET...
...A LONG TIME AGO...?
!
HOW...?
I RECENTLY... REMEMBERED.
ABOUT THINGS FROM MY CHILD-HOOD.

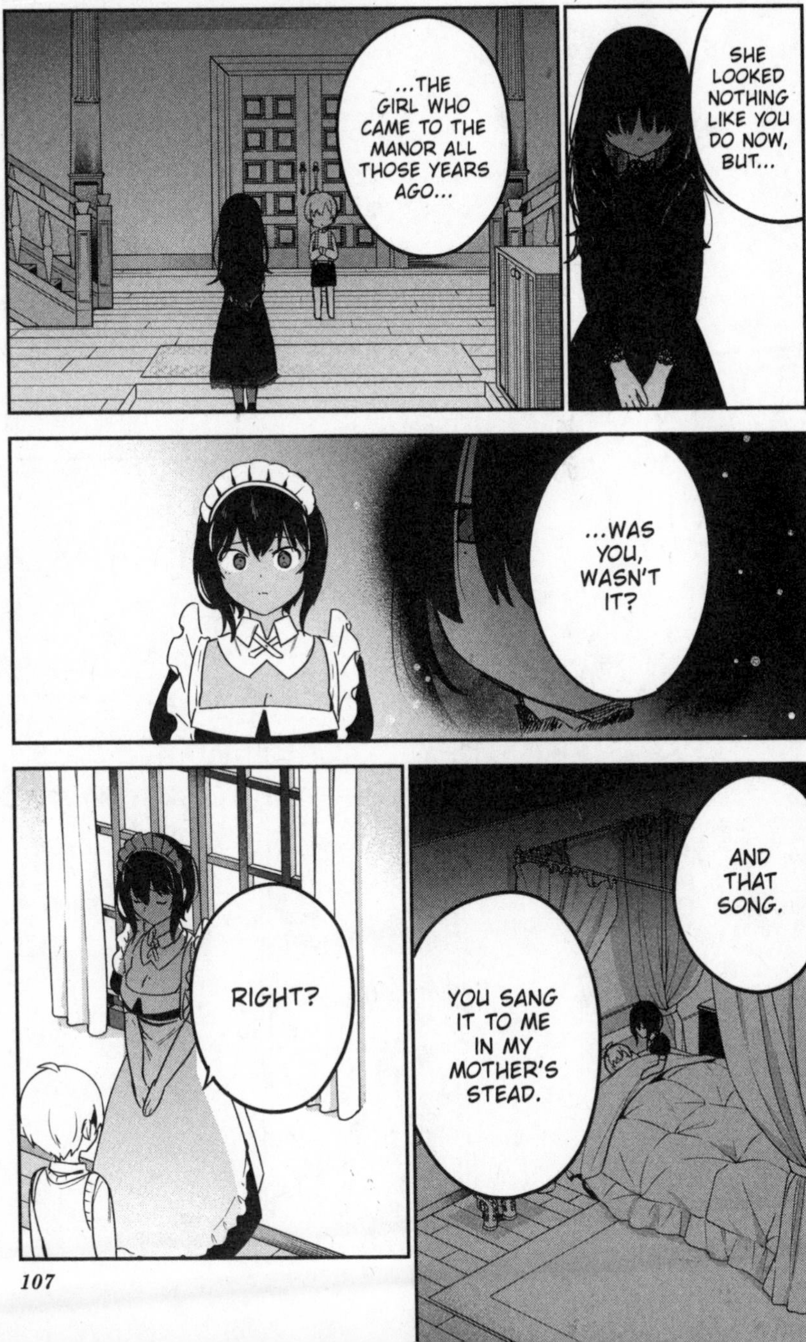
SHE LOOKED NOTHING LIKE YOU DO NOW, BUT...
...THE GIRL WHO CAME TO THE MANOR ALL THOSE YEARS AGO...
...WAS YOU, WASN'T IT?
AND THAT SONG.
YOU SANG IT TO ME IN MY MOTHER'S STEAD.
RIGHT?

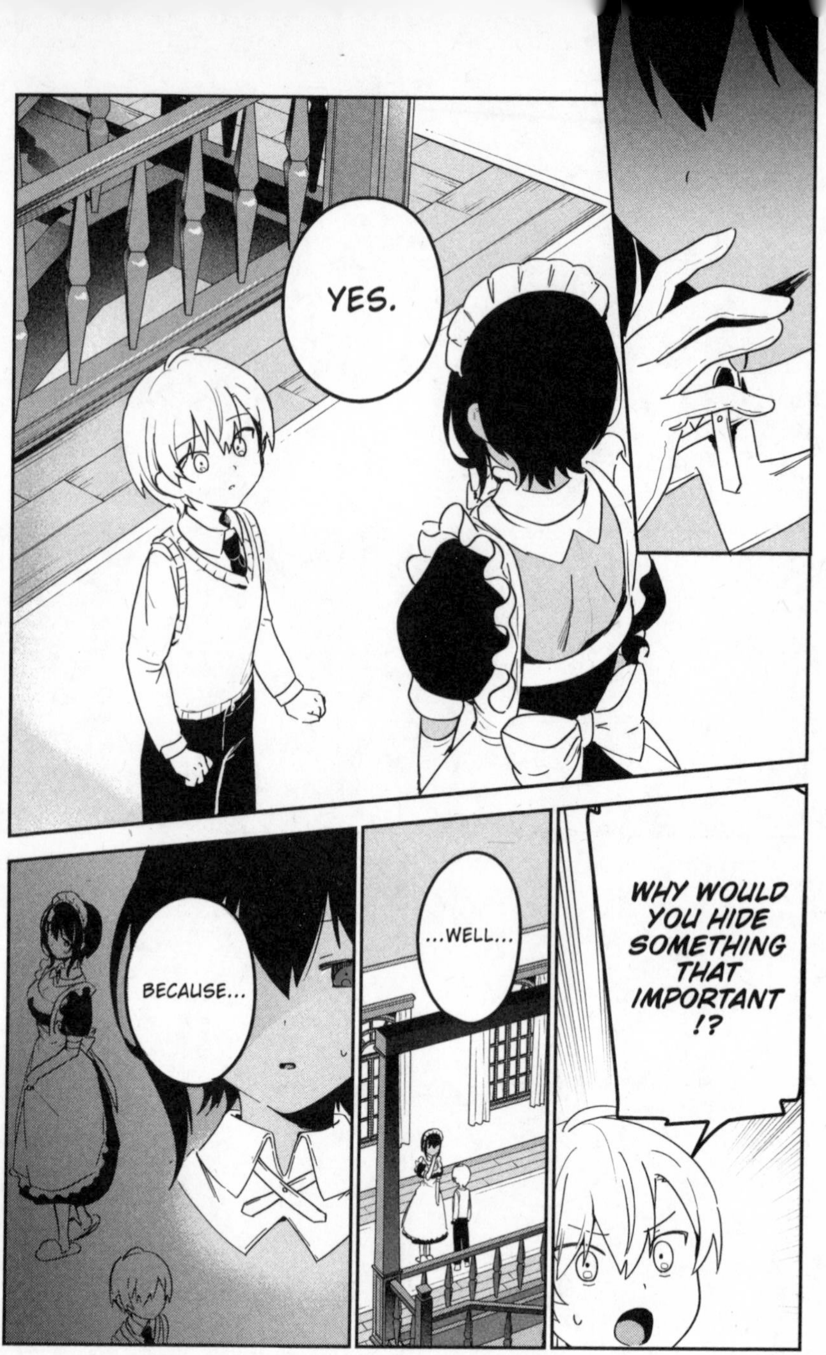
YES.
WHY WOULD YOU HIDE SOMETHING THAT IMPORTANT!?
...WELL...
BECAUSE...

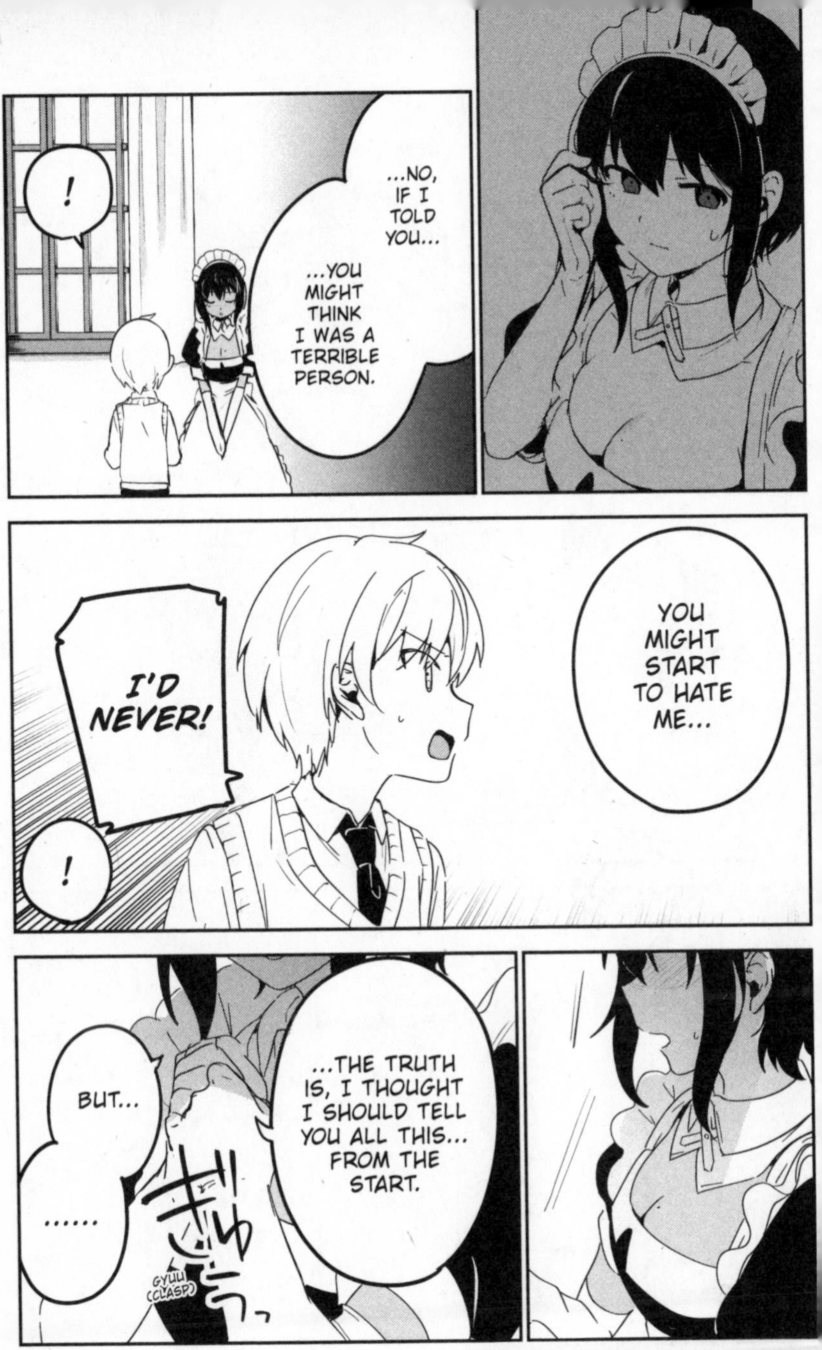
...NO, IF I TOLD YOU...
...YOU MIGHT THINK I WAS A TERRIBLE PERSON.
!
YOU MIGHT START TO HATE ME...
I'D NEVER!
!
...THE TRUTH IS, I THOUGHT I SHOULD TELL YOU ALL THIS... FROM THE START.
BUT...
......
GYUU (CLASP)

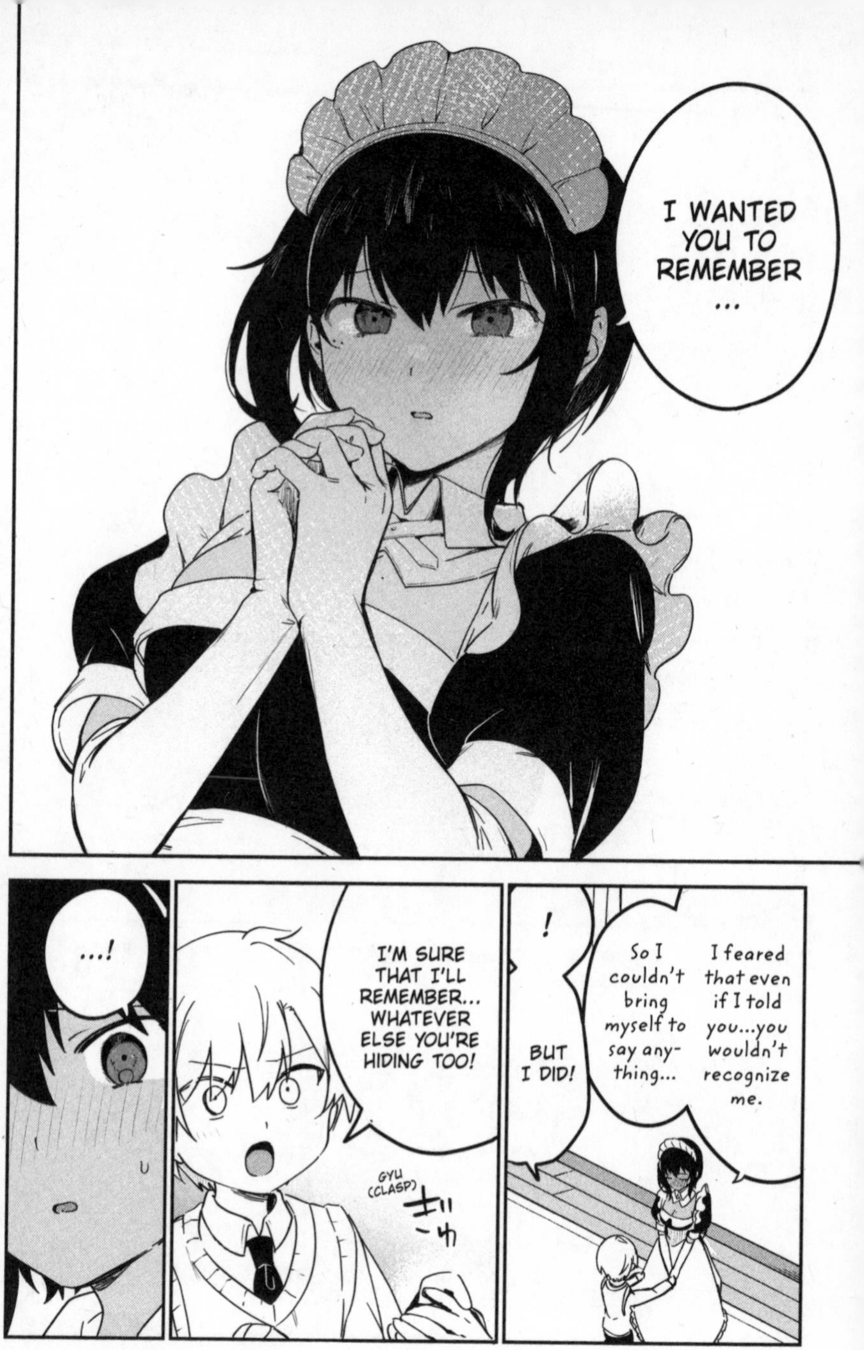
I WANTED YOU TO REMEMBER ...
I feared that even if I told you...you wouldn't recognize me.
So I couldn't bring myself to say any-thing...
!
BUT I DID!
I'M SURE THAT I'LL REMEMBER... WHATEVER ELSE YOU'RE HIDING TOO!
GYU (CLASP)
...!

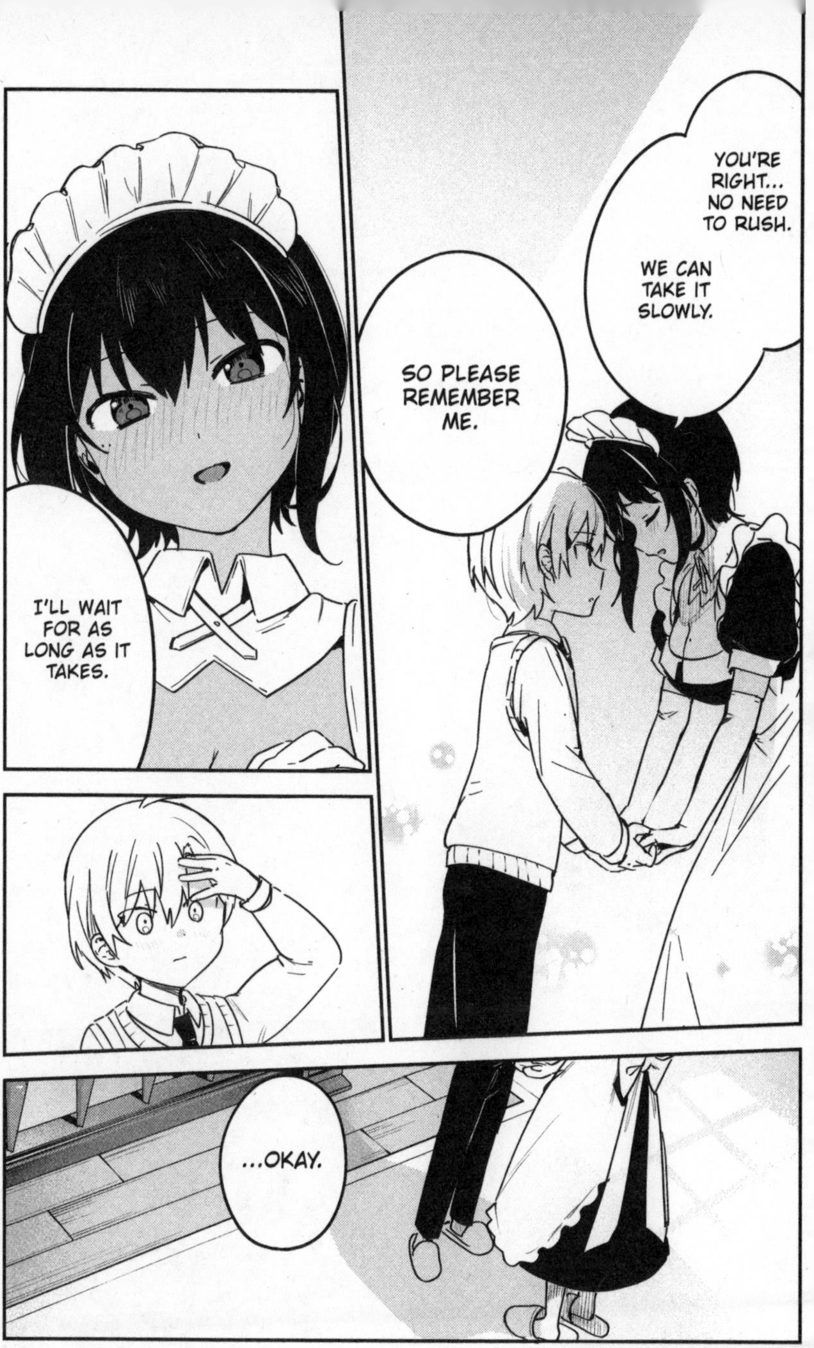
YOU'RE RIGHT... NO NEED TO RUSH.
WE CAN TAKE IT SLOWLY.
SO PLEASE REMEMBER ME.
I'LL WAIT FOR AS LONG AS IT TAKES.
...OKAY.

The Maid I Hired Recently Is Mysterious

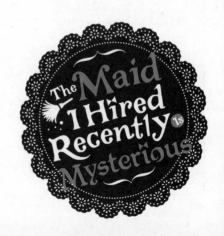

# CHAPTER 42

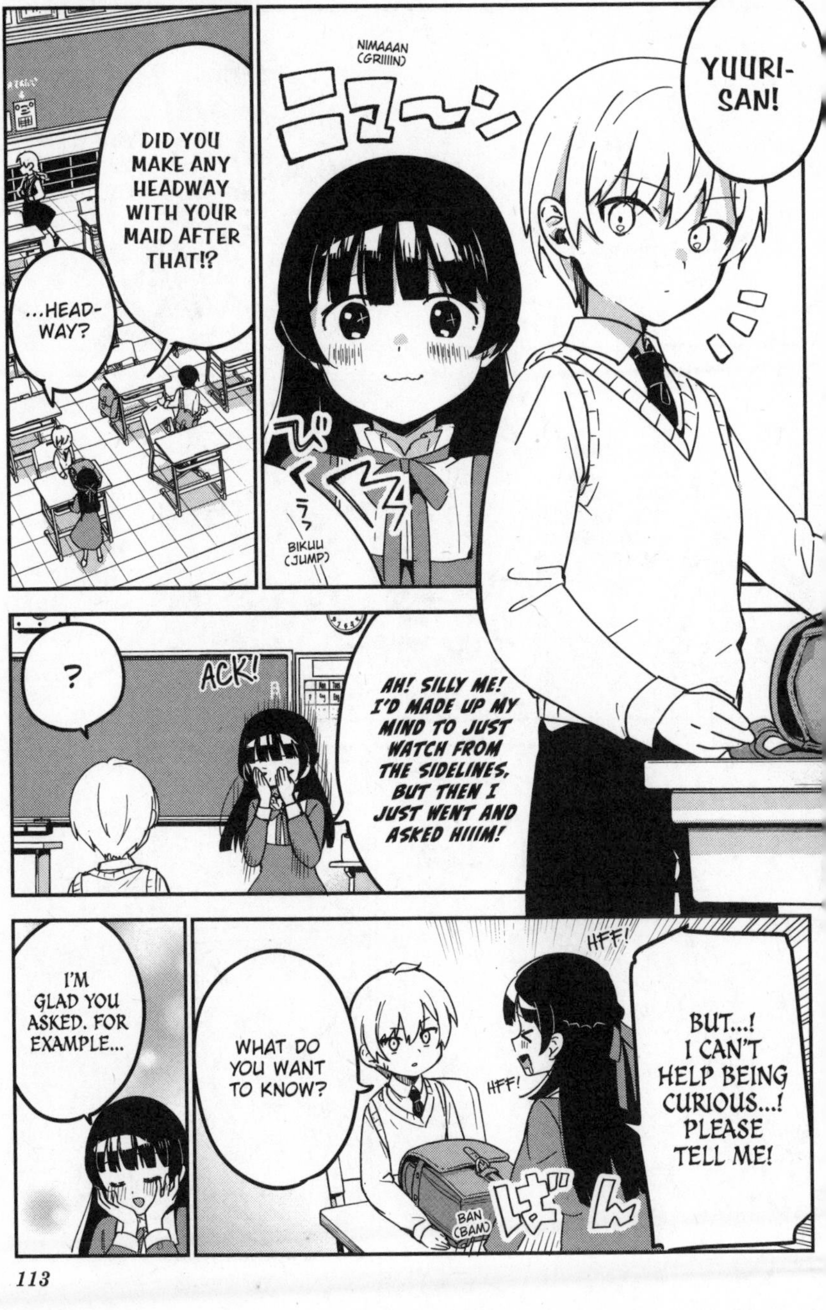
YUURI-SAN!
NIMAAAN (GRIIIIN)
BIKUU (JUMP)
DID YOU MAKE ANY HEADWAY WITH YOUR MAID AFTER THAT!?
...HEAD-WAY?
AH! SILLY ME! I'D MADE UP MY MIND TO JUST WATCH FROM THE SIDELINES, BUT THEN I JUST WENT AND ASKED HIIIM!
ACK!
?
BUT...! I CAN'T HELP BEING CURIOUS...! PLEASE TELL ME!
HFF!
HFF!
BAN (BAM)
WHAT DO YOU WANT TO KNOW?
I'M GLAD YOU ASKED. FOR EXAMPLE...

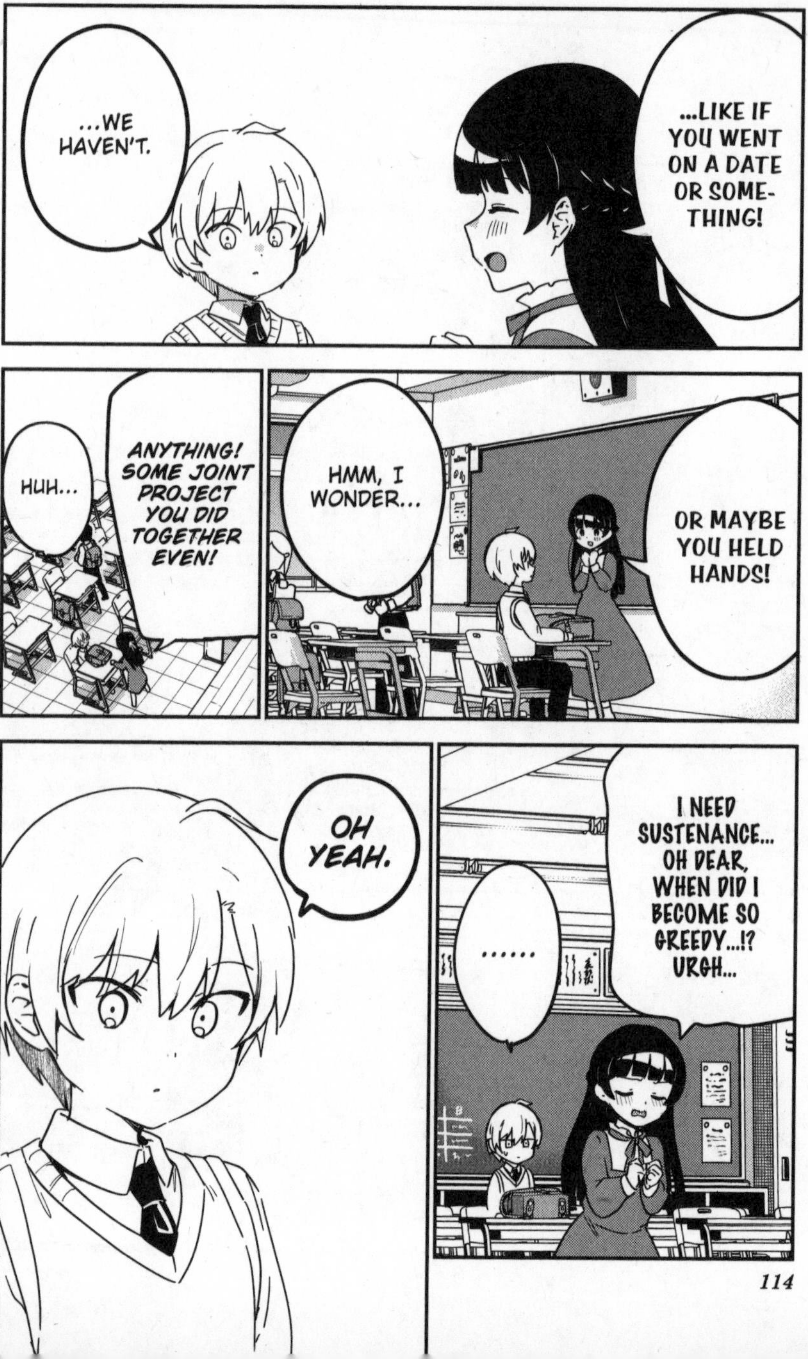
...LIKE IF YOU WENT ON A DATE OR SOME-THING!
...WE HAVEN'T.
OR MAYBE YOU HELD HANDS!
HMM, I WONDER...
ANYTHING! SOME JOINT PROJECT YOU DID TOGETHER EVEN!
HUH...
I NEED SUSTENANCE... OH DEAR, WHEN DID I BECOME SO GREEDY...!? URGH...
......
OH YEAH.

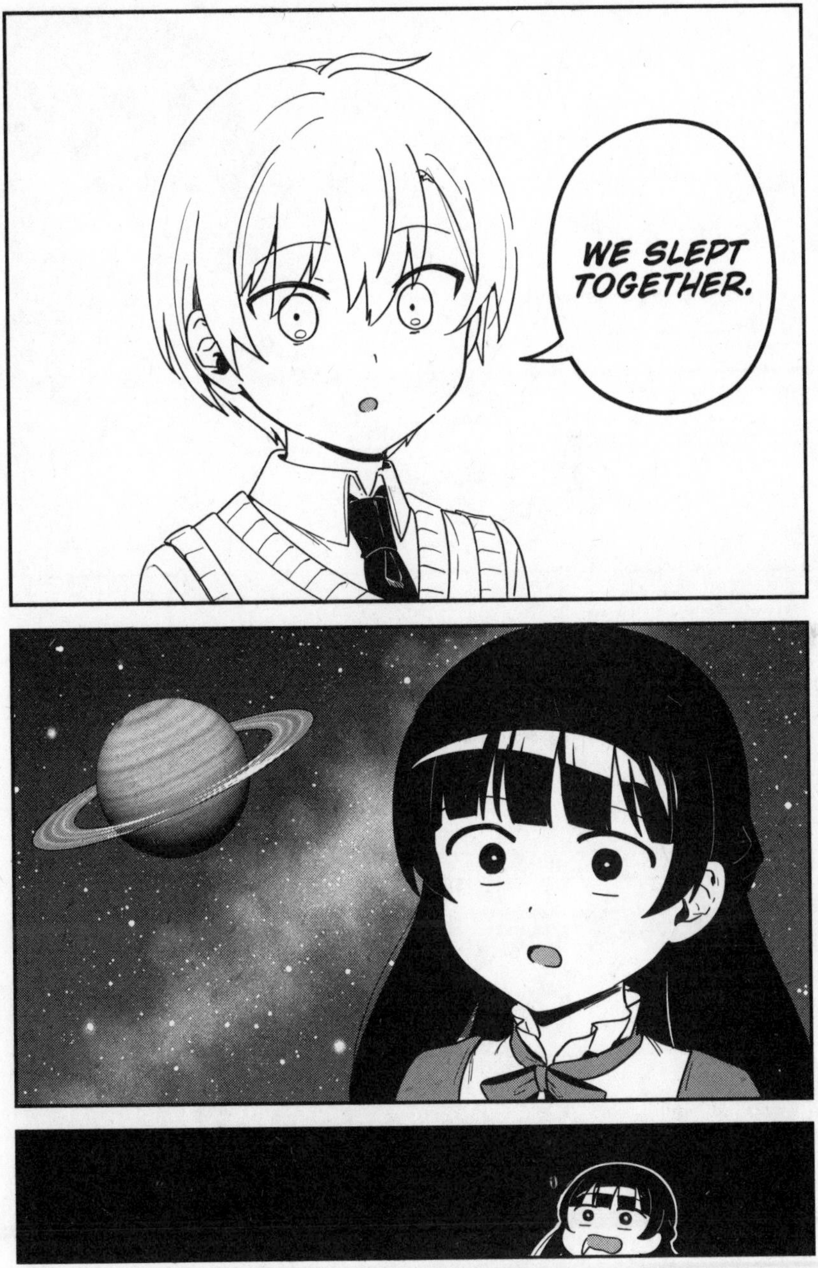
WE SLEPT TOGETHER.

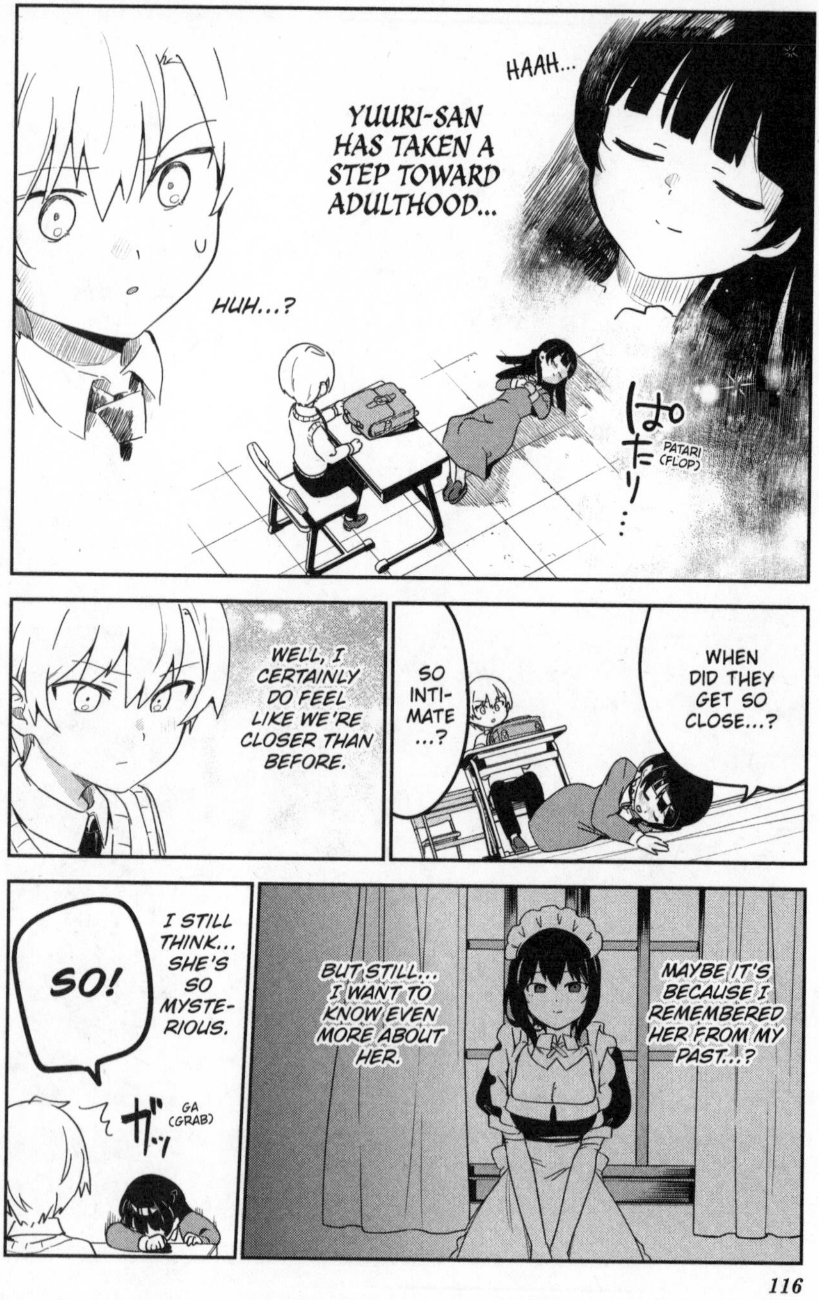
HAAH...
YUURI-SAN HAS TAKEN A STEP TOWARD ADULTHOOD...
HUH...?
ぱたり…
PATARI (FLOP)
WHEN DID THEY GET SO CLOSE...?
SO INTI-MATE ...?
WELL, I CERTAINLY DO FEEL LIKE WE'RE CLOSER THAN BEFORE.
MAYBE IT'S BECAUSE I REMEMBERED HER FROM MY PAST...?
BUT STILL... I WANT TO KNOW EVEN MORE ABOUT HER.
I STILL THINK... SHE'S SO MYSTE-RIOUS.
SO!
ガッ
GA (GRAB)

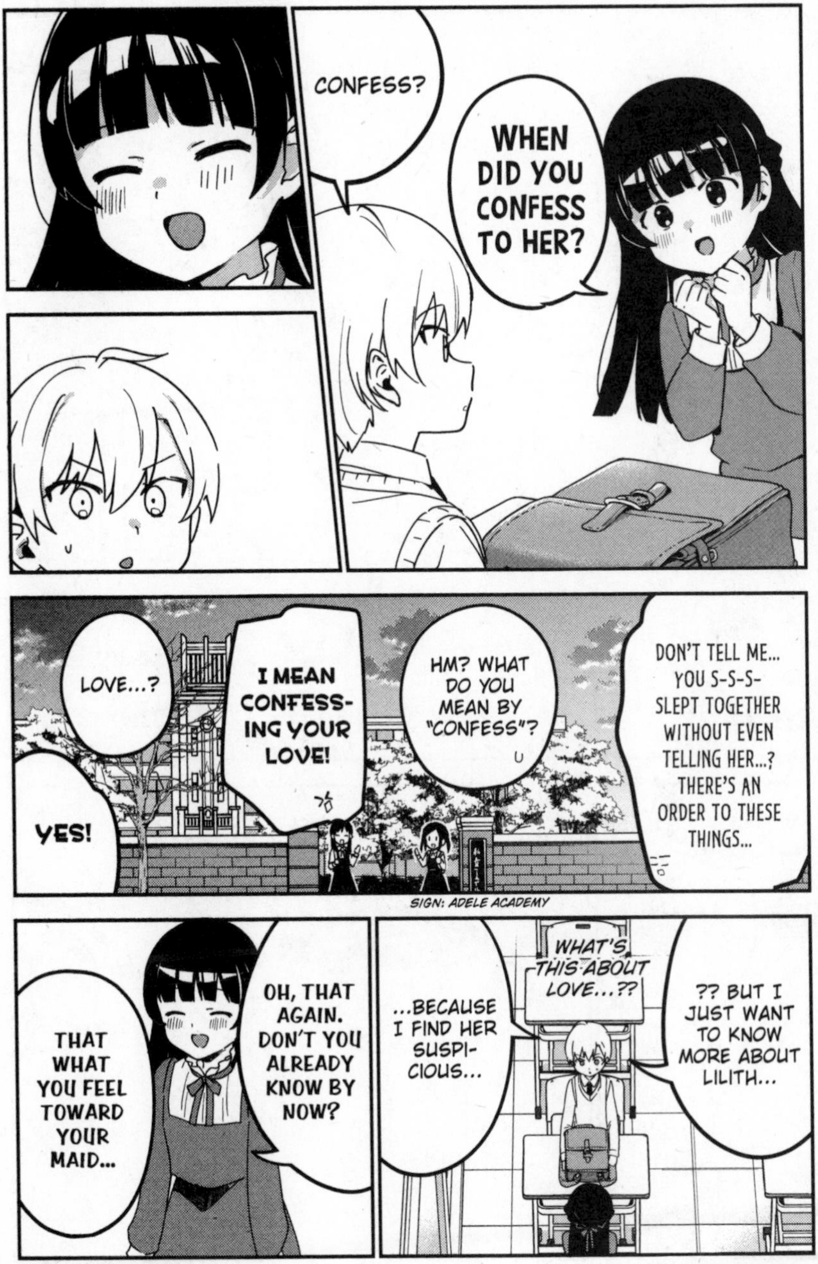
WHEN DID YOU CONFESS TO HER?
CONFESS?
DON'T TELL ME... YOU S-S-S-SLEPT TOGETHER WITHOUT EVEN TELLING HER...? THERE'S AN ORDER TO THESE THINGS...
HM? WHAT DO YOU MEAN BY "CONFESS"?
I MEAN CONFESSING YOUR LOVE!
LOVE...?
YES!
?? BUT I JUST WANT TO KNOW MORE ABOUT LILITH...
WHAT'S THIS ABOUT LOVE...??
...BECAUSE I FIND HER SUSPICIOUS...
OH, THAT AGAIN. DON'T YOU ALREADY KNOW BY NOW?
THAT WHAT YOU FEEL TOWARD YOUR MAID...

SIGN: ADELE ACADEMY

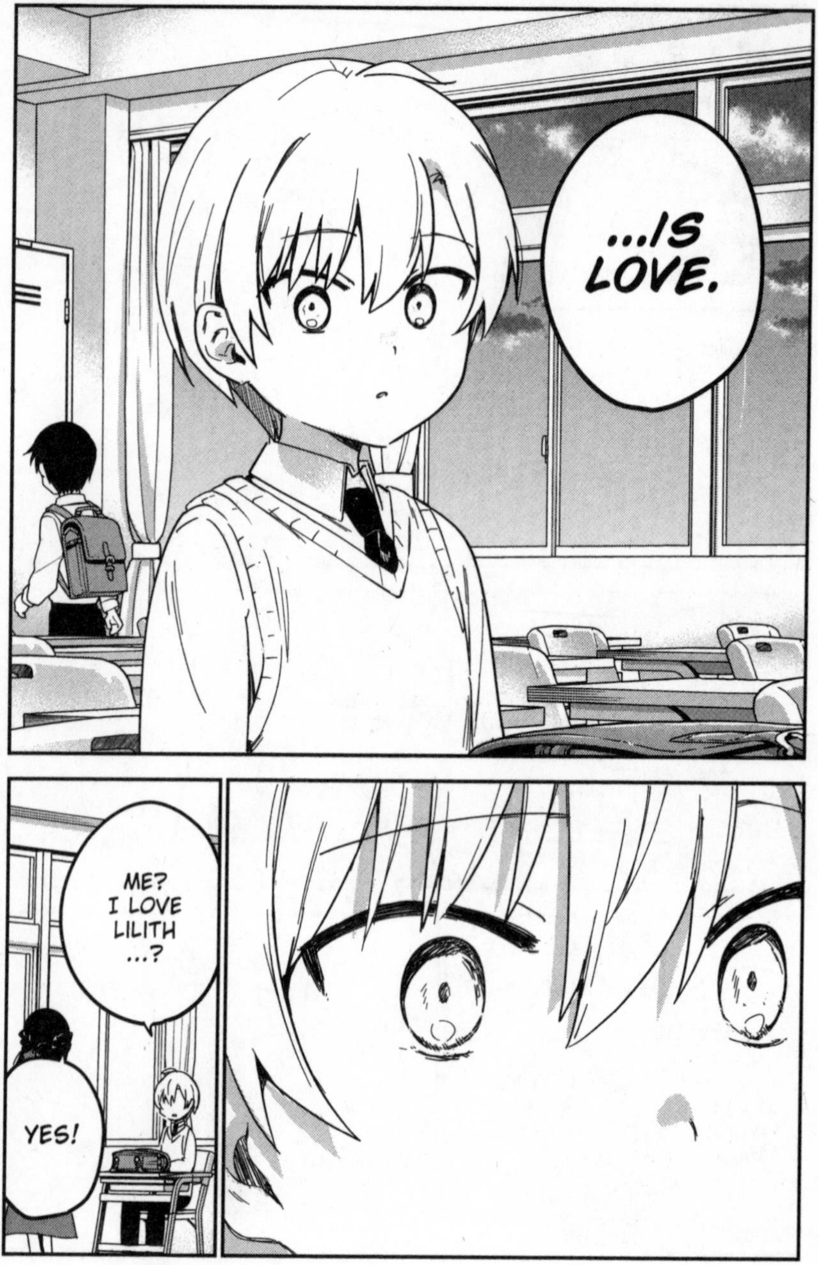
...IS LOVE.
ME? I LOVE LILITH ...?
YES!

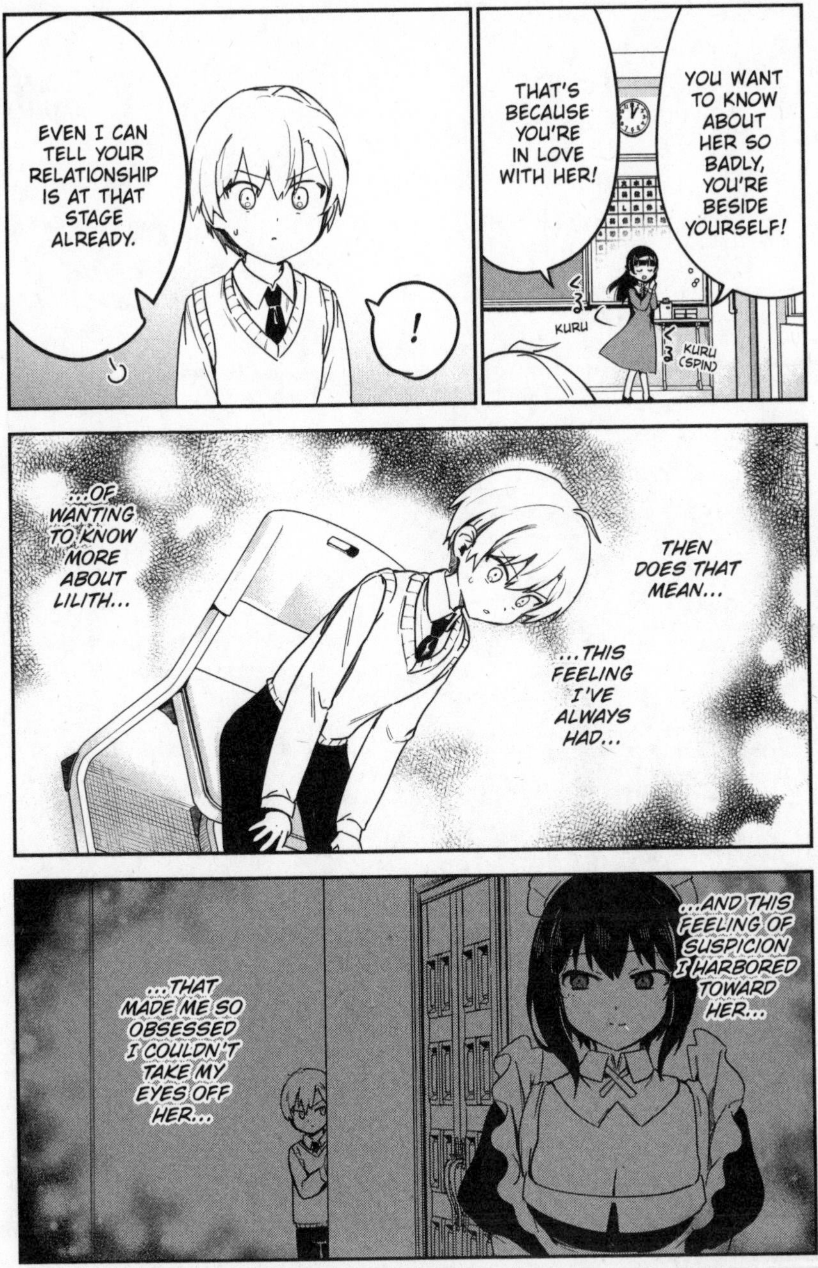
YOU WANT TO KNOW ABOUT HER SO BADLY, YOU'RE BESIDE YOURSELF!
THAT'S BECAUSE YOU'RE IN LOVE WITH HER!
KURU (SPIN)
KURU
EVEN I CAN TELL YOUR RELATIONSHIP IS AT THAT STAGE ALREADY.
!
THEN DOES THAT MEAN...
...THIS FEELING I'VE ALWAYS HAD...
...OF WANTING TO KNOW MORE ABOUT LILITH...
...AND THIS FEELING OF SUSPICION I HARBORED TOWARD HER...
...THAT MADE ME SO OBSESSED I COULDN'T TAKE MY EYES OFF HER...

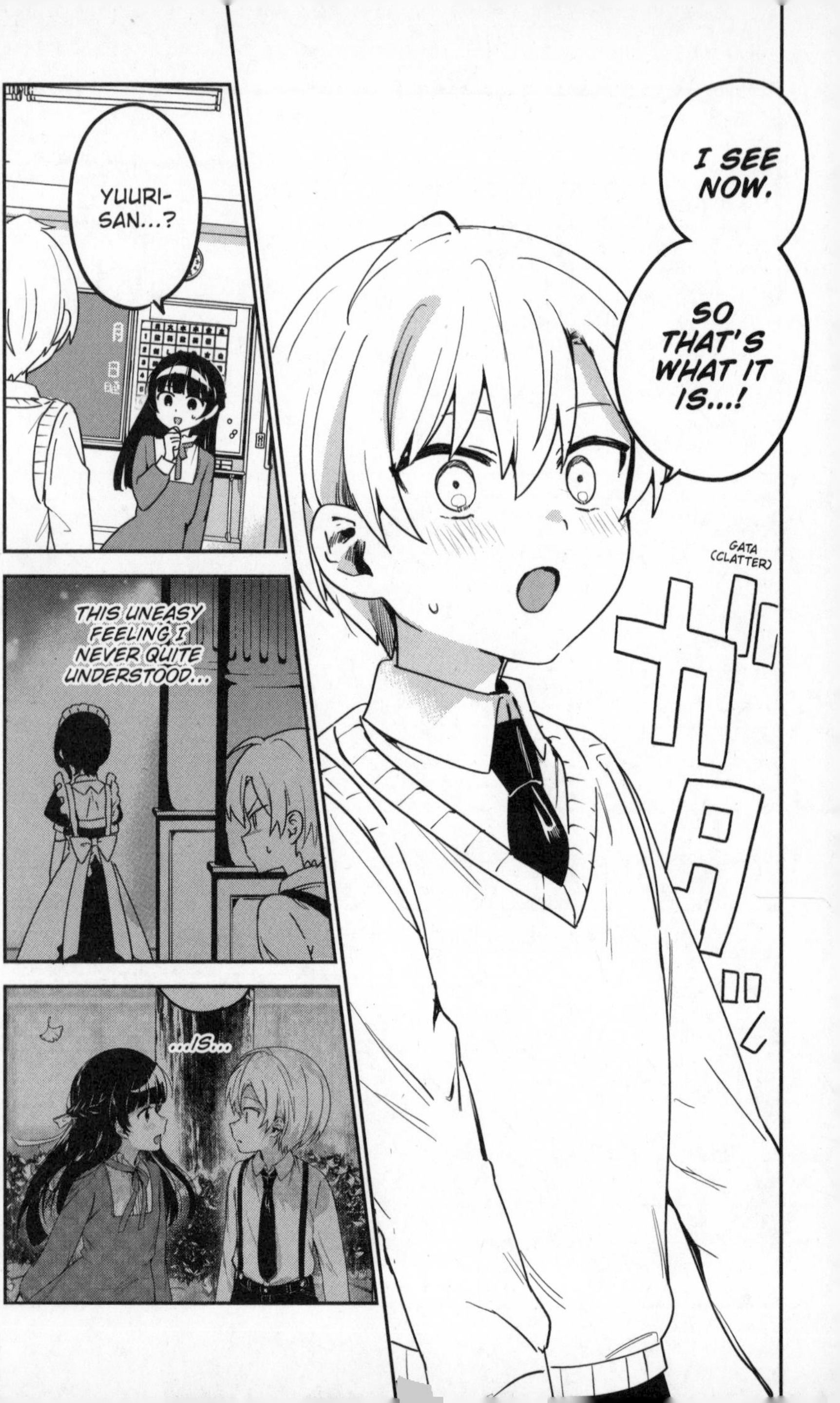
I SEE NOW.
SO THAT'S WHAT IT IS...!
GATA (CLATTER)
YUURI-SAN...?
THIS UNEASY FEELING I NEVER QUITE UNDERSTOOD...
...IS...

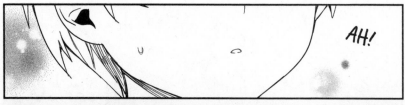

AH!
JUST AS I FELT ANXIOUS FOR NOT KNOWING ANYTHING ABOUT HER...
...LILITH MUST HAVE FELT THE SAME WAY.
SHE WAS WORRIED THAT I WOULDN'T REMEMBER HER.
THE WAY I ALWAYS SUSPECTED HER...
GU (CLENCH)
DA (DASH)
EVEN NOW...
YUURI-SAN!?

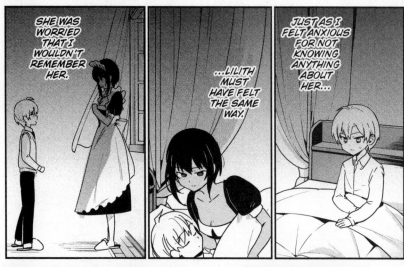

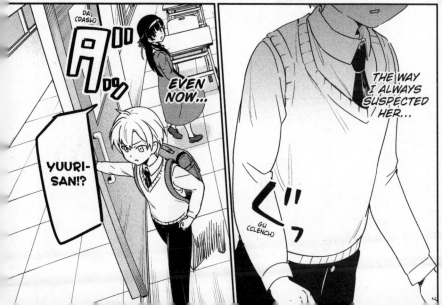

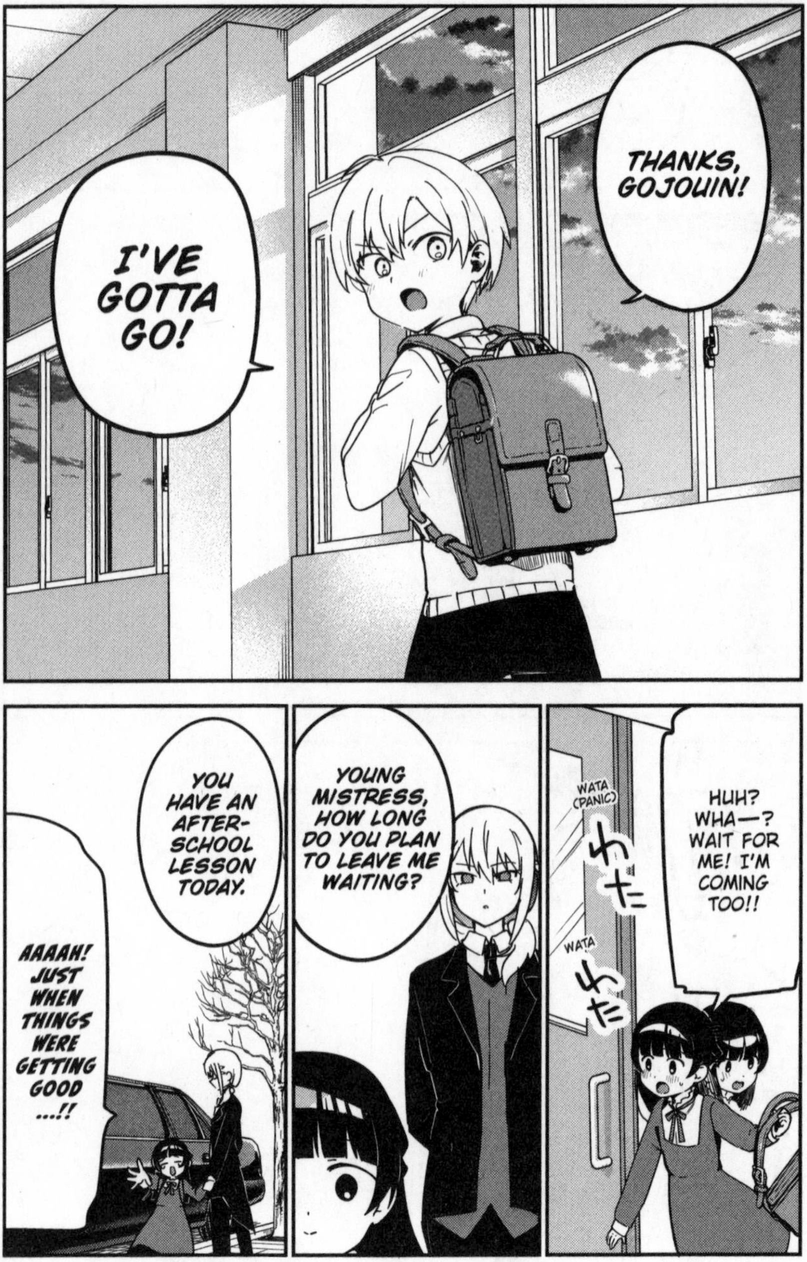
THANKS, GOJOUIN!
I'VE GOTTA GO!
HUH? WHA—? WAIT FOR ME! I'M COMING TOO!!
WATA (PANIC)
わた
WATA
わた
YOUNG MISTRESS, HOW LONG DO YOU PLAN TO LEAVE ME WAITING?
YOU HAVE AN AFTER-SCHOOL LESSON TODAY.
AAAAH! JUST WHEN THINGS WERE GETTING GOOD...!!

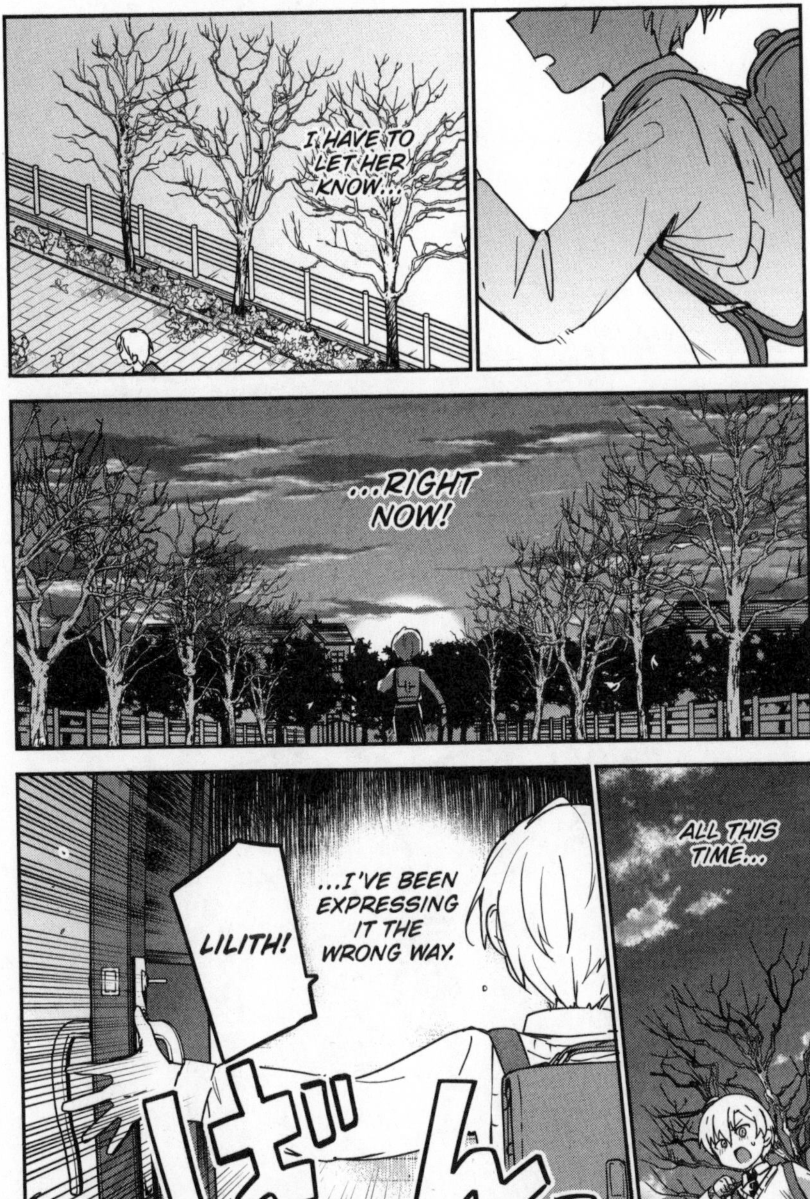
I HAVE TO LET HER KNOW...
...RIGHT NOW!
ALL THIS TIME...
...I'VE BEEN EXPRESSING IT THE WRONG WAY.
LILITH!
BAN (BAM)

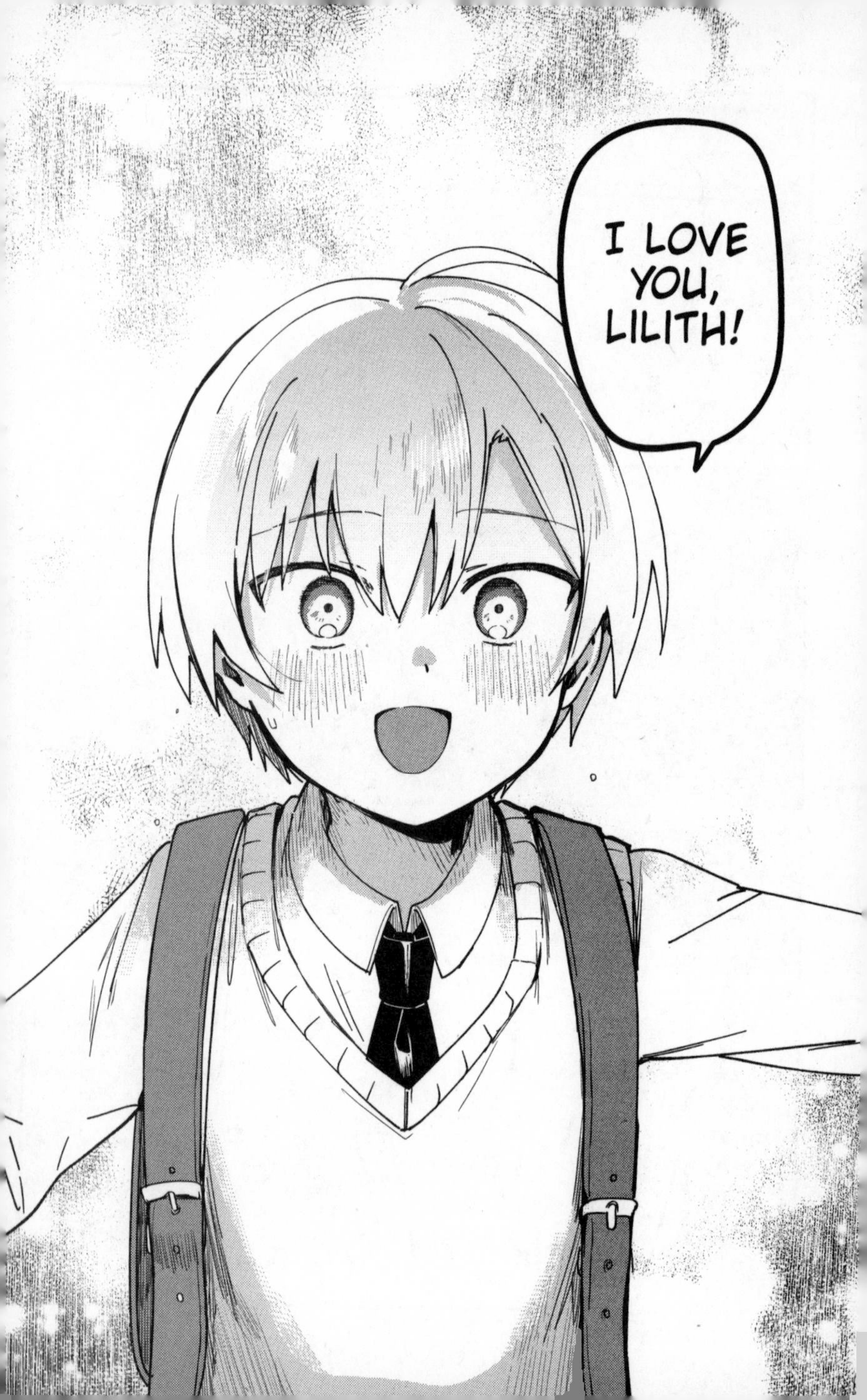
I LOVE YOU, LILITH!

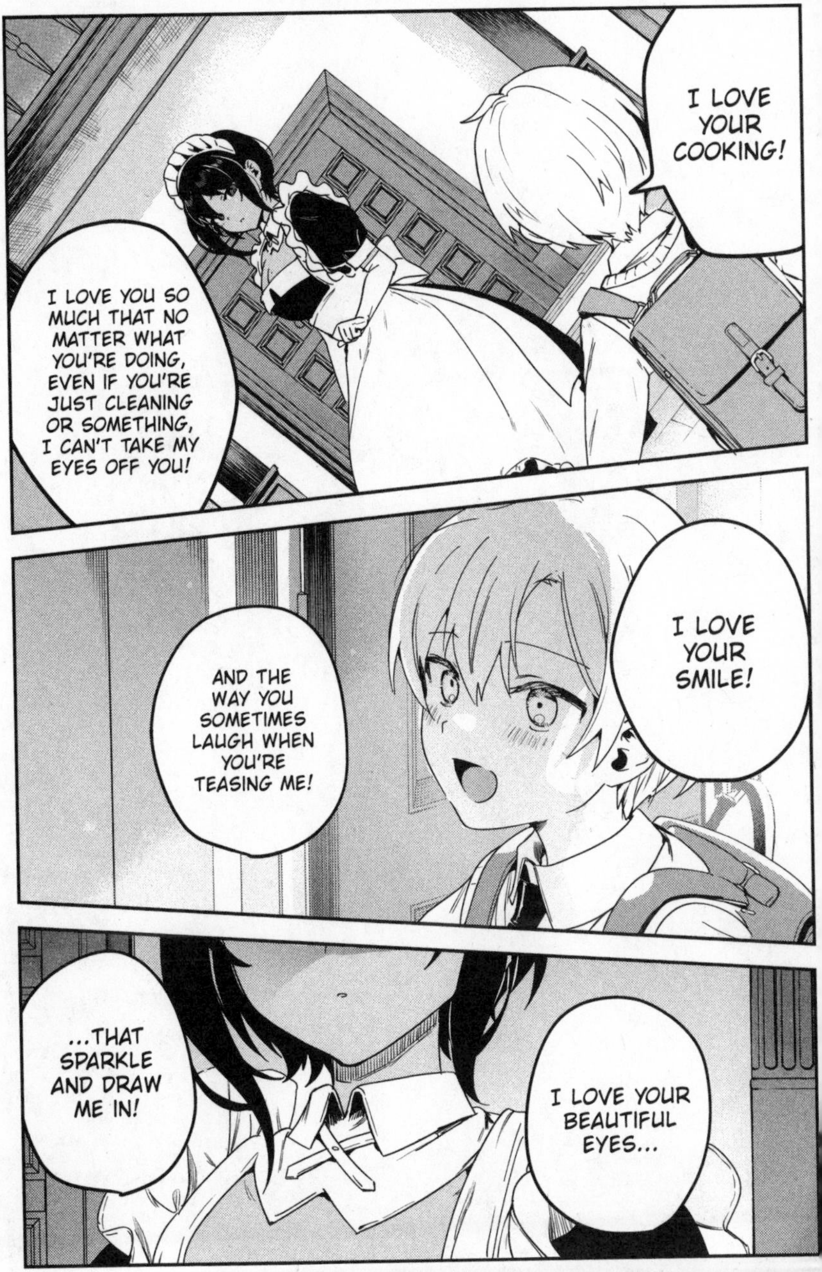
I LOVE YOUR COOKING!
I LOVE YOU SO MUCH THAT NO MATTER WHAT YOU'RE DOING, EVEN IF YOU'RE JUST CLEANING OR SOMETHING, I CAN'T TAKE MY EYES OFF YOU!
I LOVE YOUR SMILE!
AND THE WAY YOU SOMETIMES LAUGH WHEN YOU'RE TEASING ME!
I LOVE YOUR BEAUTIFUL EYES...
...THAT SPARKLE AND DRAW ME IN!

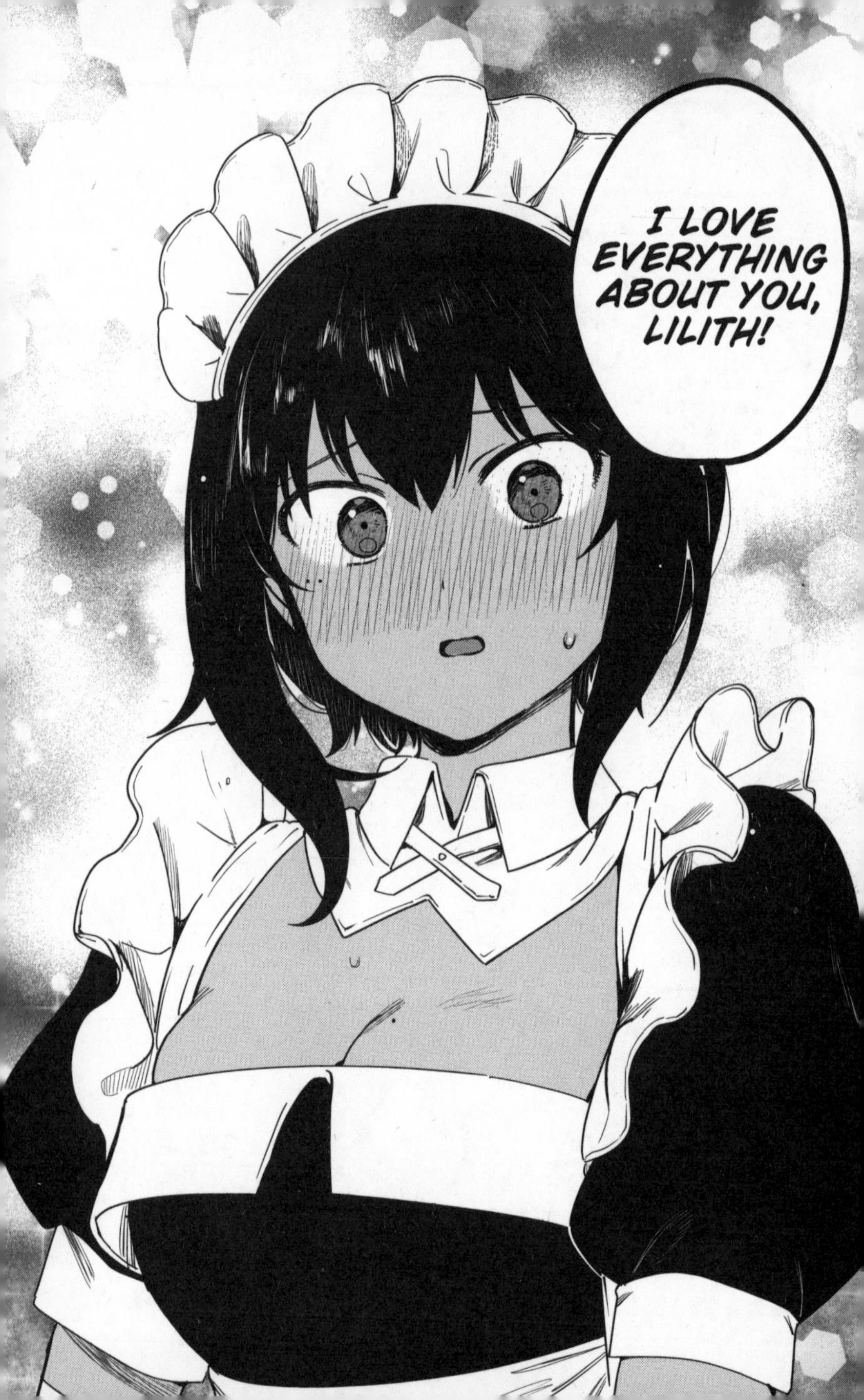
I LOVE EVERYTHING ABOUT YOU, LILITH!

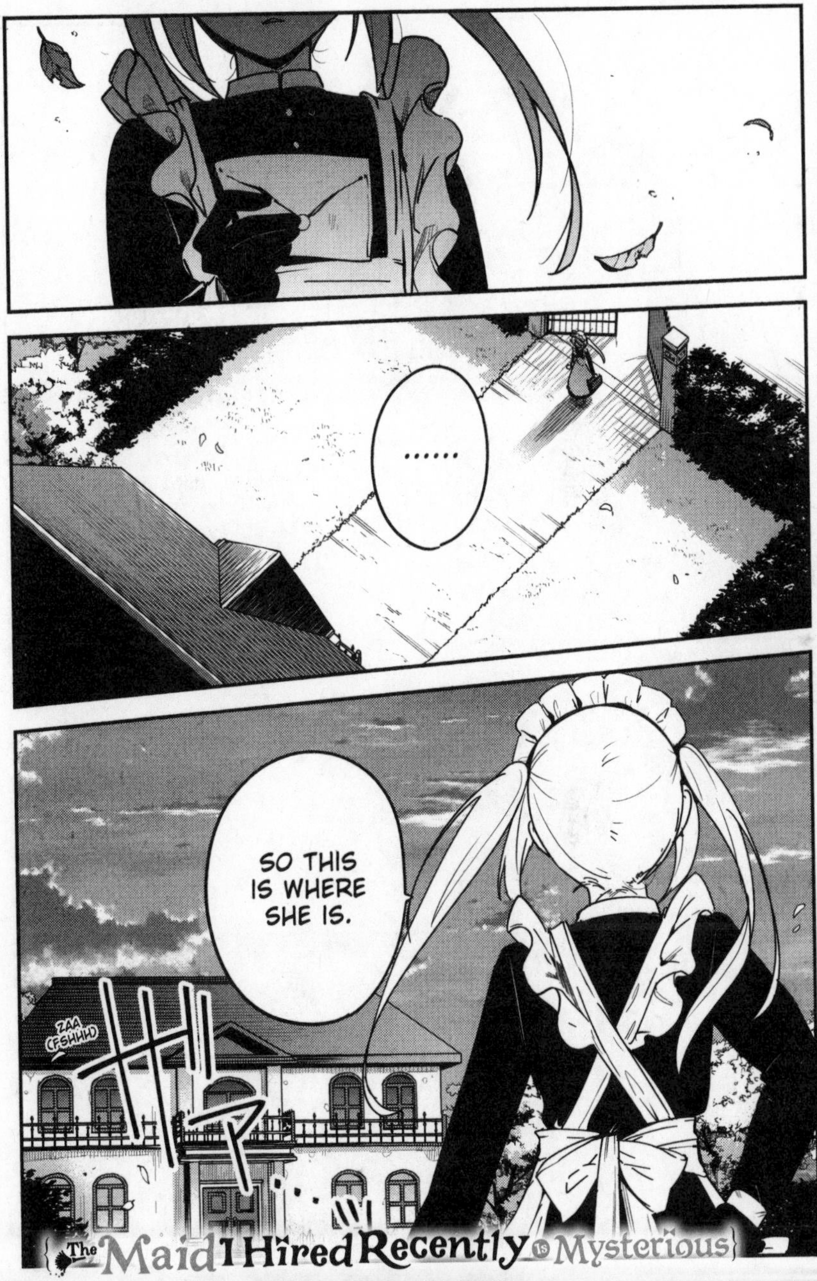
......
SO THIS IS WHERE SHE IS.
ZAA (FSHHH)
The Maid I Hired Recently Is Mysterious

VOLUME 4 END

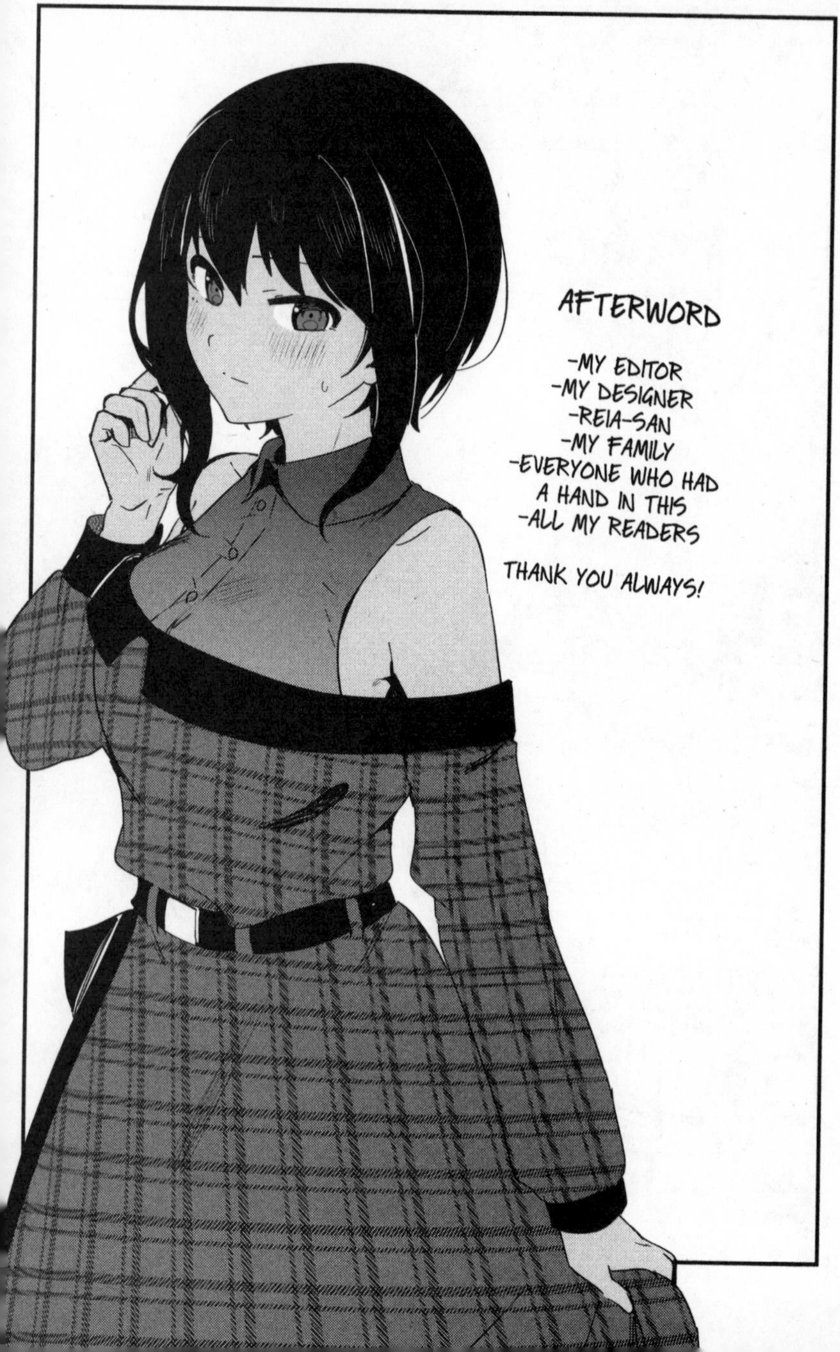
AFTERWORD
-MY EDITOR
-MY DESIGNER
-REIA-SAN
-MY FAMILY
-EVERYONE WHO HAD A HAND IN THIS
-ALL MY READERS
THANK YOU ALWAYS!

I Love

{ The Maid
I Hired Recently

~~is Mysterious~~ }!

{ The Maid I Hired Recently is Mysterious } 5

**ON SALE IN SPRING 2023!**

4 Wakame Konbu

Translation: Christine Dashiell

Lettering: Brandon Bovia

SAIKIN YATOTTA MAID GA AYASHII, Vol. 4
©2021 Wakame Konbu/SQUARE ENIX CO., LTD.

First published in Japan in 2021 by SQUARE ENIX CO., LTD.
English translation rights arranged with SQUARE ENIX CO., LTD. and Yen Press, LLC through Tuttle-Mori Agency, Inc.

English translation ©2022 by SQUARE ENIX CO., LTD.

Yen Press
150 West 30th Street, 19th Floor
New York, NY 10001

Visit us at yenpress.com
facebook.com/yenpress
twitter.com/yenpress
yenpress.tumblr.com
instagram.com/yenpress

First Yen Press Edition: November 2022
Edited by Yen Press Editorial: Jacquelyn Li, Riley Pearsall
Designed by Yen Press Design: Wendy Chan

Yen Press is an imprint of Yen Press, LLC.
The Yen Press name and logo are trademarks of Yen Press, LLC.

The publisher is not responsible for websites (or their content) that are not owned by the publisher.

Library of Congress Control Number: 2021935580

ISBNs: 978-1-9753-4741-3 (paperback)
978-1-9753-4742-0 (ebook)

1 3 5 7 9 10 8 6 4 2

WOR

Printed in the United States of America